T0350836

# Effective Complex Project Management

## An Adaptive Agile Framework for Delivering Business Value

Robert K. Wysocki

Copyright © 2014 by Robert Wysocki

ISBN-13: 978-1-60427-100-3

Printed and bound in the U.S.A. Printed on acid-free paper.

10 9 8 7 6 5 4 3 2 1

**Library of Congress Cataloging-in-Publication Data**

Wysocki, Robert K.
  Effective complex project management : an adaptive agile framework for delivering business value / by Robert K. Wysocki, PhD.
      pages cm
  Includes bibliographical references and index.
  ISBN 978-1-60427-100-3 (hardcover : alk. paper)  1.  Project management.
I. Title.
  HD69.P75W947 2014
  658.4'04—dc23
                                        2014023038

Phone: (954) 727-9333
Fax: (561) 892-0700
Web: www.jrosspub.com

# DEDICATION

My parents have long since passed, and I think of them often. I owe them the love of learning and reading that they instilled in me from the very beginning of my education. They were first generation Americans, and humble and simple people. Their worldly possessions were few. How I wish they knew how valuable their gift to me has turned out to be.

# FOREWORD

Robert Wysocki does it again, and again. Wysocki has evolved from a project management expert and guru to the preeminent thought leader on managing complexity in the 21st century.

## 21ˢᵀ CENTURY GLOBAL AND LOCAL CHALLENGES

These are tumultuous times. Businesses are faced with unprecedented challenges in the hyper-connected 21st century global economy. Extraordinary gale-force winds of change are swirling faster than ever before (see Figure A).

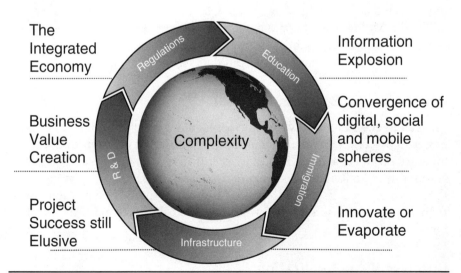

**Figure A**  The 21ˢᵗ Century Challenge. *Source: The IT Complexity Crisis: Danger and Opportunity* by Roger Sessions

## The Integrated Economy

Everyone is feeling the effects of the global integrated economy, and business analysts (BAs) are no exception. Many jobs are becoming commoditized; they can be performed by internal resources, contractors, or even outsourced resources located anywhere across the globe. Global wage scales have made U.S. employees too expensive to perform standard, repetitive tasks. Many U.S. jobs are gone and not coming back. For these reasons, basic BA tasks are often outsourced or performed by contractors.

## The Information Explosion

IT applications have also impacted U.S. jobs by automating repetitive activities, often increasing the quality and predictability of outcomes. Smart IT applications are replacing knowledge workers across industries, including BAs. The demand for new, innovative apps delivered quickly is making traditional requirements and development methods obsolete.

## Convergence of Digital, Social, and Mobile Spheres

Social/mobile media has connected us all in obvious and subtle ways, some of which we don't yet fully understand, and can't even imagine. As we saw across the Middle East, people are using social media to bring about major changes to social and political systems. BAs are using social media to enhance collaboration among key stakeholders across the globe.

## Innovation vs. Business as Usual

The call to action for today's businesses is "innovate or evaporate." For businesses to be competitive, they must be first to market with innovative, leading-edge products and services that are intuitive, easy-to-use, and offer new features. It is no longer enough for BAs to ask their business partners what they want or need. BAs must learn to foster creativity and innovation during their requirements sessions, continually asking the question: "Are we truly innovating?"

## Business Value Realization

Businesses cannot afford to waste project investments or spend precious resource time unless there are significant business benefits in terms of value to the customer and wealth to the bottom line. Enterprise BAs understand the business, their value proposition, and focus on value throughout the project. BAs work with project managers to develop release plans prioritized based on business value.

## 39% Project Success Rate

With business success riding on innovation and first-to-market speed, we must be able to deliver on time, cost, and scope commitments. However, according to the *Chaos Manifesto 2013* by The Standish Group, business change initiatives that rely heavily on IT are only 39% successful, as measured by on time, on budget, and with the full scope of functions and features.[1] What is the cost of the other 61%, the failed and challenged projects? According to Roger Sessions (2014), the cost is *USD 1.22 trillion/year in the US, and USD 500 billion/month worldwide.* So, project success equates to global competitiveness and financial stability.

> "If we could solve the problem of IT failure, the US could increase GDP by USD 1 trillion/year."
> —Roger Sessions, Leading expert on project complexity and enterprise architecture

# The Fundamentals of a Nation's Exceptionalism

As we are struggling to bring about positive change within our companies, and our companies are struggling with the challenges of the new economy, the nation states where our companies operate are under immense pressure to build and sustain the fundamental elements of a thriving economic culture. These involve investment in five major areas:

- Education—To ensure the availability of a skilled workforce;
- Immigration—To reach across the world for the best minds;
- Infrastructure—To provide the basic services for your family and your company to operate effectively and efficiently;
- Rules and regulations—To provide an environment of fairness; and
- Research and development—To continue to innovate and create.

---

[1]The Standish Group. (January, 2014). "CHAOS Manifesto, 2013: Think Big, Act Small." Online at versionone.com/assets/img/files/ChaosManifesto2013.pdf.

In the developed nations of the world, investment in these fundamentals has fallen drastically.[2] Projects are emerging at every turn to rebuild these fundamental elements of a thriving society. The result is constant change and immense complexity for individuals, families, companies, communities, states, and nations.

## Complexity

All of these forces are influenced by the unprecedented complexity that exists at all levels: globally, nationally, locally, and within projects. With complexity comes dynamic, unpredictable, adaptive change. Since projects are complex, adaptive systems operating within a complex environment, typical plan-based project and requirements management practices are insufficient when attempting to bring about speed and innovation. Roger Sessions speaks to IT complexity:

> *Large multi-million dollar IT systems are typically delivered late, over budget, and missing key functionality. Once delivered these systems have scalability, performance, reliability, and security issues. Their fragility makes them expensive to maintain and laborious to modify. The culprit is architectural complexity. Some complexity is inherent in any large system. But most systems contain considerable amounts of unnecessary complexity.*[3]

## Changing the Ways That We Do Projects

So what does all this have to do with project management? The root cause of our dismal project performance is two-fold: gaps in value-based *Enterprise Business Analysis* and *Complex Project Management*. Both of these relatively new disciplines are emerging to address our 21st century challenges. In this book, Wysocki defines the need for and offers a practical implementation approach for building a successful complex project management practice within your organization. It is a difficult and complicated endeavor to

---

[2]Friedman, Thomas. (September 4, 2011). Meet the Press. NBC News. Online at: http://www.nbcnews.com/video/meet-the-press/44391320#44391320.

[3]Sessions, Roger. (January, 2014). "The Thirteen Laws of Highly Complex IT Systems," Version 1.2, ObjectWatch Blog. Online at http://objectwatch.com/media-2013-01.

transition from a plan-based to an adaptive complex project management, but one we must traverse.

As Wysocki says, the world of traditional project management processes and practices belongs to yesterday. The convergence of complexity, uncertainty, and constant change brings new challenges to project management. Complex project management is the focus of this book. Wysocki's approach is to build a framework that can be effectively applied to align with any project, the Adaptive Complex Project Framework (ACPF).

The ACPF is THE robust decision tool that seamlessly integrates change. The ACPF contains a robust project management methodology that can be applied to all types of projects across industries. It is aligned with the most contemporary principles of innovation, agility, and lean approaches to change. The ACPF has been developed, refined, and validated more than 20 years. It represents the most forward thinking in applied complex project management.

Kathleen Hass, PMP
Consultant, IT manager, workshop developer and provider
Author, PMI® award-winning *Managing Complex Projects: A New Model*

# TABLE OF CONTENTS

# ABOUT THE AUTHOR

 **Robert K. Wysocki**, Ph.D., has more than 45 years of combined experience as a project manager, business analyst, business process consultant, information systems manager, systems and management consultant, author, and training developer and provider. He has written 23 books on project management and information systems management. One book, *Effective Project Management: Traditional, Adaptive, Extreme,* 7th ed., has been a bestseller and was recommended by the Project Management Institute (PMI®) for the library of every project manager.

In addition, Wysocki has written articles for more than 30 professional and trade journals, and made more than 100 presentations at professional and trade conferences and meetings. He has developed more than 20 project management courses, and trained more than 10,000 project managers, worldwide. From 1963 to 1970, Wysocki was a systems consultant for one of the world's largest electronics components manufacturers. In that capacity, he designed and implemented several computer-based manufacturing and quality control systems. From 1970 to 1990, he held a number of positions in state supported and private institutions in higher education as MBA Director, Associate Dean of Business, Dean of Computers and Information Systems, Director of Academic Computing, CIO, and Senior Planner.

In 1990, Wysocki founded Enterprise Information Insights (EII), Inc., a project management consulting and training practice, specializing in project management methodology design and integration, business process design, project support office establishment, development of training curriculum, and development of a portfolio of assessment tools focused on organizations, project teams, and individuals. In July, 2013, he accepted an invitation to become CEO of pmGURU, Inc., a producer and seller of online project management training.

Wysocki's client list includes AT&T, Aetna, Babbage Simmel, BMW, British Computer Society, Boston University Corporate Education Center, Centre for Excellence in Project Management, Computerworld, Converse Shoes, Data General, Digital, Eli Lilly, Harvard Community Health Plan, IBM, J. Walter Thompson, Novartis, Ohio State University, Peoples Bank, Sapient Corporation, The Limited, The State of Ohio, The State of Vermont, Travelers Insurance, TVA, University of California–Santa Cruz, US Army 5th Signal Corps, US Coast Guard Academy, Wal-Mart, Wells Fargo, ZTE, and others.

Currently, Wysocki is a Senior Consultant at the Cutter Consortium, where he is an active member of the Agile Product & Project Management Practice. He is a past Editor of the Effective Project Management Series for Artech House, a publisher to the technical and engineering professions. He was a founding member of the Agile Project Leadership Network and served as its first Vice President and President Elect, a member of the American Society for the Advancement of Project Management (asapm/IPMA-USA), the Agile Alliance, the Project Summit & Business Analyst World Executive Advisory Board, PMI, the Association for Talent Development (formerly, the American Society for Training and Development), and the Society of Human Resource Management. He was Association Vice President of AITP (formerly, DPMA) and earned a Bachelor of Arts in Mathematics from the University of Dallas, and a Master of Science and Ph.D. in Mathematical Statistics from Southern Methodist University.

Web Added Value™

At J. Ross Publishing we are committed to providing today's professional with practical, hands-on tools that enhance the learning experience and give readers an opportunity to apply what they have learned. That is why we offer free ancillary materials available for download on this book and all participating Web Added Value™ publications. These online resources may include interactive versions of material that appears in the book or supplemental templates, worksheets, models, plans, case studies, proposals, spreadsheets and assessment tools, among other things. Whenever you see the WAV™ symbol in any of our publications, it means bonus materials accompany the book and are available from the Web Added Value Download Resource Center at www.jrosspub. com.

Downloads available for *Effective Complex Project Management: An Adaptive Agile Framework for Delivering Business Value* include:

- Over 225 PowerPoint slides that may be used for teaching a course on Effective Complex Project Management, with exercises for in-class use.
- An SPT Assessment Tool that collects, analyzes, and reports the optimal balance among staff, process, and technology in an organization or a single business unit.

# 1

# INTRODUCTION TO THE ADAPTIVE COMPLEX PROJECT FRAMEWORK

*We're trying to change the habits of an awful lot of people. That won't happen overnight, but it will bloody happen.*
—John Akers, former CEO, IBM

*The dogmas of the quiet past are inadequate to the stormy present. The occasion is piled high with difficulty, and we must rise with the occasion. As our case is new, so we must think anew and act anew. We must disenthrall ourselves.*
—Abraham Lincoln, 16th President of the United States

*Markets change, tastes change, so the companies and individuals who choose to compete in those markets must change.*
—Dr. An Wang, Founder and CEO, Wang Laboratories

## CHAPTER LEARNING OBJECTIVES

Provide readers with the knowledge or ability to:

- Discuss the critical success factors (CSFs) of project success, as they relate to the Adaptive Complex Project Framework (ACPF).
- Build a project management environment that capitalizes on the reasons for project success.

1

- Understand the foundations of ACPF as a competitive weapon in dealing with complexity and uncertainty.
- Discuss the Ideation, Set-up, and Execution Phases of ACPF.
- Comprehend the importance of the relationship between ACPF performance and continuous process and practice improvement.
- Start on a journey to "becoming a chef in addition to being a cook," and know why.
- Recognize the fact that the ACPF is a lean approach to project management and why this is important.

## THE NEED FOR AN ADAPTIVE COMPLEX PROJECT FRAMEWORK

The genesis of this book came from a report by Samuel Palmisano, former CEO of IBM (IBM, 2010):

---

**IBM Report**

The significant finding from the 2010 report was that over half of the 1,541 executives from the 60 countries that were interviewed admitted that they were not prepared to support the complex and uncertain environment in which they were forced to do business and they didn't know what to do about it. Furthermore, they expected complexity and uncertainty to continue to increase.

If this isn't a clarion call to action, I don't know what is!

---

Most businesses lack the tools and staff to deal with the realities of complexity and uncertainty, and the resulting impact on market position and business growth. This book applies directly to the issues and concerns presented in the IBM report, and it spans the entire project life cycle, from ideation through solution deployment. As a companion to a book targeted to executives and those responsible for the infrastructure to support complex projects (Wysocki, 2010a), this book is a practical "how-to" publication targeted to project management consultants and practitioners.

The IBM report highlighted the efforts of a few standout organizations to manage complexity. Project management, business analysis, business process management, and systems engineering were among the enabling disciplines of the standout organizations. The IBM report provided a road map for this book.

The current business climate is one of unbridled complexity, change, and speed. Most pundits would agree that, except for the simplest of projects or projects that are repeated frequently, it is not possible to specify complete requirements at the start of the project. This situation has placed a significant challenge on organizations and their project managers in that the traditional project management tools, templates, and processes are no longer effective. Requirements are never clearly established and continue to change throughout the life of the project. These projects are called "complex." They are not simple. Cyclical, iterative, and recursive models to deal with complexity have been coming into vogue for more than 30 years. The "Agile Manifesto" (Fowler and Highsmith, 2001) formalized these models at the conceptual level and provided additional guidance for project management thought leaders.

The foundational principles of the project management paradigm are shifting, and any company that does not embrace the shift is sure to be lost in the rush. Much remains to be done as the industry has yet to find a way to favorably impact project failure rates. The ACPF, described in this book, has every promise of favorably impacting those failure rates (Standish Group, 2013). "Change or die" was never a more timely statement than in today's project management environment. *To be successful in managing complex projects, you must include, in your project management portfolio of processes, an adaptive model that continuously adjusts to changing and modifying conditions, even to the point of changing project management models mid-project.* The ACPF is currently the only robust tool that offers an orderly framework that does just that.

## A HISTORICAL PERSPECTIVE

The initial version of the ACPF was developed as part of two client engagements that date from 1994. One project involved process design; the other project involved product design. These two experiences led to the publication of the first version of the ACPF. This original version of the ACPF predates the Agile Manifesto by seven years.

The ACPF presented in this book is a second generation framework. It incorporates more than 20 years of learning and discovery from the experiences and client feedback gained from using and fine tuning the original version. The ACPF presented in this book is a matured version that is ready for prime time! It is a potent business-driven framework, which is used to define and maintain the most effective project management process for a specific project.

**This current version of the ACPF
embraces all known project management
methodologies as special cases.**

Every instantiation of the ACPF is based on the project's characteristics, and the project's internal and external environments. To expect a predefined recipe (i.e., an off-the-shelf methodology) to fulfill the needs of complex project management is not realistic and definitely not part of the ACPF. For example, despite Scrum's popularity as a powerful empirical model, an off-the-shelf version of Scrum may not be the best recipe for a specific complex project. The "feeding frenzy" around Scrum abated as managers realized that Scrum was not the "silver bullet" of agile project management practice.

The closest thing that we have to a silver bullet is access to a portfolio of vetted tools, templates, and processes from which the sponsor, client, and project team can jointly create a project management approach. This portfolio is called the "*ACPF/kit*" and it is a major focus of this book. This approach is realistic, and has proven to be very effective. The ACPF/kit is customized and will contain what your organization needs in order to align its approach to complex project management in the face of the complexity and uncertainty that dominates a dynamic business environment.

There is a need for vetted tools, templates, and processes like the ACPF/kit. According to a statistic from the Standish Group's *Chaos Manifesto* (2013), project failure rates range upwards of 65 percent. Those rates are obviously unacceptable. The same percentage was also reported by the Project Management Institute (2013). The Standish Group Report lists the most recent prioritized CSFs for project success. They are shown, in priority order, within the following box:

---

**Critical Success Factors**

1. Executive support
2. User involvement
3. Clear business objectives
4. Emotional maturity
5. Optimizing scope
6. Agile process
7. Project management expertise
8. Skilled resources
9. Execution
10. Tools and infrastructure (Standish Group, 2013)

---

See Chapter 8 for a discussion of how the ACPF directly impacts each of these CSFs.

Project failure rates are not a new problem, but little seems to be happening to bring about the change needed to improve the likelihood of project success. Project managers continue to force fit new project situations into old project management approaches, leading to a waste of time and resources.

## FOUNDATIONS OF THE ADAPTIVE COMPLEX PROJECT FRAMEWORK

The range of ACPF applications that I have seen, together with my clients, has exceeded initial expectations for its robustness. For example, the ACPF has been used in drug research and development, product design, business process improvement, state government operations, and counter terrorism operations planning. It is through these and other applications that the ACPF has matured.

The journey to the current version of the ACPF has been an agile project. Although mature and ready for prime time, it has not yet reached my desired end state. I continue to learn and discover its hidden treasures; I share them with you now and will continue to do so. The ACPF creates a totally vigorous environment within which even the most complex project can be successfully managed, so as to deliver maximum business value.

If this is your first exposure to the ACPF, welcome to the first day of the rest of an effective complex project management life! As you read, please keep an open mind. The ACPF requires a new mindset and the courage to implement it. However, from the outset, if the ACPF is used properly, it works every time!

### What Is in a Name?

This next generation ACPF continues with the name that was carefully chosen for its predecessor. Those who studied the original ACPF (Wysocki, 2010a), and adopted all or some of its features, will find a treasure of new and revamped ACPF tools, templates, and processes in this book. This ACPF moves project management processes and their attendant practices much closer to a robust solution for the complex project world than any other previous approach. But the journey is not over. Further refinements of ACPF will surely come, as it is an agile "work in progress." Your experiences and feedback are the fuel for those improvements.

### *Adaptive*

From its very beginning, the ACPF was designed to continuously *adapt* to the changing situations of a project. No other project management life cycle

(PMLC) model does this in an organized way. A change in the completeness and understanding of a solution might prompt a change in the project scope or the management approach being used. Environmental changes (both internal and external) are powerful, and will also impact change to the management approach for the project.

---

**Problem**

Suppose you are managing a project that is a year away from introducing a new product, and a major competitor just put a new product on the market that will dominate your new product. What do you do?

- Terminate your project immediately.
- Redesign your new product to be competitive.
- Switch to an incremental product roll out.

**Solution**

Use the ACPF as an approach in which decision models will help in selecting the best course of action.

---

The ability to deliberately change the approach to the management of a project in midstream is a unique property possessed only by the ACPF. Some will find this change disruptive, but experience suggests that it is necessary. The ACPF does not come with a crystal ball. There will be surprises, but the ACPF comes with a decision process to maintain a best fit alignment. Learning and discovery in the early cycles may lead to these changes. For example, starting with an initial agile approach, you and the client may discover the complete solution after only the first few iterations. Should you continue with the agile approach, or transition to a more familiar linear or incremental approach? The decision to change your project management model is complex and not to be taken lightly. The new characteristics of the solution, and the financial impact of the change, will be the bases for deciding to change the approach. Details about deciding on an approach are given in Chapters 5 and 6.

Because nothing in the ACPF is fixed, every part of it is variable and can be modified at any time to maintain alignment to the changing characteristics of the project and its environment. The client and the complex project manager (CPM) are both involved in these modifications. The changes that can be made are not taken from a predefined list of possible changes. The changes in approach are a creative response to the changing needs of the project and the business situation.

> The ACPF requires meaningful involvement of the client and the project team, acting in an open and trusting partnership, in order to effectively make these changes. Anything short of that will invite failure.

To be successful with the ACPF, you have to "think like a chef and not like a cook!" The cook can only follow a given recipe, and if an ingredient is missing in the recipe, it is useless. The cook may be at a loss as to how to continue, if at all. A chef, on the other hand, has the skills and experience to adapt to the situation and create recipes that work within the constraints of available ingredients (the portfolio of tools, templates, and processes vetted by the enterprise).

My significant other provides an excellent example of the difference between a cook and a chef. Heather makes a pumpkin cheesecake that is to die for. Late one Sunday evening she asked if I would like her to bake a cheesecake for us. That's a no brainer for me and so I said "you bet." A few minutes later I heard some rummaging around in the cupboards followed by a moan from the kitchen. She reported that there was no vanilla extract and that was an essential ingredient of her recipe. It was too late to go to the market, so I suggested she put the batter in the fridge and we'd pick up the vanilla extract in the morning. A few minutes later I could tell she had put a cheesecake in the oven to bake. Maybe she found the vanilla extract? No she hadn't. Instead she found a container of vanilla frosting and vanilla extract was one of its main ingredients. She figured out how much vanilla frosting would equal the vanilla extract called for in the cheesecake recipe and used that instead. Once she fixates on a project she is not easily dissuaded. The cheesecake was awesome! So what does this have to do with complex project management? My point is that if all you can do is blindly follow someone else's recipe for managing a project, you won't have a chance of successfully completing a complex project. The recipe author could not have anticipated every eventuality. But if you can create or modify a recipe based on the specific characteristics and environment of the project, you will have planted the seeds for complex project success.

> The traditional project manager is, in a certain sense, a cook and is captive to a specific project management model. To be a successful CPM you have to "think like a chef and not like a cook". The cook can follow a given recipe. However, if an ingredient is missing in the recipe, the cook may be at a loss as to how to continue. A chef has the skills and experience to adapt to the situation and create recipes that work within the constraints of available ingredients (the portfolio of tools, templates, and processes vetted by the enterprise).

So, you should have concluded that *adaptive* is a stronger word than you might have expected. To be adaptive means to embrace scope changes, changes to project plan or execution, as well as being open to changing to a different project management model altogether. Thus, adaptation is far more than plan revision for a chosen project management see model. To my knowledge, the ACPF is the only robust approach that is adaptive to this extent.

> **The robustness of the ACPF removes**
> **all constraints on the execution**
> **of project management.**

The bottom line in every project should be to deliver the expected business value that justified doing the project in the first place. Just as projects are unique and dynamic, so also is ACPF unique and dynamic! The responsibilities placed on the shoulders of the CPM are significant.

## *Complex*

The ACPF has demonstrated that it can deliver acceptable business value, even in the most complex and uncertain of situations. *Complex* projects are of three different types (Agile, Extreme, and Emertxe; further explained in Chapter 3). Their effective management calls for a creative and courageous commitment from not only the project manager, but also the sponsor, client, client team, and development team. These persons' roles in complex projects are different than their roles in traditional projects. And therein lies the challenge to the enterprise to effectively manage such projects and generate the business value expected from such ventures. An ACPF team is designed unlike any other (Wysocki, 2014a). ACPF teams and how they are organized are further discussed in Chapter 3.

## *Project*

*Projects* are unique and are never repeated under the same set of circumstances. So, why isn't the approach to managing them unique as well? This book does not advocate a wholesale change in management approach, but rather a thought-out approach—one that takes into account and deals with the vagaries of the project and its environment. There are project-specific, as well as organizational and environmental characteristics to account for when choosing the best fit project management approach (see Chapter 5). Any combination of the project characteristics discussed in Chapter 5 can cause a change in how the project is managed.

For example, if the project approach requires heavy client involvement, and you know from experience with a client that this is not likely to happen on the project, then you would not choose an approach like Scrum that depends on heavy client involvement. This situation means that you have to compromise and choose a less-than-ideal approach to work around the lack of meaningful client involvement. Alternatively, you might build a workshop on client involvement into the project definition phase and, based on the results of the workshop, make a mutual decision on which project management approach to use.

Or, suppose that your organizational environment is characterized by frequent reorganization and realignment of roles and responsibilities. In such an environment, sponsorship and priorities of active projects will change, which puts the project schedule and its priority in harm's way. Your best fit project management approach should be one where deliverables are introduced in increments or short intervals, rather than all at once at the end of a long project. This new strategy will reduce the risk of wasted resources and loss of business value due to the event of early termination of the project. This discussion continues in Chapter 9.

## Framework

> The ACPF is not a methodology. It is a framework for generating a unique and dynamic management approach for one-time use on a specific project. The success of that approach is measured by the delivered business value.

The ACPF is a framework that the CPM uses to create a recipe for the management of a specific project. The CPM needs to understand the situation and adapt a vetted portfolio of tools, templates, and processes—the ACPF/kit—to fit the situation. The ACPF allows for that adaptation as the project situation changes. The CPM and client are in charge of the approach, rather than the approach being in charge of the project manager, as is often the case with traditional projects.

**An effective CPM must be a chef.**
**Cooks need not apply.**

In order to place ACPF in the proper context, envision the various project management approaches as being mapped into a simple project landscape. We will review this in depth later. It is the topic of Chapter 2.

For now, it is important to understand that the complex project management environment is ever-changing and is defined by seven interdependent variables:

- The characteristics of the project itself
- The characteristics of the environment in which the project will be executed
- The skill profile of the project team
- The skill profile of the client team
- The business process life cycle
- The project management life cycle
- The hardware/software technology to support the whole endeavor

While these variables may seem overwhelming, they are not. The complexities of this multidimensional environment are explored in Chapter 5, showing you how to obtain and sustain an effective project management presence in a changing environment.

## Effective Complex Project Management Is Organized Common Sense

Every instantiation of the ACPF follows directly from the uniqueness and interaction of the variables in the project environment that were listed in the previous section. Adopting a "one-size-fits-all" mentality works if, and only if, those who developed the project management methodology were clairvoyant enough to actually design a methodology that fits any project that you would ever encounter *and* the instantiation of the seven interdependent variables. That is either impossible, or, "a solution out looking for a problem." You are probably familiar with consultants whose practices are based on adopting a "one-size-fits-all" mentality. A better approach that will work is to first understand the problem or business opportunity, and only then, design a project management approach that fits it. To design that approach, you will draw upon your ACPF/kit. The depth and breadth of that kit is an indicator of your design capabilities. Welcome to ACPF-land!

As a son of first generation Americans, who is of 100% Polish descent, I consider myself to be a pretty good problem solver. However, I like to keep things simple and intuitive, as applied to the following definition.

**The Adaptive Complex Project Framework**

The *ACPF* is a robust portfolio of vetted tools, templates, and processes that can be customized to the exact needs of the enterprise to efficiently and effectively answer the following questions:

Project Ideation Phase

1. What business situation is being addressed?
2. What do you need to do?
3. What will you do?

Project Set-Up Phase

4. How will you do it?

Project Execution Phase

5. How will you know that you did it?
6. How well did you do?

The customized ACPF environment delivers an acceptable management solution that results in achieving maximum business value within the time, cost, and resource constraints of the project.

The answers to these six questions reduces effective complex project management to nothing more than organized common sense. If it were not organized common sense, why would you want to do it at all? A good test of whether or not your project management approach makes sense lies not only in your answers to these six questions, but also in the extent to which the project team uses them. So, *effectiveness* is measured by both the delivered business value of the project and how well the management process worked.

Let's put on our new ACPF hat and take a quick look at how ACPF answers these six questions. At the highest level, the ACPF consists of three phases: Project Ideation, Project Set-Up, and Project Execution. Each phase answers one or more of the same, six questions.

## Project Ideation Phase

The ACPF project life span begins with a Project Ideation Phase. This phase marks the birth of an idea that its proposer hopes will result in a project that delivers business value. The business case is the heart of this first phase. The ACPF extends the boundaries of the project life span to include the creation of the project. To understand the ACPF requires knowing where the project came from, and why. The Project Ideation Phase launches an investigation of how an unsolved problem might be solved, or how an untapped business opportunity might be exploited. It consists of answering the first three questions as discussed below.

### 1. What business situation is being addressed by this project?

The business situation is either an unsolved problem or an untapped business opportunity. If the business situation is an unsolved problem, the solution may be clearly defined and the delivery of that solution should be rather straightforward. If the solution is not completely known, then the project management approach must accommodate the learning and discovery of that solution. That will be done through a sequence of consecutive iterations or cycles. Obviously, these are complex projects and will be a higher risk than traditional projects, simply because the deliverables are not clearly defined and may not be discovered despite the best efforts being extended. The ACPF is designed to take on such complex projects, especially when they are critical mission projects in which solutions have not been forthcoming. Obviously, these will be challenging projects that carry high risk.

If the business situation is an untapped business opportunity, the ACPF needs to provide direction in finding and evaluating ways to exploit that business opportunity. This type of project has more of a business focus than a technical focus, than would be the case in the unsolved problem situation. Both, however, are complex situations and require creativity, courage, and flexibility to achieve an acceptable result. These projects are subject to risks from external changes and technological advances. Their successful execution depends on approaches that expect change.

Despite the risks, both of these types of projects must be undertaken and the best outcome produced within the time, cost, and resource constraints. Keep in mind that your project may be competing for resources with other projects that are addressing the same problem or business situation. The importance to senior managers of finding that solution or taking advantage of that untapped business opportunity will compete with the importance of other project proposals and how they framed their costs and benefits. Complex projects require nimble management models.

### 2. What do you need to do?

Deciding what you need to do is the call to be creative and innovative. The obvious answer is to solve the problem or take advantage of the untapped business opportunity. This is all well and good, but given the present circumstances, it may not be possible. Even in those rare cases where the solution is clearly known, you might not have the skilled resources, and if you do have them, they may not be available when you need them. When the solution is not known or only partially known, you might not be successful in finding that unknown solution. In any case, you need to document what needs to be done.

To answer this question, the ACPF will draw upon the many "games" that have been developed for creative thinking. One of those games is called the ACPF Brainstorming Process (see more about this game in Chapter 4). One of the major challenges faced by the ACPF Brainstorming Process is to generate new ideas that can stand the test of delivering sustainable business value. (For a collection of similar tools and processes, see also Gray, et al., 2010.)

### 3. *What will you do?*

The answer to "what will you do?" will be framed in the project goal and objectives statements. Maybe you and others will propose partial solutions to the problem or untapped business opportunity. In any case, your goal and objective statements will clearly state your intentions to the furthest extent possible. The answer is documented with a Project Overview Statement (see Chapter 4).

### Project Set-up Phase

The Project Set-up Phase is a differentiating part of the ACPF. No other project management approach that I know of has anything similar in it. Because of the nature of every complex project, the Project Set-up Phase is a necessary component of an effective project management approach. It is based on the assumption that every project is unique, and so is the most effective way to manage it. The deliverable from the Project Set-up Phase will be the specific project management approach designed to be used for this project. It may never be used again.

> **If projects are unique, shouldn't how
> we manage them also be unique?**

### 4. *How will you do it?*

There are four steps to the Project Set-up Phase:

- Determine the project quadrant.
- Choose the best fit PMLC model template.

- Assess the project's characteristics and its environment.
- Modify the chosen PMLC model template.

These four steps answer the question and identify your approach to the project.

The term "PMLC model template" deserves some clarification. The PMLC model conjures up models like Scrum, the Feature-Driven Development model, and others. In the ACPF, these are not the models implemented, but the model you start with because it is the best fit among the PMLC model choices available to you. Once chosen, the model is adapted to the specific project conditions. The word "template" was added to the term to suggest pending changes and details.

This goes to the real heart of ACPF, for it is here that a best fit PMLC model template is chosen and adapted to the unique characteristics of the project and its internal and external conditions. Conditions are affected by the seven interdependent variables, discussed above. Further, the adapted PMLC model template is not a static entity. Change is constant in the complex project space, and so is the potential for change in the adapted PMLC model. As learning and discovery take place iteratively, the clarity of the solution and goal will change. Just as the project is unique, so are the ways that we choose to manage it.

## Project Execution Phase

If you subscribe to the *Project Management Body of Knowledge (PMBOK® Guide), 5th Edition* (Project Management Institute, 2013) you will recognize the 10 knowledge areas and 47 process groups in the details of the Project Execution Phase. This is the point where most project managers envision the start of a project. Executing an ACPF project is very different. Execution starts only after considerable preparatory work has been done to characterize the project and assess the impact of its environment. Thus, the Project Execution Phase takes the best fit project management approach delivered from the Set-up Phase and begins the project.

## 5. *How will you know that you did it?*

Your solution to the problem or untapped business opportunity will deliver some business value to the organization. That is your success criteria. It was used as the basis for project approval. That success criteria may be expressed in the form of increased revenue (IR), avoided costs (AC), or improved services (IS). *IRACIS* is the acronym that stands for these three types of business value. Whatever form that success criteria takes, it will be expressed in quantitative terms so that there is no argument as to whether you met the expected business results, or not. As part of the post-implementation audit, you will compare the actual business value realized to the estimated business value proposed in the project plan. In some PMLC models, business value might be realized in increments and be used as performance measures to validate continuing the project.

No one knows if business value will be achieved based on satisfaction of the requirements. This is the province of the sponsor and the client to validate. It is in the realm of possibility that the search for the unknown solution will not be as successful as expected. All that the project team can state is that they will do everything possible to achieve the expected business value. It should be clear here that meaningful client involvement is essential. Chapter 7 discusses client involvement in detail.

## 6. How well did you do?

There are six parts to the answer to the question of how well you and the team did on a complex project:

- How well did your deliverables meet the stated success criteria?
- How well did the development team perform?
- How well did the client team perform?
- How well did the ACPF and the project management approach work for this project?
- What lessons were learned that can be applied to future projects?
- What requirements can be further improved in the next version?

The answers to these questions are all part of the ACPF post-implementation audit. The post-implementation audit is discussed in Chapter 6.

## ACPF and *PMBOK® Guide* Compatibility

The *Project Management Body of Knowledge (PMBOK® Guide), 5th Edition* (Project Management Institute, 2013), is a portfolio of the tools, templates, and processes that should be included in every effective project management methodology, including the ACPF. Similarly, the *PMBOK® Guide* should be included in every organization's ACPF/kit (see Chapter 3). Contrary to what many project managers and their managers think, the *PMBOK® Guide* is not a methodology. It does a fairly complete and thorough job of describing the tools, templates, and processes that one would expect to use in a traditional approach to project management, but it leaves to the discretion of the enterprise how it chooses and packages those tools, templates, and processes into their own project management methodology.

The ACPF is fully compatible with the *PMBOK® Guide*, even though the *PMBOK® Guide* must be supplemented with the ACPF/kit designed specifically for the management needs of complex projects. The effective use of the ACPF/kit is supported by the business rules and decision models you will need. In other words, the ACPF is the complete environment for effective complex project management.

## ACPF Alignment

The ACPF is totally aligned to the 7 Principles of Continuous Innovation that define Radical Management (Denning, 2011), which are:

- **Principle #1: Focus Work on Delighting the Client.** The ACPF is client-focused and client-driven. That means the content, prioritization, and evaluation of the deliverables from the work must meaningfully involve the client. The client is the principle decision maker in a complex project.
- **Principle #2: Do Work through Self-Organized Teams.** The team will consist of experienced professionals who can operate without supervision. They must be given the freedom to decide with meaningful client participation what to do, and through their own discussions how and when to do it.
- **Principle #3: Do Work in Client-Driven Iterations.** The client is meaningfully involved in the entire project life span. Their input is focused on what is to be done and in what order priority. The project and client teams collaboratively decide on how and when it will be done.
- **Principle #4: Deliver Value to Clients Each Iteration.** The business value may not be actually realized for some time following deployment, but the eventual delivery of that value will be achieved.
- **Principle #5: Be Totally Open about Impediments to Improvement.** Every ACPF effort will include a risk management program because the project will encounter obstacles and must have mitigation plans in place. In the complex project world, risk of failure is often very high.
- **Principle #6: Create a Context for Continuous Self-Improvement by the Team Itself.** At the completion of each iteration, a checkpoint will

review not only the solution performance, but also the team's performance. Lessons learned is a critical part of that checkpoint.

- **Principle #7: Communicate through Interactive Conversations.** An open and honest exchange of information between client and development team is essential. Both parties play a critical role. For the client, it is the business expertise that helps guide the solution. For the project team, it is the effectiveness of the process used to discover the solution.

ACPF is also aligned to the 7 Lean Principles (Poppendieck and Poppendieck, 2003). The ACPF is robust and not constrained to any domain, such as software development. It works well in both product and process development. Experience has borne that out. The 7 Lean Principles are:

- **Eliminate waste.** If a process step does not add business value, it is defined as "waste." Something that is laying around and not being used is a waste. Find out what the client wants and deliver it ASAP. The ACPF utilizes just-in-time planning as one tool, and colocated teams is another tool, for minimizing the waste associated with creating plans that are never executed or frequently changed.
- **Amplify learning.** The ACPF, like all agile processes, uses iteration in the project execution phase, and through iteration, learning and discovery about the solution takes place. The ACPF is different from all other empirical agile processes (like Scrum) in that it includes experimentation as part of its iteration strategy. It does this using "probative swim lanes," whereas other agile processes utilize only "integrative swim lanes" based on observations from previous iterations.
- **Decide as late as possible.** The ACPF processes create learning and knowledge. Decisions should be based on as much information as can reasonably be gathered. Keep all options open until a decision must be made. Then, make it based on as much information that has been gathered to that point. Just-in-time planning is a defining characteristic of ACPF.
- **Deliver as fast as possible.** Clients learn from the ACPF process just as developers do. Giving the client deliverables ASAP gives them additional input on which to base further learning and discovery efforts.
- **Empower the team.** The team must work in an open, honest, and creative environment and not be shackled by heavy process and procedure. Their environment appears informal and unfettered by management constraints, but from a creative standpoint is the most effective

way to search out a heretofore undiscovered solution. They are clearly a self-directed team. The ideal ACPF team environment will be a hyper-productive environment (Tendon and Muller, 2014). These are rare.

- **Build integrity in.** The success of a deliverable, when the client says it is exactly what they had in mind, speaks to integrity. The ultimate market success of the final deliverables also speak to integrity.

- **See the whole.** Specialists are often fixated on the success of their piece of the solution and give little thought to the overall effectiveness of the whole solution. That tunnel vision has to take a back seat in any effective agile process, including the ACPF. The ACPF focuses on creating maximum business value, always! "Seeing the whole" means reaching back to the Project Ideation Phase and the rationale for the project.

## Using the ACPF in Your Organization

A collaborative workshop will help your team and our professional staff design and implement an ACPF environment specific to your organization's needs. The workshop is designed to answer these questions:

- **Where are you now?** This is a definition of the current state of project management in your organization. Usually, a needs analysis or a strengths, weakness, opportunities, and threats analysis is appropriate for answering this question.

- **Where do you want to go?** This is a definition of the end state of project management processes, practices, and expected business value. An ACPF Brainstorming Session (described in Chapter 4) is the preferred approach.

- **How will you get there?** This is accomplished through a series of exercises done by your team under the guidance of a trained facilitator and their team. Implementation planning is included. Developing the answer is the heart of the workshop.

- **How will you know that you got there?** As part of the workshop deliverables, your team will have defined success criteria against which the performance of the end state will be continuously evaluated over time.

These questions are part of the Blended Training/Consulting Workshop described in Chapter 8. See the Web Added Value (WAV™) section of the publisher's website at www.jrosspub.com for additional details.

## PUTTING IT ALL TOGETHER

The ACPF is a bold step forward in project management approaches. To be successful requires that you reach inside yourself and summon up all the creative juices and out-of-the-box thinking that you possibly can. The ACPF requires the same from the client. They must be meaningfully involved in an ACPF project if it is to be successful. The ACPF is not for the faint of heart. It requires seeing the project as the unique entity that it is, and drawing upon a vetted collection of tools, templates, and processes to craft the best fit management approach for your project.

There is no silver bullet. So, don't expect one. There is no recipe. So, don't look for one. But take comfort in the fact that you are about to become a chef, and not just a cook! If you apply what is offered by the ACPF, you will be prepared to effectively manage any project from the perspective of generating expected business value, no matter how complex and uncertain the project might be. I have "been there and done that" many times, and found that the ACPF works all the time!

# 2

# THE COMPLEX PROJECT LANDSCAPE AND BUSINESS CHALLENGES

*Define the problem before you pursue a solution.*
—John Williams, CEO, Spence Corporation

*Things are not always what they seem.*
—Phaedrus, Roman writer and fabulist

*In complex situations, we may rely too heavily on planning and fore-
casting and underestimate the importance of random factors in the
environment. That reliance can also lead to delusions of control.*
—Hillel J. Einhorn and Robin M. Hogarth,
Center for Decision Research,
University of Chicago Business School

## CHAPTER LEARNING OBJECTIVES

This chapter will provide readers the knowledge or ability to:

- Understand the complex business environment and the evolving roles and responsibilities of complex project management within that environment.
- Discuss the Objectives, Strategies, and Tactics model and how it links complex project management to the strategic plan of the enterprise.

- Have a working knowledge of the project landscape, the four types of projects that populate that landscape, and the ability to classify a project into the appropriate quadrant.
- Recognize a complex project and complex project management.
- Understand the organization and power of the complex project team and its member interactions.
- Understand the disciplines that define a Complex Project Manager (CPM).
- Know the differences between the Iron Triangle and the Adaptive Complex Project Framework (ACPF) Scope Triangle, and how the Scope Triangle promotes more effective complex project management.

To be successful in today's project world calls upon the sponsor, project manager, development team, client manager, and client team to forge a partnership that is very different than the one that characterized the project management models dating from the 1960s. In this chapter, we establish today's project world and provide a basis for crafting project management approaches that make sense, given the vagaries and dynamics of the business situation.

Projects cannot be viewed as islands unto themselves any longer. Projects are investments aligned to the strategic plan of the enterprise, and for completeness must be approved and managed within that context. In this holistic view of projects, program and portfolio managers are then seen as enablers of the strategic plan. Their decision environment is also holistic, and for many, that will be a revelation. The ACPF prepares these stakeholders to function effectively from tactical, to operational, to strategic levels. That is a unique characteristic of the ACPF.

So, we will begin our journey with an understanding of the business environment from the top, and continue to drill down into that environment until we reach the individual project level.

At the project level, we will establish the project landscape and project management types, and specific Project Management Life Cycle (PMLC) model templates. This is the foundation on which an enterprise can build a version of the ACPF specific to their needs.

## THE COMPLEX AND UNCERTAIN BUSINESS ENVIRONMENT

The contemporary project environment is characterized by high speed, high change, lower costs, complexity, uncertainty, and a host of other factors. This presents a daunting challenge to the C-level managers and their project managers, who are the enablers of the tactics that comprise the strategic plan of the enterprise.

Figure 2.1 illustrates the business environment from the highest levels, down to and including the project level. Processing it and making it your own is fundamental to our discussion of projects, programs, and portfolios in the proper context of the enterprise. It "takes a village" to effectively manage an ACPF and generate sustainable business value. Defining that village, and how each of its citizens interact and depend upon one another, is critical to the success of an ACPF.

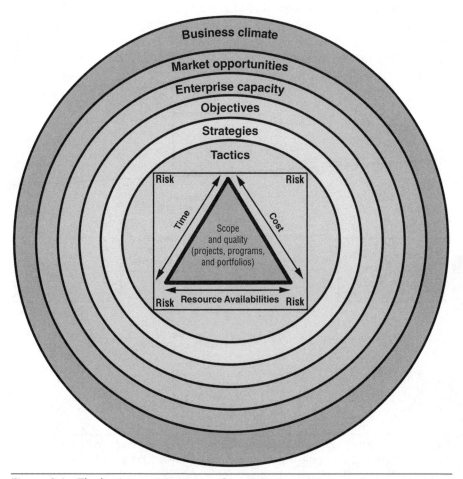

**Figure 2.1**    The business environment. *Source:* Adapted from Wysocki, 2014a.

## Business Climate

The feeding frenzy that has arisen from the relentless advances of technology and the Internet has had several disruptive effects on the business climate. These effects are global, and have unknowingly put many businesses in harm's way. The Internet is the gateway for anyone, anywhere, to create and sell their products and services! Business sustainability now depends on how effective a business can erect barriers to entry for new competitors, and how it can "out-create and out-pace" the competition. Anyone, regardless of their physical location, can be a competitor. Even if you don't sell in the international markets, your competitors can and do, so you are pulled into the global marketplace and may not even be aware of it. Your business decisions must consider actual and potential global impact.

As the enterprise develops its business case, it must pay close attention to Porter's Competitive Forces model. Figure 2.2 is an application of Porter's (1980) model to the Workforce and Business Development Center (WBDC) Case Study in Appendix B.

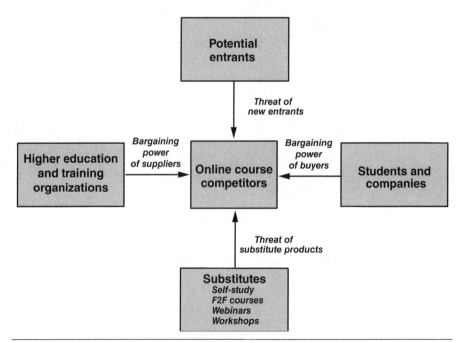

**Figure 2.2**  Porter's competitive forces applied to the case study: WBDC model.
*Source*: An application of the model introduced in Porter, 1980.

Specifically, our business case must answer the following questions:

- Who are the potential competitors in our market?
- Who are our suppliers?
- Who are our customers?
- What are the substitute products and services?

Our objective is to create barriers to entry into our markets. The ACPF can be instrumental in achieving those objectives. (See Chapter 4 for a detailed discussion on developing the business case.)

## Market Opportunities

Market opportunities will come and go, and not on a schedule that organizations can predict or even be able to accommodate. Whatever project environment your organization embraces, it must be able to respond immediately. The opportunities can be internal (problem solving and process improvement to maintain or improve market position) and external (new product, service, and processes for meeting the needs of an expanded customer base). The ACPF is an environment characterized by flexibility, rapid response, openness, and creativity. It is lean and has eliminated all non-value added work. This is the business landscape that the ACPF was designed to exploit. The ACPF is the first project management approach of its kind to do so.

## Enterprise Capacity

Management can entertain all sorts of new business opportunities and envision processes and practices that work perfectly, but someone has to pay attention to the ability of the enterprise to deliver on these dreams. In most organizations, human resource capacity, among all other resources, usually happens by accident rather than as the result of a human resource management system that aligns resources to the strategic plan of the organization. Resource availability was first added to the "Iron Triangle" and reintroduced as the "Scope Triangle" (Wysocki, et al., 1995). That Scope Triangle occupies the center of the business environment as illustrated in Figure 2.1.

Market opportunities can only be exploited within the capacity of the enterprise to support them. Two of the big questions for senior management are how to spend current enterprise resources for maximum business value, and how to grow those resources to align with future strategic portfolios.

Enterprise capacity is both a constraining factor and an enabling factor. As a constraining factor, what the enterprise should do is limited by what the enterprise can do in the near term and finally leads to what the enterprise will do. As a counter measure to the constraining factor, the enterprise needs to assure the alignment of not only resource supply, but also resource availability against the business demands for those resources. So enterprise capacity is a dynamic tool that can be adjusted as a deliverable from the planning exercises. Expanding or enhancing resources will reduce schedule contention between resources, but that is a business decision that arises during the fulfillment of the strategic plan.

As an enabling factor, resource managers collaborate with functional business managers and line of business (LOB) managers to creatively solve resource availability problems and enable the exploitation of new business opportunities. These collaborative efforts result in the commissioning, scope revision, rescheduling, postponement, and termination of projects, programs, and portfolios. This is the reality imposed upon the ACPF. We have no choice but to deal with it!

## Objectives, Strategies, and Tactics Model

The remaining parts of the business environment are contained in a system that I developed from business experiences, beginning in 1963 as a systems consultant at Texas Instruments. Figure 2.3 is a graphic illustration of the current Objectives, Strategies, and Tactics (OST) model. (It has gone through several revisions in the past 50 years.) The OST model has its roots in a product/service planning process developed and used by Texas Instruments in its Corporate Research and Engineering Division. I have taken those product planning processes and practices, and brought them into current standards and expectations, imbedding them in the ACPF. The Project Overview Statement (POS), discussed in Chapter 4, is a deliverable from that updating effort. Clearly, the ACPF is a game-changer for every project/program/portfolio manager and for enterprises transitioning to a project-based structure.

The OST model is a key component of the ACPF. The OST model is the hinge pin that connects the projects, programs, and portfolios of the enterprise to its strategic plan. Furthermore, it provides a basis for the decision model, which has the purpose of maintaining the alignment of the projects, programs, and portfolios to the strategic plan. The criterion that the ACPF recommends be used in that decision model is the expected business value that the projects will return to the enterprise.

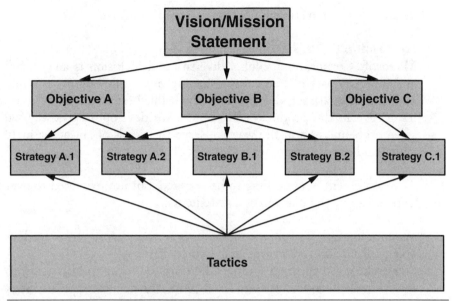

**Figure 2.3**    The Objectives, Strategies, and Tactics model. *Source:* Adapted from Wysocki, 2014a.

Recognize that there is risk attached to those expected values. The more complex and uncertain the project, the higher the risk of not finding a solution; or, if a solution is found, it may not deliver the expected business value. Complex projects are looking for acceptable solutions, and what will finally be delivered is conjecture tempered by risk. So is the difference between the delivered business value and the expected business value.

At each ACPF Project Performance Review, each active project is reviewed for performance against the plan, and will change as the senior managers adjust project investments to maximize expected business value. The project status can change. Project priorities might change. Projects could be judged as complete, terminated, or postponed, or have their schedules extended or reduced in scope. For an ACPF, this means using models that anticipate such changes and still deliver some business value at the completion of each iteration, cycle, or phase, regardless of the project's future.

## Vision and Mission Statements

At the highest level, the vision and mission statements embody the business strategy. Vision and mission can be statements about a desired end state for the enterprise. However, they will be more an end state to be pursued, than an end state to be achieved.

Here are a few vision statements that you may recognize:

- **Ford Motor:** One team. One plan. One goal.
- **Microsoft Corporation:** Global diversity and inclusion is an integral and inherent part of our culture, fueling our business growth while allowing us to attract, develop, and retain this best talent, to be more innovative in the products and services we develop, in the way we solve problems, and in the way we serve the needs of an increasingly global and diverse customer and partner base.

The vision statement is something to be pursued, but not expected to ever end. Here are a few popular mission statements:

- **Washington Gas:** To provide the best energy value: A superior product and quality service at a competitive price.
- **Star Trek:** Space, the final frontier. These are the voyages of the Starship *Enterprise*. Its five-year mission: To explore strange new worlds, to seek out new life and new civilizations, to boldly go where no man has gone before.

The mission statement is a high-level blueprint of success that acts as a guide to the enterprise as it pursues its vision through its OST plan.

---

**Case Study: Establishing a Workforce and Business Development Center**

The full case study is presented in Appendix B. The vision and mission statements for the WBDC in that case study are:

**Vision:** To implement a disruptive innovation for sustainable economic recovery.

**Mission:** To establish a self-supporting WBDC that integrates the learning environment, entrepreneur/business environments, and student/worker environments into a cohesive framework for career and professional development, new business formation, business process improvement, and business growth.

---

## Objectives

Objectives flow directly from the vision and mission statements. The enterprise will know how it stands with respect to its vision and mission, and how it should proceed toward closing the gap with its desired end state. They are expressed through the objectives statement. They are the first expression of operational level details of the enterprise. Objectives of the enterprise are likely to be multi-period, multi-year, or continuous statements designed to achieve an end state or condition.

Objectives might never be attainable (eliminating world hunger, for example), or they might be achievable over long periods of time (finding a cure for polio or a prevention for the common cold, for example). Any of these are good examples of objectives. The missing ingredient is how to get there. Strategies and their aligned tactics describe near-term progress toward that journey.

---

**Case Study: Establishing a Workforce and Business Development Center**

**Objective 1:** Support the entrepreneurial needs for new business formation.

**Objective 2:** Support business needs for process improvement and growth.

**Objective 3:** Support the career and professional development needs of students and workers.

**Objective 4:** Support the needs of WBDC-owned businesses.

**Objective 5:** Establish a Business Incubation Center as the integrating infrastructure for meeting the above needs.

---

These five objectives from the WBDC Case Study are high-level statements with multi-period implications to subordinate strategies and tactics. Objectives are generated by senior level executives as directives to the operational, functional, and LOB managers.

## Strategies

There will be many approaches to the realization of each objective. Each approach is called a strategy, which usually ranges over multiple planning time horizons. Strategies are developed by senior management during its strategic planning meetings. Operational, functional, and LOB managers will often be invited to submit strategies for consideration by senior management.

Take the example of an objective to find a cure for the common cold. Strategies might include investigating possible food additives, modifying the immune system prior to birth, or finding a drug that establishes a lifetime immunity to the cold. Many of these strategies require a more technical orientation than senior managers might possess, and will be offered by operational and functional managers with the appropriate expertise. Each strategy launches a portfolio of tactics to achieve the strategy, and hence the objective(s) to which it is aligned. An effective ACPF instantiation in an organization will include a process where anyone in the organization with an idea to share will be able to submit project ideas.

Each strategy has a Strategy Manager. They are responsible for managing their strategy until all projects, programs, and portfolios in their Strategy Portfolio are completed. The general responsibilities of a Strategy Manager include:

- Strategy Portfolio planning and management.
- Encouraging project idea submissions and evaluating them for inclusion.
- Monitoring Strategy Portfolio performance to a maximum delivered business value.
- Adjusting project plans to align with resource capacity and availability.
- Negotiating resource utilization between and among all Strategy Managers.

---

**Case Study: Establishing a Workforce and Business Development Center**

**Objective 1.** Support the entrepreneurial needs for new business formation.

Strategy 1.1: Design the Entrepreneurial process infrastructure.

Strategy 1.2: Design the process for investigating new business ideas.

Strategy 1.3: Design the process for conducting new business validation studies.

---

## Tactics

Tactics usually start out as a list of ideas submitted to a Strategy Manager for consideration as a single project, program, or portfolio. Ideas are evaluated for the contribution they can make to business value. The ideas are prioritized, combined into projects, and populate a program or portfolio under the Strategy Manager. For best results, a project should be completed within a budget cycle. Because of the complexities and uncertainties involved in complex projects, strategic planning is a continuous process within an ACPF instantiation. This is a departure from common conventions, but is part of every ACPF instantiation.

Many of my clients will include a high-level description of the approved tactics in their final Strategic Plan. These descriptions are the POS introduced in Chapter 3, and discussed in detail in Chapter 4.

> **Case Study: Establishing a Workforce and Business Development Center**
>
> **Objective 1.** Support the entrepreneurial needs for new business formation.
>    Strategy 1.1: Design the entrepreneurial process infrastructure.
>       Tactic 1.1.1: Create the Service Level Agreement.
>       Tactic 1.1.2: Create the Membership Application.

## THE PROJECT LANDSCAPE

In order to accurately apply the ACPF, we need a clear definition of what constitutes a project. The major shortcoming of most traditional definitions of a project is that they don't focus on the real purpose of a project—to deliver business value to the organization. They are focused on the triple constraints (scope, time, and cost). Many examples exist of projects that meet the triple constraints, but the client is not satisfied with the results. So, I offer a definition of an ACPF project that is clearly based on the reason for doing a project:

> An *ACPF project* is a sequence of finite
> dependent activities of which successful
> completion results in the delivery of business
> value, as estimated in the business case that
> was developed to validate the project.

In the face of the volatile and rapidly changing business environment, business managers have to make sense out of the project landscape. Not all projects are the same from the standpoints of complexity and uncertainty, and how they should be managed will differ in the face of that uncertainty and complexity.

Project management processes need an approach to get the project successfully through this maze. I like simple and intuitive models, so I have defined a project landscape around two characteristics: *goal* and *solution*. Every project must have a goal and a solution. You could use a number of metrics to quantify these characteristics, but the simplest and most intuitive will be two values: clear or not clear. Two values for each characteristic generate the four-quadrant matrix shown in Figure 2.4.

I don't know where the dividing line is between *clear* and *not clear*, but that is not important to this landscape. These values are conceptual, not quantifiable, and their interpretation is certainly more subjective than objective. A given project can exhibit various degrees of clarity with respect

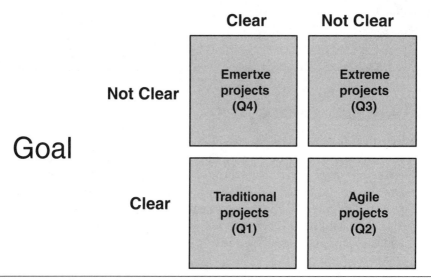

**Figure 2.4**   The complex project landscape.

to the goal and solution. The message in this conceptual and qualitative landscape is that the transition from quadrant to quadrant is continuous and fluid.

As an example, say that the project goal is to cure the common cold. Is this goal statement clear and complete? Not really. The word *cure* is the culprit. Cure could mean any one of the following:

• Prior to birth, the fetus is injected with a DNA-altering drug that prevents the person from ever getting a cold.
• As part of everyone's diet, they take a daily dose of the juice from a tree that grows only in certain altitudes in the Himalayas. This juice acts as a permanent barrier and prevents the onset of the common cold.
• Once a person has contracted a cold, they take a massive dose of tea made from a rare tree root found only in central China, and the cold will be completely cured within 12 hours.

So, what does *cure* really mean? As another example, consider this paraphrasing of a statement made by President John F. Kennedy during his

Special Message to Congress on urgent national needs on May 25, 1961: "By the end of the decade, we will have put a man on the moon and returned him safely to Earth." Is there any doubt in your mind that this goal statement is clear and complete? When the project is finished, will there be any doubt in your mind that this goal has or has not been achieved?

And, what about solution clarity? For example, how would the moon landing project goal be accomplished? I was fortunate to have worked on the propulsion part of that project and know for a fact that the engineers who were also working on that project did not have much of an idea of what type of a propulsion system would work. Whatever the solution would be, it was about as unclear as it could be. Our project was to find one. There were several possibilities being considered. My team was investigating an onboard nuclear reactor. The ACPF was still 30 years in the future; it could have been helpful.

Every project that ever existed or will exist falls into only one of the four quadrants of Figure 2.4 at any point in time. This landscape is not affected by external changes of any kind. It is a robust landscape that will remain in place, regardless. The quadrant in which the project lies will provide an initial guide to choosing a best fit PMLC model template and adapting its tools, templates, and processes to the specific characteristics of the project. As project work commences, and the goal and solution clarity changes, the project could change quadrants and perhaps the PMLC model template will then change as well. However, the project is always in just one quadrant. The decision to change the PMLC model template for a project already underway may be a big change and needs to be seriously considered. Costs, benefits, advantages, and disadvantages are associated with a mid-project change of the PMLC model template. (See Chapter 5 for further detail and advice.)

## WHAT IS A COMPLEX PROJECT?

Imbedded within the project landscape are projects whose characteristics require special approaches for their effective and successful management. These are the complex projects that populate Quadrants 2, 3, and 4. They are very different from one another as is the most effective approach to their management (see Chapter 5).

An intuitive picture of what constitutes a complex project is shown in the spider diagram in Figure 2.5. These nine dimensions describe the complex nature that underlies every complex project. Note also that complex projects are unique and can be very different from one another. That tells

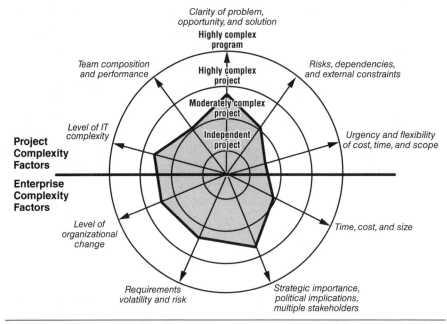

**Figure 2.5**   Dimensions of project complexity. *Source*: Adapted from Hass, 2009.

me that our project management approaches to these different projects will also be very different. The ACPF uniquely provides us with the decision model that will guide the client and project manager through this challenging management adventure.

## Characteristics of Complex Project Management

There are five specific characteristics to call to your attention because they relate directly to the kinds of project management approaches that will deliver business value when managing complex projects. They are:

- High speed
- High change
- Low cost
- Increasing complexity
- Increasing uncertainty

### *High Speed*

The faster products and services get to market, the greater will be the resulting value to the business. However, we are not going to trade speed for quality. Current competitors are watching and responding to unmet opportunities, and new competitors are waiting and watching to seize upon any opportunity that might give them a foothold or expansion in the market. Any weakness or delay in responding may just give them that advantage. The need to be fast translates into a need for the project management approach to not waste time—to rid itself, as much as possible, of spending time on non-value-added work. The ACPF is a lean framework that responds to the need for high speed.

*High speed* means the project management approach must be based on "lean principles." The ACPF is designed to eliminate all non-value-added work.

The window of opportunity for products is always narrowing and constantly moving. Organizations that can quickly respond to those opportunities are organizations that have found a way to reduce cycle times and eliminate non-value-added work as much as possible. Taking too long to roll out a new or revamped product can result in a missed business opportunity. Project managers must know how and when to introduce multiple release strategies and compress project schedules to help meet these requirements. Even more importantly, the project management approach must support these aggressive schedules. That means that these processes must protect the schedule by eliminating all non-value-added work. A business simply cannot afford to burden the project management processes with a lot of overhead activities that do not add value to the final deliverables, or that may compromise their effectiveness in the markets served.

Effective project management is not the product of a rigid or fixed set of steps and processes to be followed on every project. Rather, the choice of project management approach is based on having done due diligence on the project specifics and defined an adaptive approach that makes business sense.

## High Change

High change requires PMLC models that not only accommodate change but *embrace* change. Moving from the unclear to the clear state with respect to solutions and goals flows from PMLC model templates, where learning and discovery takes place iteratively. Traditional project management PMLC models are change intolerant. The nature of complexity and uncertainty is more the cause of high change than is any ignorance on the part of the client. The business world is dynamic. It does not stand still just because you are managing a project. The best fit project management approach must recognize the realities of frequent change, accommodate it, and embrace it. In the complex project world, solutions and goals move from unclear to clear as a result of learning and discovery. The extent to which change is expected will affect the choice of a best fit PMLC model template.

---

*High change* means the project management approach must include a "just-in-time" planning approach:

- Planning for future events that may not occur is a waste of time.
- The ACPF processes change requests only at the completion of a cycle using a Bundled Change Request Process.

---

Change is constant! I hope that does not come as a surprise. Change is always with you and seems to be happening at an increasing rate. Every day you face new challenges and the need to improve yesterday's practices. For experienced project managers, as well as "wannabe" project managers, the road to breakthrough performance is paved with uncertainty and the need to be courageous, creative, and flexible. If you simply rely on a routine application of someone else's methodology, you are sure to fall short of the mark. In the pages that follow, I have not been afraid to step outside of the box and outside of my comfort zone. Nowhere is there more of a need for change and adaptation than in the approaches we take to managing complex projects.

## Low Cost

With the reduction in management layers and the emergence of "flat" structures (a common practice in many organizations), the professional staff needs to find ways to work smarter, not harder. Project management includes a number of tools and techniques that help professionals manage increased workloads. Your staff needs to have more room to do their work in the most productive ways possible. Burdening them with overhead activities for which they see little value is a sure way to failure.

---

*Low cost* means the project management approach must minimize "non-value-added work." These approaches must be lean.

---

### Increasing Complexity

All of the simple projects have been done. They have left a rich heritage of experiences, and the ACPF records those for use in future simple projects. Those projects that remain are getting more complex with each passing day. At the same time that problems are getting more complex, they are getting more critical to the success of the enterprise. They must be solved. We do not have a choice. They must be managed, and we must have an effective way of managing them. The ACPF shows you how to create commonsense project management approaches by adapting a vetted set of tools, templates, and processes to even the most complex of projects.

### Increasing Uncertainty

With increasing levels of complexity come increasing levels of uncertainty. The two are inseparable. Adapting project management approaches to handle uncertainty means that the approaches must not only accommodate change, but also embrace it and become more effective as a result of it. Change is what will lead the team and the client to a state of certainty with respect to a viable solution to its complex problems. In other words, we must have project management approaches that expect change and benefit from it. The ACPF shows you how to create commonsense project management approaches by adapting a vetted set of tools, templates, and processes to even the most uncertain of projects.

> *Increasing levels of complexity and uncertainty* mean the project management approaches must allow for creativity, flexibility, and adaptability on the part of the complex project team.

## WHAT IS A COMPLEX PROJECT TEAM?

A complex project team bears little resemblance to a traditional project team. The traditional project team consists of the development team members and a project manager. Such a team will not be appropriate for a complex project. Figure 2.6 identifies the members of a typical complex project team.

The first thing to note in Figure 2.6 is the degree to which the members are interlinked. They depend on an open and honest working relationship among all of their members. The business systems engineer and the business

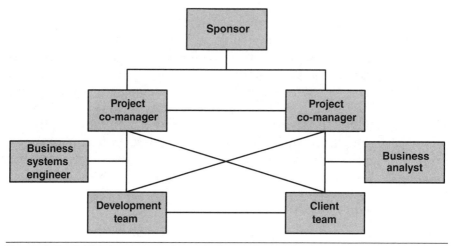

**Figure 2.6**   A high-level view of a typical complex project team.

analyst are consultants to the team. Both of them will have familiarity with the parts of the business that affect or are affected by the project.

The development team needs no further explanation, but the client team can be more complex than one might first envision. The client team can be from a single business unit where the activities of those teams would be quite straightforward. Where multiple business units are involved in the same project, the situation can become more complex from a management standpoint. The complexity begins at the requirements elicitation phase and continues to the end of the development efforts. Competing and contradictory requirements will often arise. In extreme cases, multiple solutions might be needed to resolve contradictory requirements. See Chapter 4 for suggestions on how to handle these conflicting situations.

Whenever the "complex project team" is mentioned, it is the team shown in Figure 2.6 that is being referenced.

## WHAT IS A COMPLEX PROJECT MANAGER?

A CPM comes in two flavors: One is client-facing; the other is development-facing. The real difference, though, is that they always come in pairs. Complex projects are always managed by co-managers who share responsibility and authority. Insist on the co-manager model in every complex project!

**A *complex project manager* is a chef, not a cook.**

I introduced the metaphor "Be a chef, not a cook!" in Chapter 1. For the sake of keeping this discussion self-contained, let me briefly explain how the metaphor applies to complex project management. A cook is trained and experienced to follow recipes developed by someone else. A chef is that someone else. If the cook is missing an ingredient, they may be helpless as far as their ability to complete their assigned task. They will either cobble something together that may work but probably won't, or they default on their assignment all together. On the other hand, if a chef is missing an ingredient, they search the pantry for a substitute ingredient to complete their assigned task with minimal or no disruption. Another way of looking at the difference is that the cook follows a defined process, while a chef can call on their creative skills and extensive portfolio of tools, templates, and processes whenever the situation calls for it.

Clearly, a CPM must be a "chef" to effectively manage a complex project. If you are a "cook," you need to become a chef to protect your career. In general, a competent CPM is a knowledge worker who can be either a generalist or a specialist. The co-manager of the development team will be a generalist while the co-manager of the client team will be a specialist. The need for special skills should be based on project characteristics and provided by team members who are the specialists. While there are a number of disciplines that an individual CPM might possess, I believe that every CPM must possess some degree of skill, capability, and experience in all five specific disciplines. Those disciplines are the core disciplines of a CPM. They are:

- Project Management (PM)
- Business Analysis (BA)
- Business Process Management (BPM)
- Systems Engineering (SE)
- Information Technology (IT)

Figure 2.7 illustrates these five dimensions with an example profile.

The primary tactical and operational needs of the enterprise are couched in these five disciplines. Each discipline is currently present in varying skill levels in every CPM, depending on their work history and experiences. Figure 2.7 is the landscape of the CPM position family across the five disciplines with an example given by the polygon. The professional depicted by the polygon is strongest in PM, IT, and SE, with lesser skills in BA and BPM. There will be projects for which this particular CPM profile will be a good fit to the project's needs. Based on this profile, process design and process improvement projects are two types of projects for which this CPM is particularly well-suited.

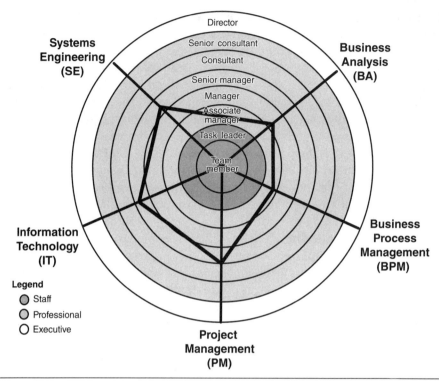

**Figure 2.7**   CPM position family landscape with an example profile

## Where Do Complex Project Managers Come From?

Right now, most CPMs are accidents of their experience rather than the product of a planned professional development program. That is unacceptable in an ACPF environment. To be really effective in managing complex projects, the organization will have to reverse that situation. A cadre of CPMs must be developed to align with current and future project staffing needs. That means having a professional development program that anticipates future demands, and counsels and prepares CPMs to be ready to meet that demand as it materializes. Future demand is a changing target, and so is the profile of the CPM cadre at any point in time. Maintaining the alignment of supply and demand over time is a major challenge.

## How Should We Develop Complex Project Managers?

The Project Support Office (PSO) is the best home for professional development of the CPM position family. The PSO occupies the best vantage point for:

- Understanding the skill and competency demands of current and future projects.
- Knowing the skill and competency profile of current and future project managers and project team members at any point in time.
- Knowing the availability of skilled project professionals now and into the future.
- Analyzing the supply of skills and competencies, as compared to the demand for skills and competencies.
- Knowing the skill and competency gaps, and how to reduce them with training and experience acquisition.

Only the most sophisticated Human Resource Management System (HRMS) or Human Resource Information Systems (HRIS) can sufficiently meet the information needs that drive the management and staffing needs of the complex project portfolio. Comparing and contrasting the commercially available HRMS and HRIS tools are beyond the scope of this book.

## THE ACPF SCOPE TRIANGLE

The ACPF Scope Triangle is the heart of the business environment, as Figure 2.1 shows. You may have heard of the term *Iron Triangle*. It refers to the relationship between scope, time, and cost. These three parameters form the vertices of a triangle and are an interdependent set. If any one of them changes, at least one of the other parameters must also change in order to restore balance to the project. That is all well and good, but in the complex project landscape there is more to explain. Despite their differences, every complex project is constrained by the same parameters:

- Scope
- Time
- Cost
- Quality
- Resource availability
- Risk

Except for risk, these constraints form an interdependent set—a change in one parameter can require a change in one or more of the other parameters in order to restore the equilibrium of the project. In this context, the set of five parameters, plus risk, form a system that must remain in balance for the project to be in balance. Figure 2.8 illustrates this system. Because they

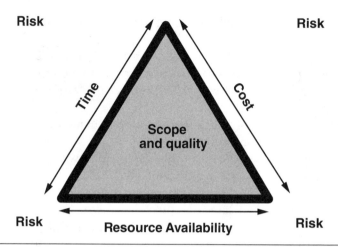

**Figure 2.8**　The ACPF Scope Triangle.

are so important to the success or failure of the project, each parameter is discussed individually in this section.

## Scope

*Scope* is a statement that defines the boundaries of the project. Scope tells not only what will be done, but also what will not be done. In the information systems industry, scope is often referred to as a *functional specification*. In the engineering profession, it is generally called a *statement of work*. Scope may also be referred to as a *document of understanding, scoping statement, project initiation document,* or *project request form*. Whatever its name, this document is the foundation for all project work to follow. It is critical that the scope be correct. Chapter 4 describes the ACPF POS document.

> In a complex project, scope is variable.

If the solution is not clearly defined, scope is only a desired end state, and is therefore variable. Scope can increase as the result of learning and discovery, and client requests. Scope can also decrease as a result of learning and discovery that eliminates certain functions and features of the original end state definition.

Beginning a project on the right foot is important, and so is staying on the right foot. It is no secret that a project's scope can change. You do not know how or when, but it will change. Detecting that change, and deciding how to accommodate it in the project plan, are major challenges for the CPMs.

## Time

The client specifies a time frame or deadline date within which the project must be completed. To a certain extent, cost and time are inversely related to one another. The time a project takes to be completed can be reduced, but costs increase as a result.

*Time* is an interesting resource. It can't be inventoried. It is consumed, whether you use it or not. The objective for the project manager is to use the future time allotted to the project in the most effective and productive ways possible. Future time (time that has not yet occurred) can be a resource to be traded within a project or across projects. Once a project has begun, the prime resource available to the project manager to keep the project on schedule or get it back on schedule is time. A good project manager realizes this, and protects the future time resource jealously.

## Cost

The dollar cost of doing the project is another variable that defines the project. It is best thought of as the budget that has been approved by the sponsor to fund the project. This is particularly important for projects that create deliverables that are sold either commercially or to an external customer.

*Cost* is a major consideration throughout every PMLC model template. The first consideration occurs at an early and informal stage in the life of a project. The client can simply offer a figure about equal to what he or she had in mind for the project. Depending on how much thought the client put into it, the number could be fairly close to or wide of the actual cost for the project. Consultants often encounter situations in which the client is willing to spend only a certain amount for the work. In these situations, you do what you can with what you have. In more formal situations, the project manager prepares a proposal for the projected work. That proposal includes an estimate (perhaps even a quote) of the total cost of the project. Even if a preliminary figure has been supplied by the project manager, the proposal allows the client to base his or her go/no-go decision on these estimates.

---

**Advice**

- If the client cuts the budget, you cut the scope.
- If the client adds scope, you require more budget and/or time.

## Quality

The following two types of *quality* are part of every project:

- **Product quality**—The quality of the deliverable from the project. As used here, "product" includes tangible artifacts like hardware and software, as well as business services or processes. Think of quality as being "suitable for use."
- **Process quality**—The quality of the project management process itself. The focus is on how well the project management process works, how it can be improved, and how the team uses it.

## Resource Availability

*Resources* are finite assets such as people, equipment, physical facilities, or inventory that have limited availabilities; they can also be scheduled or leased from an outside party. Some resources are fixed; others are variable only in the long term. In any case, resources are central to the scheduling of project activities and the orderly completion of the project.

For development projects, people are the major resource. Another valuable resource for systems projects is the availability of computer processing time (mostly for testing purposes), which can present significant problems to the project manager with regard to project scheduling.

## Risk

*Risk* is not an integral part of the Scope Triangle, but it is always present and spans all parts of the project both external as well as internal. Therefore, risk does affect the management of the other five constraints. In a complex project, risk can be very high. In any instantiation of an ACPF project management model, a strong risk management program and someone to manage it will be critical.

## Envisioning the ACPF Scope Triangle as a System in Balance

Projects are dynamic systems that must be kept in equilibrium. Not an easy task, as you shall see!

The area inside the triangle in Figure 2.8 represents the scope and quality of the project. Lines representing time, cost, and resource availability bound scope and quality.

The project plan will have identified the time, cost, and resource availability needed to deliver the scope and quality of a project. In other words, the project is in equilibrium at the completion of the project planning session and approval of the commitment of resources and dollars to the project. That will not last too long, however. Change is waiting around the corner.

The ACPF Scope Triangle offers a number of insights into the changes that can occur in the life of the project. For example, the triangle represents a system in balance before any project work has been done. The sides are just long enough to encompass the area generated by the scope and quality statements. Not long after work begins, something is sure to change. Perhaps the client calls with a request to add an additional feature that was not envisioned during the planning sessions. Perhaps the market opportunities have changed, and it is necessary to reschedule the deliverables to an earlier date. Or, a key team member leaves the company and is difficult to replace. Any one of these changes throws the system out of balance.

In a complex project, either the goal or the solution, or both, cannot be known until the project is nearly complete. That presents some interesting management challenges to the client and the project manager. Those challenges revolve around the business value delivered by the final solution and the final goal.

The project manager controls resource utilization and work schedules. Management controls cost and resource level. The client controls scope, quality, and delivery dates. Scope, quality, and delivery dates suggest a hierarchy for the project manager as solutions to accommodate the changes are sought.

## Applying the ACPF Scope Triangle

There are only a few graphics that I want you to burn into your brain because of their value throughout the entire complex project life cycle. The ACPF Scope Triangle in Figure 2.8 is one such graphic. It will have at least two major applications: as a problem resolution strategy, and as a reference for the Project Impact Statement (place this in your ACPF/kit), which is created as part of the scope change process.

### *Problem Resolution Strategy*

The ACPF Scope Triangle enables you to ask the question, "Who owns what?" The answer will give you an escalation pathway from project team, to resource manager, to client, to sponsor. The client and senior management own time, budget, and resources. The project team owns how time, budget, and resources are used. Within the policies and practices of the enterprise, any of these may be moved within the project to resolve problems that have arisen. In solving a problem, the project manager should try to find a solution within the constraints of how the time, budget, and resources are used.

The next step in the resolution strategy would be for the project manager to appeal to the resource managers for problem resolution. The resource manager owns who gets assigned to a project, as well as any changes to that assignment that may arise.

The final step in the problem resolution strategy is to appeal to the client and perhaps to the sponsor for additional resources. They control the amount of time and money that has been allocated to the project. Finally, they control the scope of the project. Whenever the project manager appeals to the client, it will be to get an increase in time or budget, or some relief from the scope by way of scope reduction.

### Scope Change Impact Analysis

Scope is variable in the complex project landscape. What starts out as the scope of a complex project is usually not the final scope that is delivered. The second major application of the ACPF Scope Triangle is as an aid in the preparation of the Project Impact Statement. This is a statement of the alternative ways of accommodating a particular scope change request of the client. The alternatives are identified by reviewing the ACPF Scope Triangle and proceeding in much the same way as a problem resolution strategy.

A common application of the prioritized ACPF Scope Triangle variables occurs whenever a change request is made. The analysis of the change request is documented in a Project Impact Statement. If the change is to be approved, there will be several alternatives as to how that change can be accommodated. Those alternatives are prioritized using the matrix format, given in Figure 2.9.

## Business Challenges in a Complex and Uncertain Global Climate

As pointed out in the IBM CEO Report (IBM, 2010), and cited in Chapter 1, the business world is a complex and uncertain world. Complexity and uncertainty are trending upward. To be successful, the enterprise must:

- Embody creative leadership.
- Reinvent customer relationships.
- Build operational dexterity.

| Priority / Variable | Critical (1) | (2) | (3) | (4) | Flexible (5) |
|---|---|---|---|---|---|
| Scope | | | | X | |
| Quality | | | X | | |
| Time | X | | | | |
| Cost | | | | | X |
| Resource Availability | | X | | | |

**Figure 2.9**  Prioritizing ACPF Scope Triangle.

## Embody Creative Leadership

Creativity is the key to successfully capitalizing on complexity and uncertainty. It requires an enterprise culture and infrastructure that encourages creativity and does not erect procedural and unnecessary barriers to its realization. The courage may involve a step into the unknown—a disruptive innovation, perhaps. So, in addition to creativity, the team will need a good dose of courage. All of this will be embodied into Step 1 of the ACPF: Develop the Business Case (discussed in Chapter 4).

## Reinvent Customer Relationships

In the complex project space, no one has a corner on the knowledge market. It would be a mistake to exclude anyone who might have something to contribute. Err on the side of inclusion rather than exclusion. The critical members of the complex project team will sort themselves out through a natural selection process. All subject matter experts (SMEs) need to be part of the complex project team. The complex project team includes developers, clients, and customers at certain times in the Complex Project Set-up Phase. The voice of the customer will not be heard by the complex project team unless they are somehow part of the complex project team. The continual use of focus groups is one way to meet this requirement.

## Build Operational Dexterity

In the complex project space, every business process is a work in progress. Again, no one is a complete SME, but a team can collectively be that SME.

## PUTTING IT ALL TOGETHER

It should be clear that when we talk about complex projects and complex project management, we are in a rarefied landscape where success and effectiveness of our management models is far from satisfactory. The *Chaos Manifesto Report* (The Standish Group, 2013) provides documented results that stand as testimony to high project failure rates. The reported performance is unacceptable and must stop! The ACPF fills that need.

But the ACPF does not come for free. It is not a silver bullet. It speaks of a robust environment that is designed to be customized to the culture and needs of your organization. Your instantiation of the ACPF will be unique to your organization. It is my expectation that this book will provide the encouragement and impetus for making a serious effort at building that infrastructure. Each organization is different, and so each design, development, and implementation plan will be different. My advice is to commission a task force and get busy. Delays are costly!

# 3

## OVERVIEW OF THE ADAPTIVE COMPLEX PROJECT FRAMEWORK

*It is a mistake to look too far ahead. Only one link of the chain of destiny can be handled at a time.*
—Winston Churchill, UK Prime Minister

*There is no data on the future.*
—Laurel Cutler, Vice Chairman, FCB/Leber Katz Partners

### CHAPTER LEARNING OBJECTIVES

This chapter will provide readers the knowledge or ability to:

- Understand the Ideation, Set-up, and Execution Phases of the Adaptive Complex Project Framework (ACPF).
- Understand the robustness and adaptability of the ACPF.
- Understand the role of the ACPF/kit and its contents.
- Explain the twelve steps of ACPF process flow.
- Gain a working knowledge of the Linear, Incremental, Iterative, Adaptive, and Extreme Project Management Life Cycle (PMLC) model types that populate the complex project landscape.
- Understand the PMLC model templates as they relate to the five types of PMLC models.

- Gain familiarity with the decision process for changing PMLC model templates during complex project execution.
- Know how to use the ACPF for the Proof of Concept, revision of the version plan, and embed the ACPF in traditional project management (TPM).

If you are not convinced that we have a desperate business situation, you are not paying attention. We have a serious problem, and it is time to learn and discover how to create a serious solution!

The ACPF is a robust project management environment that thrives on business challenges and creativity of the team, with the change process as the driver to solution discovery and the courage of conviction. It embraces all project management methodologies, from the simplest linear models (like Waterfall) to the most complex agile models (like Scrum). Included in the ACPF is a:

- Customized brainstorming process that begins with an idea and concludes with a project to be proposed.
- Decision model and process for choosing and continuously adapting the best fit project management approach, tailored to the specific characteristics of the project and the changing environment in which the project is executed.
- Portfolio of specific PMLC model templates to be chosen and customized for the project situation.
- Portfolio of vetted tools, templates, and processes for building and continuously adapting the chosen PMLC model template to fit the changing project situation.

In this sense, the ACPF is the closest we can practically get to a silver bullet. So, in addition to providing a model for managing complex projects using RUP, Scrum, and several others, the ACPF is a structure that includes all project management methodologies as special cases. For that reason, the ACPF stands alone among complex project management processes and practices.

The full realization of the ACPF is itself an ongoing agile project. The instantiation documented here is a significant step forward in that journey. My immediate goal is to have the ACPF become a major addition to your portfolio of tools, templates, and processes and to be implemented. Feedback from practice is essential as ACPF process improvement will be a continuous effort. So, I view the ACPF as a work in process. It will get better as those who use it provide feedback on their experiences. I would appreciate any feedback from your experiences. My goal is ACPF implementation and improvement.

In this chapter, we take a high-level tour through the three phases of the ACPF. The details of each phase are presented in Chapters 4, 5, and 6.

## BACKGROUND OF THE ADAPTIVE COMPLEX PROJECT FRAMEWORK

In the early 1990s, before I introduced the initial version of the ACPF, I had the occasion to be concurrently working on two independent client engagements. One was a new product design project; the other was a process improvement project. The only thing that these two projects had in common was that neither client could define the final solution needed to achieve their clearly stated goals. The goals of each project were perfectly clear, but not how to achieve those goals (a.k.a., the solutions). Today, we would correctly label these projects as "Quadrant 2" complex projects.

Clearly, some type of agile approach was needed for both of them. However, neither of these projects were exclusively software development projects, and at that time, all of the existing agile approaches were designed for software development projects. Some project managers would adapt their software development processes to fit. The results were mixed, and the deliverables were generally compromised. I felt compelled to develop a robust management approach that worked for both of these non-software development projects.

That situation got me to start thinking about the fact that we define projects as unique and finite experiences that will never be repeated under the same circumstances. That statement is obviously true. But what is not so obvious is, why then isn't the best project management approach to these unique projects also unique? We do not live in a "one-size-fits-all" project management environment. I don't think we ever really did. Some organizations attempted to dictate the use of a single methodology only to fail miserably. They learned a painful and expensive lesson.

What came out of those two 1990 engagements was surprising, since the two projects started out looking like they could use the same project management approach, but in fact, went in entirely different project management directions. That got me started on the journey that eventually led to the development of the ACPF in 1994, and, after 20 years of experience with it, to the development of the second generation of the ACPF. This book reports the second generation and the status of my continuing journey.

## What Does the ACPF Contain?

The ACPF contains all of the ingredients you will need to create a "recipe" for delivering a successful complex project. The portfolio of ingredients consists of vetted tools, templates, and processes. We will have occasion to refer to it often and will call it the *ACPF/kit*.

Every ACPF project:

- Begins with the statement of an unsolved business problem/opportunity.
- Builds a business case to validate investment in the project.
- Gathers the high-level requirements of an acceptable solution.
- Chooses a best fit PMLC model template.
- Assesses the characteristics of the business problem/opportunity.
- Assesses the impact of the internal and external situation.
- Adapts the chosen PMLC model template to align with the situation.
- Executes the project.
- Maintains alignment of the adapted PMLC model template to the changing nature of the project until the project is complete.

---

**Contents of the ACPF/kit**

The *ACPF/kit* is a portfolio of vetted tools, templates and processes that an organization will use to create and maintain a PMLC model. These are templates for the successful management of a specific project. An ACPF/kit might contain:

- Bodies of knowledge (PMBOK, Prince2, Microsoft Solutions Framework)
- A specific portfolio of PMLC model templates (Scrum, Feature-driven development, Rational Unified Process)
- Tools, templates, and processes
- Customized reports (Project Overview Statement, Project Proposal, Earned Value Analysis, Milestone Trend Charts, Burn Down Charts)
- Business process models
- A process improvement program
- A professional development program
- Problem solving models
- Decision-making processes
- A RASCI matrix
- Whatever else is needed by the organization

---

First, it is important to remember that the ACPF is not a methodology. If you are like a cook and need someone to hand you a recipe in order to manage your project, the ACPF is not for you because it does not contain any recipes and are no one is going to tell you what to do. However, if you are like a chef and are prepared to build a recipe for the best fit approach to managing your project, then the ACPF is the best choice for you. In fact, at this writing, the ACPF is the only documented choice you have.

The ACPF includes the ACPF/kit, in which the contents will be familiar to most project managers. The inventory of an organization's ACPF/kit will be unique to the needs of each organization. Your complex project teams will utilize this ACPF/kit to define, analyze, plan, and continuously adapt the best fit PMLC model template to a specific project. This effort continues across the entire project life span. In order to meet the needs of the chef, the ACPF must embrace all project management process templates with a rationale for selecting and adapting from among them to build the best fit approach. And, the ACPF does that quite effectively. As the collection of project management processes increases, so does the breadth and depth of your ACPF/kit. For each organization, the further development of their ACPF/kit is a process improvement project. It will never be finished. Like a fine Bordeaux wine, your ACPF environment will only improve with age.

## ACPF Process Flow Diagram

If you think of the ACPF as a decision model whose purpose is to design a project management model in addition to executing that project management model, you will have a good start on understanding the ACPF and how it can revolutionize all your approaches to complex project management. My beginning assumption is that projects are unique, and so is the best way to manage them. There are no recipes, but only project management experts who can design recipes for these unique and constantly changing projects. These are the "chefs" of ACPF project management. ACPF does not accommodate those who can only follow a recipe, i.e., the "cooks." Effective complex project management is not accomplished by following a predefined recipe. Effective complex project management can only come from first having designed the project management approach for a specific project, and then following it with the assumption that it will probably change before the project is complete. But that is the nature of an ACPF guided project! So, an ACPF project manager must be a creative and courageous leader, and certainly not a follower.

The ACPF consists of three dependent phases: Project Ideation (Steps 1-3), Project Set-up (Steps 4-7), and Project Execution (Steps 8-12). Figure 3.1 illustrates these three phases and their 12 Steps, and the feedback relationship that links Step 11 in the Project Execution Phase to Step 5 in the Project Set-up Phase.

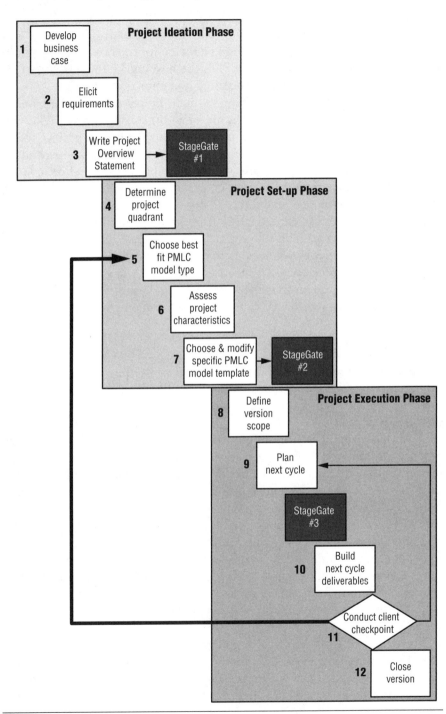

**Figure 3.1** The ACPF process flow diagram

- The **Project Ideation Phase** begins the ACPF with an untested idea to solve a recognized problem or take advantage of an untapped business opportunity, and ends with a brief explanation of a project to be proposed. StageGate #1 is received at the approval of the Project Overview Statement (POS) and the granting of the authority to begin the Project Set-up Phase.
- The **Project Set-up Phase** is where the decision is made as to what is the best fit project management methodology and how it needs to be adapted to be the best fit approach for the specific project at hand. StageGate #2 is received at the approval of the modified PMLC model and the granting of the authority to begin the Project Execution Phase.
- The **Project Execution Phase** is where the project is executed using the best fit approach that was defined during the Project Set-up Phase, and contains a feedback loop to maintain that alignment over the project life span. StageGate #3 is received when the High-level Project Plan is approved and the budget authorized to launch the project.

The ACPF consists of three dependent StageGates:

- **StageGate #1:** The deliverable from the Project Ideation Phase is the POS. One purpose of the POS is to gain sponsor approval to continue to the Project Set-up Phase. Minimal resources will be required to complete the Project Set-up Phase. That means that the business case has demonstrated the validity of the project from the perspective of the likely business value that will be delivered from a successful project.
- **StageGate #2:** The approval granted in StageGate #2 is for the feasibility of the PMLC and the granting of resources to complete the project plan. It is not approval to do the project. That comes later.
- **StageGate #3:** StageGate #3 approval is the last approval prior to executing the project plan for TPM projects or the next cycle plan for a complex project.

Each StageGate is a milestone event in the project life span and presents an opportunity for review by senior management, sponsor, and client.

## Project Ideation Phase

A simple and intuitive process must be in place so that anyone in the enterprise with an idea for generating business value will be encouraged to come forward with their idea without any prejudging and with minimal documentation.

## Step 1: Develop a Business Case

Driven by the sponsor, with the participation of the client and perhaps the project manager, a business case is developed and documented. The process to develop a business case consists of the following:

- Define the problem or untapped opportunity.
- Identify alternative solutions.
- Gather data relevant to each alternative solution.
- Analyze, prioritize, and choose an alternative.
- Document the chosen alternative.

There is nothing new here. Every ACPF project is initiated by a business case. It establishes the what, why, and business value of a project. To do that, it will contain at least the above actions and may be further customized to align with specific enterprise processes and practices. A simple model for developing the business case is discussed in Chapter 4.

## Step 2: Elicit Requirements

In an ACPF project, elicitation of requirements is a two-part effort. The first part gathers a high-level list of the necessary and sufficient requirements that an acceptable solution must meet. This list is often documented in the POS in the Ideation Phase, Step 3: Write the POS. The second part of the Elicit Requirements step is found in the ACPF Execute Phase, Step 8: Define the Version Scope. In Step 8, the high-level requirements are decomposed to provide a better understanding of the functions and features that define them. This is the requirements breakdown structure (RBS), which describes what must be done, but not how. The RBS is then further decomposed into the work breakdown structure (WBS). The WBS defines how the deliverables will be built. The RBS and WBS are developed iteratively over the cycles of an ACPF project.

For simpler situations, a conditions of satisfaction (COS) can be used for the first part. For more complex situations, one of the many approaches to requirements elicitation can be used. The COS and a selected list of elicitation processes are discussed in Chapter 4.

## Step 3: Write a Project Overview Statement

This is a five-part, *one-page* document that includes:

- Statement of business problem or opportunity
- Project goal
- Project objectives or high-level solution requirements
- Quantitative business value and success criteria metrics
- Risks, assumptions, obstacles.

The POS is written in the language of the business, so that anyone in the organization who has the occasion to read it will understand it.

## Project Set-up Phase

The POS is an input to the process that decides whether the project justifies further investigation. If it does, the authorization and resources are allocated by the sponsor for project planning. With the POS as input, the remaining Steps for the Project Set-up Phase consist of classifying the project; choosing the best fit project type from among the Linear, Incremental, Iterative, Adaptive, and Extreme types; within the chosen type, a specific PMLC model template is chosen and adapted to fit the project characteristics and the internal/external environments.

The Project Set-up Phase consists of four steps. This is radically different than the approach used in many organizations. In fact, it may happen without any conscious effort. Their portfolio of project management methodologies is limited to just a few choices, and Set-up happens with little analysis and ceremony.

---

**Warning**

Standard Waterfall and Scrum are the only two project management methodologies in many organization's PMLC model template portfolios. For the ACPF to be effective, this is too constraining.

---

### Step 4: Classify the Project

Based on the initial understanding of the goal and solution, the project is classified into the appropriate quadrant of the four-quadrant project landscape shown in Figure 3.2. Further explanation of these four project quadrants is given in Chapter 5.

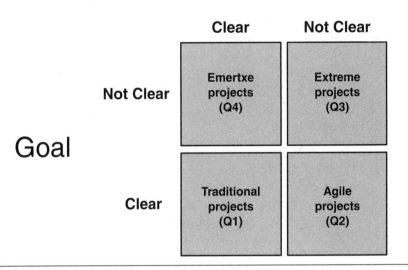

**Figure 3.2**   The project landscape

### Step 5: Choose the Best Fit PMLC Model Template

There are several choices of specific PMLC model templates chosen from among Linear, Incremental, Iterative, Adaptive, or Extreme types (see Figure 3.3). These five project management types are further defined in Chapter 5. Each enterprise will have its own PMLC model portfolio for each of these five project management types. That will include specific PMLC model templates like Waterfall, Scrum, and others (see Figure 3.4). The larger and more complex the organization, the richer their PMLC model template portfolio will be.

With the exception of home grown models, some subset of the 12 specific PMLC model templates shown in the right-most panel of Figure 3.4 will be the portfolio of models in use in most organizations. The contents of this portfolio should be carefully chosen and built. The specific PMLC model templates will have to cover a potentially wide range of project types.

Once the portfolio of PMLC model templates is chosen, the next task for the organization is to build the skilled cadre of project managers and developers that will be able to utilize their portfolio of PMLC model templates. This is not only a matter of delivering training, but also the scheduling of that training and the participants to be trained. This has to be aligned with

## Solution

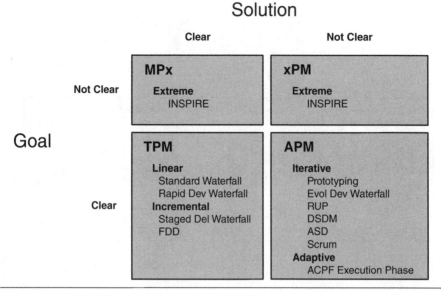

**Figure 3.3**    Five project management categories mapped into the four quadrant project landscape

the need for complex project managers and their development team members: How many will be needed, and when will they be needed? That puts the human resource managers in the position of having to forecast needs by skills and competencies. Do not underestimate the challenges they will face. That is a major effort and requires a career and professional development program that aligns with the forecasted portfolio of project types that will be encountered by the organization. See Chapter 8 for a discussion of how this program might be defined. I will return to Figure 3.4 in Chapter 5, with a detailed discussion of Steps 4 and 5.

### Step 6: Assess Project Characteristics

There are several variables that can impact how the chosen PMLC model template is adapted for use. In addition to the specific characteristics of the project, the internal business environment and the external marketing environment are included, and their impact on the chosen PMLC model template determined. See Chapter 5 for more details on this impact.

### Step 7: Modify PMLC Model Template

Projects are dynamic. They can change for a variety of reasons, including changes in business conditions and priorities, as well as other internal and

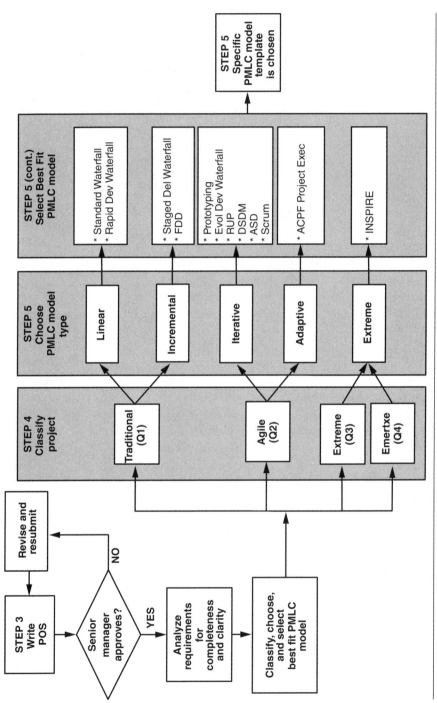

**Figure 3.4**    Specific PMLC model templates mapped into the project management categories

external environmental factors listed in the details of Step 6 as discussed in Chapter 5. That translates into a need to continuously review the chosen PMLC model template for adaptations, and even for reconsideration. For example, at some point in an iteration during a Scrum project, the client says: "Aha, now I see what the complete solution will look like!" and the project manager replies, "And I know how we can build that solution." Does that mean that Scrum should be abandoned in favor of a Staged Delivery Waterfall model, for example? That question is difficult to answer because there are so many moving parts to consider. For example, some of the more obvious implications are:

- Changes to resource requirements and development team membership
- Schedule changes due to resource availabilities
- Cost of abandonment of Scrum and replacement by a Staged Delivery Waterfall model
- Budget implications

These added costs need to be balanced against the benefits of such a change, which could include:

- Pricing changes to products/services
- Sales and marketing implications to product/service rollout dates
- Cost avoidance implications

Revise the management model(s) accordingly and prepare a business proposal that will increase revenues, avoid costs or improve service, and evaluate the business proposal-based specific quantitative metrics.

## Project Execution Phase

At this point, reflect on your current comfort level with project execution using the ACPF. For example:

- Do you know how your project aligns with the strategic plan, especially its priority?
- Do you know how well your adapted PMLC model template fits the project, and where potential problems and obstacles might arise?
- Is your approach a lean approach, based on just-in-time planning?
- Have you made a good start on the risk mitigation plan and appointed a team member to manage it?

A specific PMLC model template has been chosen and modified, and it is time to start project work. At this point in the ACPF process flow, the initial recipe is complete and it is time to deliver.

The Project Execution Phase consists of five steps that will be familiar to most project managers. The only new feature that you will encounter in Project Execution, compared to traditional models, is the feedback loop from Step 11: Client Checkpoint, to Step 5: Choose the Best Fit PMLC model template. This feedback loop is unique to the ACPF. Plus, it contributes to the lean principles that the ACPF protects. Taken together, these two steps and their history track the status of the goal and solution convergence to clarity and completeness. Armed with that information, the project team is prepared for Step 10.

### *Step 8: Define Version Scope*

The POS, including the project objectives, is a high-level description of what this ACPF version is all about. In anticipation of possible future projects that might extend the delivered business value, I call this a "Version." The Version scope includes some preliminary planning activities like cycle lengths, number of cycles, and cycle objective statements to help the sponsor and the client, which are related to the project.

### *Step 9: Plan the Next Cycle*

The Version Scope statement is the basis for identifying cycles of learning, discovery, and deployment. In the simple case where the project is a traditional project, there will only be one cycle in this project. In more complex projects, there will be any number of cycles including an unspecified number of cycles. Across all project types, cycle length can vary from a few hours (prototyping) to several months (Staged Delivery Waterfall). Goal and solution clarity are the major factors in determining cycle length.

### *Step 10: Build the Next Cycle Deliverables*

The deliverables from a cycle plan are fixed and are not affected by any scope change requests. Any suggestions for scope change are stored in the scope bank and considered in Step 11. Once the deliverables are produced or the cycle duration is reached, the cycle ends. Any incomplete deliverables are returned to the project scope bank for reprioritization and possible consideration in some later cycle. There are a few situations that would cause a deviation from the cycle plan. These are discussed in Chapter 6.

## Step 11: *Conduct Client Checkpoint*

This is a critical milestone in the life of the project. The Client Checkpoint includes an analysis of:

- The cumulative planned versus actual requirements delivered from all completed cycles.
- The scope bank, which contains the prioritized list of requirements not yet met.
- Separate prioritized lists of future Probative Swim Lanes and Integrative Swim Lanes (see Chapter 6).
- A review of the adapted PMLC model template for any needed changes.
- The decision about the next cycle and its requirement content.

## ACPF Feedback Loop from Client Checkpoint to Choose PMLC Model Type

The feedback loop from the Project Execution Phase: Conduct Client Checkpoint to the Project Set-up Phase: Choose Best Fit PMLC model type (shown in Figure 3.1) is a unique feature of the ACPF. This feature will be new to most readers. No other known PMLC model includes this option.

The sole purpose of the feedback loop is to keep Project Execution aligned with the unique and changing nature of the project. The uniqueness of the project makes such a feedback loop essential to successful complex project execution. It arises from the fact that the less we know about the solution, the less we know about the best way to manage the project. As knowledge about the solution changes, the way the project is managed might change as well. Our initial choice of a PMLC model template might turn out at some later cycle to be the wrong choice for future cycles. While the initial choice was based on what was known about the solution at that time, learning and discovery of the goal and solution might render that decision invalid.

What it communicates is that changes that emerge during Project Execution can result in a reconsideration of the PMLC model template choice. Those changes can be simple or significant. Complex project management presents its own unique set of challenges and risks, but I don't want the management methodology to be a barrier to success.

Changing the PMLC model template mid-project is not a decision to be taken lightly. There are several competing factors to weigh. Here are some of the possible reasons for revisiting the choice of the PMLC model template:

- **A radical change in the priority of the project:** This happens more frequently than one would expect. We might be great starters, but we are often lousy finishers. Projects are reprioritized, interrupted, postponed, rescoped, and even canceled, and the resources reassigned to other projects. These changes are often the result of politics, reorganizations, change of sponsors, and peer pressure rather than the result of sound business decisions. The best protection against the risk of investment loss is to use a PMLC model template that produces production-ready deliverables as often as possible. That means adopting models that have a cycle length as short as possible, and that produce production level deliverables as often as possible.
- **A significant proposed scope change:** Market forces and changes are not always predictable; we know that they will occur, but not when. These can often cause significant changes in scope, either by reducing scope or greatly expanding the scope in order to counteract the market changes. This will occasion the revisiting of the model choice with the prospect of a better fit, given the new conditions. Understand that scope change is not the enemy in a complex project as it is in a traditional project. The solution is not known and must be learned and discovered through iteration. That means there will be several false starts and redirections. The more *aha's*! the team gets, the better the progress towards an elusive solution. So, change is not only encouraged, it is essential. Special design features are built into the Plan Next Cycle step to minimize the false starts and misunderstood directions. See the discussion of *Integrative Swim Lanes* and *Probative Swim Lanes* in Chapter 6.
- **The loss of a scarce resource**: This loss can have devastating effects on an in-process ACPF project. If the risk management plan did not identify this as a risk, the impact can be even bigger and can stop a project dead in its tracks. The short-term solution is to go to the market and hire a consultant with the same skills that were lost. Every project that utilized the same scarce resource will have the same problem. The impact might be a scope reduction to remove the need for that lost resource, and perhaps a switch of the PMLC model template choice to fit that reduced scope. A good risk management plan should identify this risk and have a mitigation plan in place. Popular mitigation plans include shadowing and use of outside contractors.
- **Actions of a competitor**: Increased functionality, price reductions, and other actions of a competitor can stop your ACPF project. Sometimes an incremental release strategy may be the best strategy as a hedge against a competitor's actions. Getting to market faster can establish a foothold that the competitor will find hard to counter.

- **The entry of a new competitor**: The new competitor might be a company that operates from the dining room table in a small apartment anywhere in the world. They may be offering a product or service that looks exactly like the one you are offering, but at a much lower price. As you design your ACPF environment, think in terms of creating barriers to entry.
- **The release of a new technology**: The entire market will be impacted and speed to market will be affected. There is also a strategy that gets you to market without incorporating the latest technology: only implement it in the next release, once the technology has matured.

## Adapting or Changing the PMLC Model Template During Project Execution

Changing the PMLC model template during the Project Execution Phase is not a decision to be taken lightly for the following reasons:

- **The cost of abandonment**: Here you will abandon one PMLC model template and switch the remaining Project Execution to a different PMLC model template. In this case, cost is not just measured in dollars. In complex project situations, knowledge gained during project execution is not necessarily documented. It may exist only in the experiences of the client and development teams. It is intrinsic to the ACPF project experience and used whenever appropriate. Changing PMLC model templates during Project Execution risks losing that knowledge and any future benefits that may derive from it. Yes, you might put a practice in place to document that knowledge. That's OK, but now it adds:
  - The actual dollar cost of creating that documentation, which is OK if the PMLC model template is changed.
  - Non-value-added work if the PMLC model template is not changed, which is counter to the "lean" principles of ACPF.
- **The impact on resource requirements and committed schedules**: This has all sorts of implications to the continuation of Project Execution. These include:
  - The new PMLC model template may require fewer or less experienced development team members.
  - The client team and/or the development team may not have any experience with the new PMLC model template and be taken

outside of their comfort zone. To relieve their anxiety, it may require holding some type of workshop. A workshop takes time and money.

- **The impact on the schedules of other projects**: Changing the PMLC model template during the Project Execution Phase can have a significant impact not only on your project schedule, but also on the project schedule of any other project that utilizes the same resources. The concern is more focused on the immediate plan, which should not be detailed beyond the next cycle, if there is one:
  - If the current PMLC model template being used is a Linear or Incremental model, the remaining schedule and complete plan will be seriously impacted, as can the schedules of any projects utilizing the same resources.
  - If the current PMLC model template is an Iterative or Adaptive model, the impact will be somewhat greater because of the increased complexities and uncertainties.

Not every change of the PMLC model template results in added costs, non-value work, or delays in the schedule. There are a few benefits:

- **The use of a simpler PMLC model template**: Usually the change in PMLC model templates will be to simpler models (i.e., from an agile PMLC to a traditional PMLC model template). This allows the new model to take advantage of some of the planning and scheduling benefits of the now-known, complete solution. The time between increments or cycles can be reduced, and that contributes to being lean.
- **The use of less experienced and skilled team members**: This can have a big impact on resource cost reduction. The use of distributed development team members may now be an option, where it was an inconvenience for agile projects.
- **Risk reduction**: The simpler model will have a lower risk, and hence a higher probability of project success.

## *Step 12: Close the Version*

Closing a Version is no different than closing a traditional project. There will have been acceptance criteria that the client and sponsor deem to have been met, followed by a list of closing activities. If it is an ACPF project, the closing activities will also include an evaluation of the scope bank contents at the time work was completed on the current version. The final scope bank contents will be input to the decision to proceed with a Version 2 solution.

## Variations

The ACPF is truly flexible and adaptive in that it can be used, and has been used, in a variety of different situations. As its name implies, it will work well in a number of situations other than those we have discussed so far. In the sections that follow, we will explore some of the many variations and applications of the ACPF during Project Execution.

Flexible and adaptive approaches are more powerful than you might anticipate. Another way of saying that is: "The ACPF is organized common sense tempered with a good dose of creativity." If any step or process does not make sense, change it so that it does make sense. The last thing I want to hear is that "the ACPF does not do that" or "I can't do that with the ACPF." That would defeat the purpose of designing the ACPF to be a robust approach to managing projects.

We have also seen how the ACPF not only anticipates these adaptations, but also expects them. We have already discussed that the ACPF is not a recipe to be blindly followed. Instead, the ACPF offers a structured framework—a strategy—for thinking about how best to manage a project. However, the ACPF is far more adaptable than even the situations in the preceding chapters have indicated. There are three additional adaptations that I want you to be aware of because they have occurred on my watch and are relevant. The first two demonstrate how the ACPF can be used as a proof-of-concept tool and within revising the version plan.

---

**Note about the ACPF**

You will probably find many other reasons to adapt the ACPF. Feel free to do that. The ACPF is not a rigid structure to be followed without question. The bottom line has always been to do what is right for the client. If that flies in the face of some established process or procedure, you need to take a serious look at your process or procedure. It may not be serving your needs, at least for this project. You may need to build a case for your sponsors and managers.

---

At the end of every ACPF cycle, you can deliver a production version of the known solution. It may have enough business value to be released, but that is not even necessary. Organizational velocity with respect to change and the support capabilities of the project team are major determinants of the release plan. The process can stop at any time, and the solution deployed.

Organizations will probably have a release plan in place (quarterly, semi-annual, or annual), and your ACPF release strategy should be aligned to it.

## *Proof of Concept*

There will be situations where the business case has not been sufficiently made to get approval to do the project. In much the same way that we have used prototyping to help with client definition of functionality, we can use the same concept in the first cycle by making the first cycle of ACPF a proof-of-concept cycle. The proof of concept could entail any of the following:

- The creation of an iconic prototype
- A feasibility study
- The writing of use cases
- Storyboarding
- Cash flow, break even analysis, return on investment, or other analysis
- Any other activity to demonstrate potential business value.

However, it is very important that you not drag this activity out too long. Client interest and the interest of the approving manager for the idea will wane. You need to strike quickly while the iron is hot and the window of opportunity is open.

## *Revising the Version Plan*

There will be situations where the initial version scope misses the mark. The more complex and uncertain the project, the more likely this will happen. You will see evidence of this miss via a significant number of discoveries and lessons learned coming in the first few cycles. These discoveries and lessons can create a big disconnect between the original direction of the project and the corrected one that is now indicated. In other words, continuing on the course suggested by the original version scope is a waste of time and money. Remember that you built a mid-level WBS and are making your cycle plans around that WBS. Too many changes brought on by learning and discovery may render much of the WBS out of sync. The need to revise the version plan is clearly a subjective decision. I would err on the side of revision rather than sticking with a plan that may be heading in the wrong direction. The "ACPF-ist" (my term to denote those who practice ACPF) is hard-pressed to do anything that may be a waste of the client's time or money. The ACPF-ist would conclude that the plan is off course and should be abandoned immediately. The correct action is to revise (or even replace) the current version plan and basically start over.

---

**Advice**

At this early point in the project, results may not be forthcoming as planned. Do not be afraid to kill the plan. In almost every case, you will be making the correct decision. Abandonment is costly, but not as costly as wasting resources and time on a project that is going nowhere.

---

## *Imbedding the ACPF in Traditional Project Management*

So far, we have only considered applications of the ACPF for the entire project. The ACPF is more adaptive than that! Figure 3.5 is an example that has come up several times in its short history. So far, the ACPF has been easily accommodated as shown in Figure 3.5.

In the ACPF TPM Hybrid example, we have a project that meets the goal through five high-level solution requirements. With one exception, the five requirements are clear and their delivery completely defined. If it weren't for Requirement E's lack of clarity, TPM would be a perfect fit. Well, in this case you can have your cake and eat it too.

As shown in Figure 3.5, requirements A through D are clearly defined and documented, but Requirement E is not. For the purposes of this example,

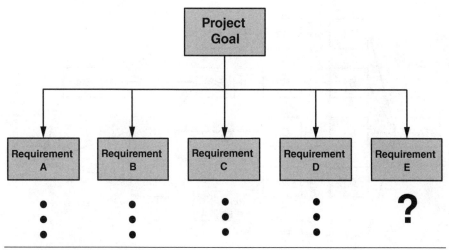

**Figure 3.5**   ACPF TPM hybrid

the unclear requirement will temporarily be treated as a task in the precedence diagram, shown in Figure 3.6. The example is very simple, but it illustrates the point.

Under the condition that the unclear ACPF Activity is a task, this is a complete precedence diagram for the project and can be treated as such. Due to the fact that the ACPF Activity is a very high-level task, it will have several predecessors and several successors, but it can be inserted in a precedence diagram and have a schedule developed. Depending on how much task duration can be assigned to the ACPF Activity, a complete project schedule can be established. In practice, you can calculate the Early Start and Late Finish of the ACPF Activity so that the project completion date would not be compromised. The Early Start for the ACPF Activity is the latest of the Early Finishes of tasks D2 and E2. The Late Finish for the ACPF Activity is the Late Start for task D3. Using these calculated Early Start and Late Finish dates as the actual scheduled start and end dates for the ACPF Activity means it is on the critical path. The ACPF Activity is an ACPF Project. Its start and end date are now determined. The client can set the budget for finding the solution for delivering the ACPF Activity. All of the parameters are now set for the ACPF Activity to be met, using an ACPF approach. We now have an ACPF project embedded in a traditional project.

Actually, ACPF can be imbedded in any Linear or Incremental PMLC model template. For example, in a Staged Delivery Waterfall PMLC model template, one of the swim lanes could be an ACPF Project. Barring any constraining dependencies between the ACPF Swim Lane and any other swim

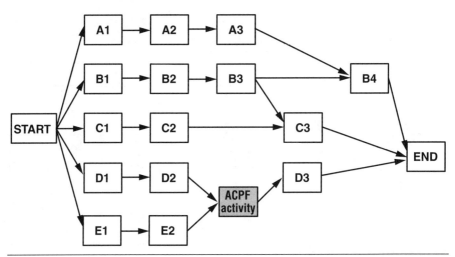

**Figure 3.6**   The precedence diagram for an ACPF/traditional hybrid

lane, the ACPF Project will begin as soon as the first swim lane begins, and end when the last swim lane is complete.

## PUTTING IT ALL TOGETHER

My intention from the beginning of developing the ACPF was to provide the project manager and client with a tool that would guide their thinking toward constructing a best fit project management approach unique to each project, and adapting that decision as the project work commences. I have done that, and will continue to develop the ACPF so that it can easily align with the changing project environment in your organization. With that goal in mind, let's look briefly inside each of the ACPF process steps given in Figure 3.1. Chapter 4 is a detailed "how to" discussion of the ACPF Ideation Phase. Chapter 5 is a detailed "how to" discussion of the ACPF Project Set-up Phase.

The ACPF is not limited to any specific PMLC, software development life cycle, business process, or domain, and in that sense, is a robust and timeless project management approach. It might help by viewing the ACPF as a decision model and thought process that provides a guide as to how a specific project is best managed, and following that decision by assembling the tools, templates, and processes to execute that management approach. The portfolio of applicable management models is dynamic. In most cases, that portfolio is limited to the vetted tools, templates, and processes within the needs, competencies, and capabilities of the organization. Finding an outside provider to assist in meeting some of those needs is part of the equation, too.

# 4

---

# ADAPTIVE COMPLEX PROJECT FRAMEWORK: PROJECT IDEATION PHASE

---

*The creativity ... that emerges from the company comes*
*from the many ideas of the people who are here.*
—John Rollwagen, CEO, Cray Research

*A recent study of product innovation in the scientific instru-*
*ments and tool machinery industries indicates that 80 percent*
*of all product innovations are initiated by the customer.*
—Eric von Hippe, management consultant

## CHAPTER LEARNING OBJECTIVES

This chapter will provide readers the knowledge or ability to:

- Identify and analyze an idea for solving an unsolved problem or exploiting an untapped business opportunity, and build the business case for justification of its promotion to project status.
- Understand the concept of Adaptive Complex Project Framework (ACPF) business requirements as a necessary and sufficient set for achieving project business value.
- Know how to generate a one-page, general description of a project.

The Ideation Phase of the ACPF is usually not part of the project life cycle. A more common practice is to begin the project life cycle with some form of project charter statement. The ACPF takes a more holistic approach. Including Ideation in the ACPF project life cycle provides an understanding of how the project aligns with the business of the organization and its priority with respect to the generation of that business value. You will come to realize that it is a powerful tool for complex project management decision making that is not shared by other methodologies. This uniqueness gives the ACPF a powerful and far more effective capacity for successfully managing any type of project from inception to the end of the useful life of its deliverables.

Few project management books discuss the decision processes and practices over the entire project life span. A *complex project* is a dynamic entity that changes for all sorts of reasons, both predictable and unpredictable, and for that reason the best management approach will also be dynamic and change along with the changing project conditions that arise. This places several challenges on the sponsor, the project manager, the client manager, the client team, and the development team. They must be constantly vigilant and ready to embrace change. The purpose of these changes is to maintain alignment between the changing nature of the project and how it is managed. The goal of the ACPF is to deliver maximum business value with respect to the strategic plan of the organization.

## ADAPTIVE COMPLEX PROJECT FRAMEWORK: PROJECT IDEATION PHASE

An ACPF project begins with an idea for solving a critical yet unsolved problem, or to take advantage of an untapped business opportunity, but it can also begin with nothing more than knowledge that there is a problem or untapped business opportunity. Figure 4.1 highlights the three steps that are executed during the Ideation Phase of a complex project. The approach discussed below is simple and intuitive. Once an idea is submitted: 1) a business case is developed, 2) high-level requirements are elicited, and 3) a Project Overview Statement (POS) is prepared.

## STEP 1: DEVELOP THE ACPF BUSINESS CASE

Most project management methodologies start with the project as given, and proceed from there. Those methodologies often start with writing the POS. The ACPF is not like other project management methodologies. The ACPF is a holistic framework and embraces the entire project life span. That

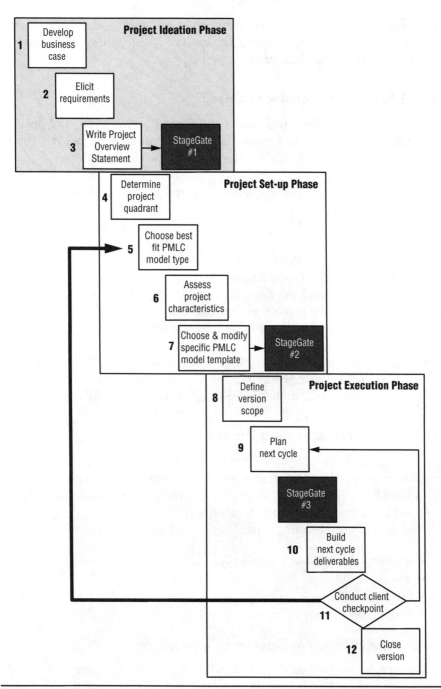

**Figure 4.1**   Project Ideation Phase

begins with the very roots of a possible project—with an idea where a problem or an unmet need is identified and analyzed for business feasibility. Step 1 ends with the identification of a specific project.

## What Is an ACPF Business Case?

A *business case* is a document that identifies an unmet need, and provides evidence and justification for initiating or continuing a project investment to address that need. An ACPF business case typically includes:

- A statement of a critical need and the overall justification for a project to address that need
- A description of the product, process, or service that the project will deliver
- How the project aligns with the business strategy
- A financial analysis comparing alternative project ideas
- A prioritization of the alternatives and the preferred option
- The scope of the project and its deliverables
- The incremental business value that will result.

There are several models and processes that could be used to develop the business case. One stands out that aligns very well to the ACPF (Maul, 2011). I have adapted it to be the best fit for use in the ACPF.

## The ACPF Brainstorming Process

Figure 4.2 is a high-level view of how the ACPF has incorporated and expanded the typical brainstorming process and mapped it across the Project Ideation Phase. Figure 4.2 is an ACPF adaptation of a model originally developed by (Gray, Brown, and Macanuto, 2010).

The ACPF Brainstorming Model consists of four main phases:

- Definition of the problem or business opportunity
- Divergent Phase
- Emergent Phase
- Convergent Phase

### *Define the Problem or Business Opportunity*

The ACPF is designed so that an idea can originate anywhere and be submitted by anyone in the organization. The person proposing the idea must

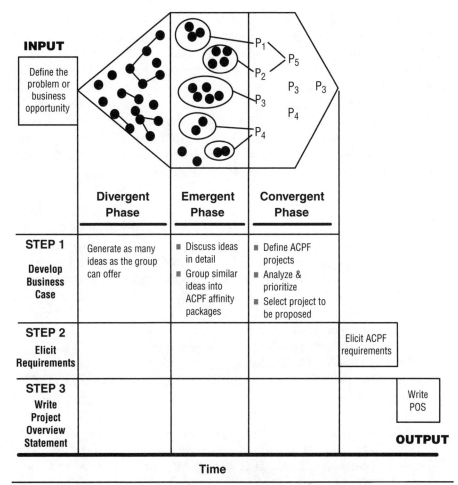

**Figure 4.2**    ACPF Brainstorming Model imbedded in the Project Ideation Phase

get the endorsement and support of a manager, who will often become the sponsor. This is the first step in the process of developing a business case. A sponsor (usually an executive from the client organization who will fund the project) makes a request of senior management to undertake a project to solve a mission critical problem, or take advantage of a significant yet untapped business opportunity. Whether it be a problem or an opportunity, the organization is presented with a major challenge. The challenge arises from the fact that the problem remains unsolved, and it is unclear how to take advantage of the untapped business opportunity. That uncertainty is a fundamental characteristic of complex projects.

A representative from the development organization is assigned to work with the client sponsor. In keeping with the principles underlying the ACPF, this individual from the development organization will become one of the co-project managers, and someone from the sponsor's business unit (the client) will become the other co-project manager. That could be the sponsor or a responsible business analyst, but it usually is a line manager from the affected business unit(s). Whoever is chosen, they must represent the sponsor's interests and have decision-making authority for the business unit(s) they represent. These co-managers are equally responsible for the project from inception through completion (i.e., the project life span).

## Divergent Phase

The purpose of the Divergent Phase is to elicit as many ideas as the brainstorming group can produce. No evaluation is done at the time, except for clarification. The more ideas that can be generated, the better the final result. No idea is too extreme to be rejected. One idea might not be used, but it may be the catalyst for other ideas. The best way to start the Divergent Phase is with a brainstorming session. What is presented here is a variant of the familiar brainstorming session that most people will be familiar with. This variant is far broader and comprehensive than you may have experienced so far:

- Assemble any individuals, whether they are team members, consultants, or others, who may have some knowledge of the problem or business opportunity area. A team of 8-12 should be sufficient. They don't need to be experts. In fact, it may be better if they are not experts. You need people to think creatively and outside of the box. They may not be aware of any risks associated with their ideas, and that is good at this early stage. Experts tend to think inside the box and focus on why something can't be done, rather than on why it should be done. How it will be done is a decision better left during the Set-up and Execution Phases.
- The session begins with everyone recording an idea, reading it to the brainstorming group, and placing it on the table face up so everyone can see it. No discussion (except clarification) is permitted. Silence and pauses are fine. This allows any group member to think about the suggestions that have been submitted, and what they have heard and seen, and maybe that will spur another idea. Families of ideas can be generated like those shown linked together in Figure 4.2.
- After all the ideas are on the table, and no new ideas seem to be forthcoming from the brainstorming group, the Divergent Phase is declared

closed by the facilitator. A Divergent Phase can be completed in less than two hours.

---

**Brainstorming Group Operating Rule**

When a group member puts an idea on the table for consideration, they surrender ownership of the idea. It becomes the property of the entire group. It no longer makes any difference where it came from, and that should not even be part of any later discussions regarding the idea.

---

## Emergent Phase

The purpose of the Emergent Phase is to collect and consolidate the brainstormed ideas into packages of similar ideas (i.e., affinity packages) as a prelude to defining specific action items:

- Discuss the ideas that have been submitted. Try to combine ideas, or revise ideas based on each member's perspective. Ideas are grouped into affinity groups, or packages of similar ideas, if you prefer. Some ideas may not be similar enough to be placed in a package. Don't discard any ideas. They might have value that has not yet been recognized.
- In time, primitive solutions will begin to emerge from these packages. Don't rush this process, and by all means test each idea with an open mind. Remember that you are looking for a solution that no individual could identify, but that you hope the group is able to identify through their collective efforts. There is a synergy that comes from a well-run Emergent Phase.
- An Emergent Phase can be completed in 2-3 hours, but don't cut it short if it is still producing good affinity packages.

## Convergent Phase

The purpose of the Convergent Phase is to use the affinity groups or packages as the foundation for projects, and perhaps group similar packages into projects, and then analyze, prioritize, and finally select the project to be proposed. Referring to Figure 4.2, the Convergent Phase consists of these activities:

- Define the ACPF project or projects (P1 through P4).
- Analyze and prioritize the alternative projects (P5, P3, P4).
- Select the first project to be proposed (P3).

The Convergent Phase is the first time that projects begin to take shape. Even though a single project is chosen, the list still can have residual value if the chosen project does not appear to be delivering business value. You may want to come back to this list for another pick.

## Define the ACPF Project or Projects

Whether you use the ACPF Brainstorming Process or feasibility studies, you should have generated a few alternatives, and it is time to explore them in more depth in your search for the best alternative. There are several variables that you might use to profile each alternative project. Here are some suggestions:

- Risk
- Duration
- Cost
- Team size and skills
- Expected business value

## Analyze the Alternative Projects

The analysis of alternative projects examines their business value. The objective is to prioritize them and select the best. There are several approaches for analyzing the financial aspects of a project. While the sponsor should perform this analysis, it is often done by a project manager. The approaches I have chosen are easily understood and give enough insight into the financials of the project at this early stage in its life span.

Some organizations require a preliminary financial analysis of the project before granting approval to perform the detailed planning. Although such analyses are very rough because not enough information is known about the project at this time, they will offer a trip wire for project-planning approval. In some instances, they also offer criteria for prioritizing all of the POS documents that senior management will be reviewing.

At one time, IBM required a financial analysis from the project manager as an attachment to the POS. At the time, they were my client and allocated four hours for the project manager to complete the financial analysis. Project managers are typically not professional financial analysts, and four hours was not much time. So, the resulting analysis was cursory at best, but it did lend some information relevant to financial feasibility.

The following are brief descriptions of the types of financial analyses you may be asked to provide. Keep in mind that the project manager may not be a financial analyst, and requiring an in-depth financial analysis may be beyond their ability.

## Cost and Benefit Analysis

Cost and benefit analyses are always difficult to do because you need to include intangible benefits in the decision process. As mentioned earlier in the chapter, things such as improved client satisfaction cannot be easily quantified. You could argue that improved client satisfaction reduces client turnover, which in turn increases revenues, but how do you put a number on that? In many cases, senior management will take these inferences into account, but they still want to see hard-dollar comparisons. Opt for the direct and measurable benefits to compare against the cost of doing the project and the cost of operating the new process. If the benefits outweigh the costs over the expected life of the project deliverables, senior management may be willing to support the project.

## Breakeven Analysis

Breakeven analysis is a timeline that shows the cumulative cost of the project against the cumulative revenue or savings from the project. At each point where the cumulative revenue or savings line crosses the cumulative cost line, the project will recoup its costs. Usually, senior management looks for an elapsed time less than some threshold number. If the project meets that deadline date, it may be worthy of support. Targeted breakeven dates are getting shorter because of more frequent changes in the business and its markets.

Breakeven analysis is a technique that is useful to get a good initial input regarding the investment pattern for any project. It involves simply adding up the project's predicted annual cash flows, i.e., the year-wise income minus expenses for the project in question. The breakeven point for a product is calculated using the formula:

**Breakeven point = (fixed cost)/(selling price – variable cost)**

The graph shown in Figure 4.3 will clarify. Breakeven analysis does not add the cash flows for the time period still remaining in the total project once this initial investment has been recovered. Breakeven analysis is simple to use. It does not take depreciation into consideration.

Advantages of breakeven analysis are:

- It is simple to use.
- It is a standard technique used worldwide.
- It can be used effectively for high risk situations.

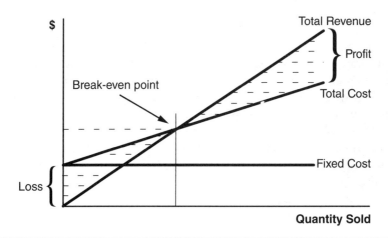

**Figure 4.3**   Breakeven analysis

Disadvantages of breakeven analysis are:

- Breakeven analysis normally ignores the time value of money, i.e., inflation or the discounted cash flow.
- Little consideration is taken of the cash flow situation after the breakeven period.
- The breakeven analysis method, if used by itself, can give rise to wrong decision making for investment, due to the disadvantages listed above.

Breakeven analysis is a good indicator for Initial Investment analysis, but it must be used in conjunction with other investment appraisal techniques.

### *Return on Investment*

Return on investment (ROI) analyzes the total costs as compared with the increased revenue that will accrue over the life of the project deliverables. Here, senior management finds a common basis for comparing one project against another. They look for the high ROI projects or the projects that at least meet some minimum ROI.

The ROI technique considers only the total cash profit or cash flow (income minus expenses). It does not consider depreciation or the time value of money. To arrive at the project's ROI:

- The cash flow for each year is added without discounting it, and this total cash flow for the complete project is divided by the number of years to get the average return per year.

- The average return per year is then divided by the initial investment made in the year 0, and multiplied by 100 to get the project's ROI.

## *Cost-Benefit Ratio*

The cost-benefit ratio (CBR) is the ratio of quantifiable benefits to the costs incurred in achieving the benefits. In theory, benefits can be in financial terms covering the revenue generation and cost savings, fulfillment of social objectives, intangible and nonquantifiable, improving quality, boosting the morale of the team, etc.

Let us represent benefits as B and costs as C. The CBR is C/B. Inflows can be linked to benefits, and outflows to the costs incurred. Mathematically speaking, a ratio can be either greater than 1, less than 1, or 1 itself. If the ratio is less than 1, it is much better as benefits are more than the costs incurred to achieve them. A ratio greater than 1 will imply that we get fewer benefits in comparison to the costs incurred. The ratio 1 implies no gain or loss.

In the case of non-revenue generating projects, a CBR ratio can be computed by taking the ratio of the total cost savings to cost incurred for affecting the savings (for instance, by providing an opportunity to managers to opt for leaving the company by giving them a good compensation package).

## Prioritize the Alternative Projects

The first tactical step in every portfolio management model involves prioritizing the projects that have been shown to be aligned with the portfolio strategy. Proposed projects are usually grouped into funding categories or aligned under objectives, or under the strategies that align under objectives.

Each group defines a potential portfolio. When finished, each group will have a list of prioritized projects. Dozens of approaches could be used to establish that prioritization. Some are nonnumeric; others are numeric. Some approaches are very simple; others can be quite complex and involve multivariate analysis, goal programming, and other complex computer-based algorithms. My approach is to identify methods that can easily be implemented without any prerequisite knowledge or experience, and which do not require a computer system for support, although sometimes a simple spreadsheet application can reduce the labor intensity of the process. This section describes the models commonly used for establishing priorities:

- Forced ranking
- Q-Sort
- Must-Do, Should-Do, Postpone
- Criteria weighting

- Paired comparisons
- Risk/benefit matrix

## Forced Ranking

The forced ranking approach is best explained by way of an example. Suppose that five projects have been proposed. Number the projects 1 through 5 so that you can refer to them later. Suppose that the brainstorming team has six members (A, B, C, D, E, F), and they are each asked to rank the five projects from most important (1) to least important (5). They can use any criteria they wish, and they do not have to describe the criteria they used. The results of their rankings are shown in Table 4.1.

The individual rankings from each of the six members for a specific project are added to produce the rank sum for each project. Low values for the rank sum are indicative of projects that have been given high priority by the members. For example, Project 4 has the lowest rank sum, and is therefore the highest priority project.

Ties are possible in forced ranking. In fact, the preceding example has a tie between Project 2 and Project 3. Ties can be broken in a number of ways. For example, I prefer to use the existing rankings to break ties. In this example, a tie is broken by taking the tied project with the lowest rank score and moving it to the next lowest forced rank. For example, the lowest rank for Project 2 is 2, and for Project 3 is 1. Therefore, the tie is broken by giving Project 3 a rank of 3, and giving Project 2 a rank of 4.

Forced ranking works well for small numbers of projects, but it does not scale very well. It will work well if a few alternatives (like in a business case) are being compared in an effort to pick one to proceed to the project level.

## Q-Sort

In the Q-Sort model (see Figure 4.4), projects are first divided into two groups: high priority and low priority. The high-priority group is then di-

Table 4.1   Forced ranking of five solution ideas

| Project Idea #1 | A | B | C | D | E | F | Rank Sum | Forced Rank |
|---|---|---|---|---|---|---|---|---|
| 1 | 2 | 1 | 3 | 2 | 1 | 4 | 13 | 2 |
| 2 | 4 | 3 | 2 | 3 | 4 | 3 | 19 | 3 |
| 3 | 5 | 4 | 1 | 5 | 3 | 1 | 19 | 3 |
| 4 | 1 | 2 | 4 | 1 | 2 | 2 | 12 | 1 |
| 5 | 3 | 5 | 5 | 4 | 5 | 5 | 27 | 5 |

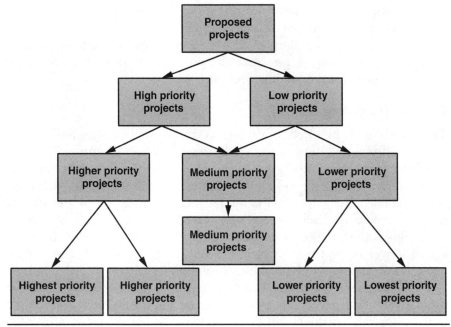

**Figure 4.4**    An example of the Q-sort model

vided into two groups: higher priority and medium priority. The low-priority group is also divided into two groups: low priority and medium priority. The next step is to divide the higher-priority group into two groups: highest priority and higher priority. The same is done for the low-priority group. The decomposition continues until all groups have eight or fewer members. As a last step, you could distribute the medium-priority projects to the other final groups.

The Q-Sort method is simple and quick. It works well for large numbers of projects. It also works well when used as a small group exercise using a consensus approach.

## Must-Do, Should-Do, Postpone

The Must-Do, Should-Do, Postpone approach (and variations of it such as MoSCoW) is probably the most commonly used way of ranking. As opposed to the forced rank, in which each individual project is ranked, this approach creates a few categories, such as Must-Do, Should-Do, and Postpone. The person doing the ranking only has to decide which category the project belongs in. The agony of having to decide relative rankings between pairs of projects is eliminated with this approach. The number of categories is arbitrary, as are the names of the categories.

This method is even simpler than Q-Sort. If the number of projects is large, you may need to prioritize the projects within each of the three groups in order to make funding decisions.

## Criteria Weighting

There are literally hundreds of criteria weighting models. They are all quite similar, differing only in the minor details. I give one example of criteria weighting, but several others apply the same principles. A number of characteristics are identified, and a numeric weighting is applied to each characteristic. Each characteristic has a scale attached to it. The scales usually range from 1 to 10. Each project is evaluated on each characteristic, and a scale value is given to the project. Each scale value is multiplied by the characteristic weight, and these weighted scale values are added. The highest result is associated with the highest-priority project.

Figure 4.5 shows a sample calculation for one of the proposed projects for the portfolio. The first column lists the criteria against which all proposed projects for this portfolio will be evaluated. The second column lists the weight of that criterion (higher weight indicates more importance to the scoring algorithm). Columns 3 through 7 evaluate the project against the given criteria. Note that the evaluation can be given to more than one level. The only restriction is that the evaluation must be totally spread across the levels. Note that the sum of each criteria is 1. Using the Contribute to Goal B row as an example, multiply the rating (0.2) times the value of *Very Good (8)* to get a score of 1.6, and then multiply the rating of (0.8) times the value of *Good (6)* to get a value of 4.8. Add the values 1.6 and 4.8 to calculate the total rating of Contribute to Goal B as 6.4, shown in column 8. So the eighth column is the sum of the levels multiplied by the score for that level. This process is totally adaptable to the nature of the portfolio. The criteria and criteria weight columns can be defined to address the needs of the portfolio. All other columns are fixed. The last two columns are calculated based on the values in columns 2 through 7. Column 9 is the product of the criteria weight (6 for the example) and the expected level weight (6.4 for the example), which gives an expected weight of 38.4. This is the score used to rank this project among the other candidate projects.

## Paired Comparisons Model

In the paired comparisons model, every pair of projects is compared. Using whatever criteria s/he wishes, the evaluator chooses which project in the pair

| Criteria | Criteria Weight | Very Good (8) | Good (6) | Fair (4) | Poor (2) | Very Poor (0) | Expected Level Weight | Expected Weighted Score |
|---|---|---|---|---|---|---|---|---|
| Fit to Mission | 10 | 1.0 | | | | | 8.0 | 80.0 |
| Fit to Objectives | 10 | 0.2 | 0.6 | 0.2 | | | 6.0 | 60.0 |
| Fit to Strategy | 10 | | | 1.0 | | | 4.0 | 40.0 |
| Contribute to Goal A | 8 | | | | 1.0 | | 2.0 | 16.0 |
| Contribute to Goal B | 6 | 0.2 | 0.8 | | | | 6.4 | 38.4 |
| Contribute to Goal C | 4 | | 0.5 | 0.5 | | | 5.0 | 20.0 |
| Uses Strengths | 10 | | | | 0.6 | 0.4 | 1.2 | 12.0 |
| Uses Weaknesses | 10 | 0.7 | 0.3 | | | | 7.4 | 74.0 |
| | | | | | | | | 340.4 |

**Figure 4.5**   Criteria weighting

is the higher priority. The matrix in Table 4.2 is the commonly used method for conducting and recording the results of a paired comparisons exercise.

## Risk/Benefit Matrix

Another scoring model is the risk/benefit matrix (Figure 4.6). There are many ways to do risk analysis, from subjective methods to very sophisticated mathematical models. The model that I am introducing is a very simple, quasi-mathematical model. The probabilities of success are divided into five levels. Actually, any number of levels will do the job. Defining three levels is also quite common. In this model, you assess two probabilities: the *probability of technical success* and the *probability of business success*. These are arranged as shown in Figure 4.6.

Each project is assessed in terms of these probabilities. The probability of idea success is estimated as the product of the two separate probabilities. To

Table 4.2   An example of paired comparisons

|   | 1 | 2 | 3 | 4 | 5 | SUM | RANK |
|---|---|---|---|---|---|-----|------|
| 1 | X | 1 | 1 | 0 | 1 | 3 | 2 |
| 2 | 0 | X | 0 | 0 | 1 | 1 | 3 |
| 3 | 0 | 1 | X | 0 | 0 | 1 | 3 |
| 4 | 1 | 1 | 1 | X | 1 | 4 | 1 |
| 5 | 0 | 0 | 1 | 0 | X | 1 | 3 |

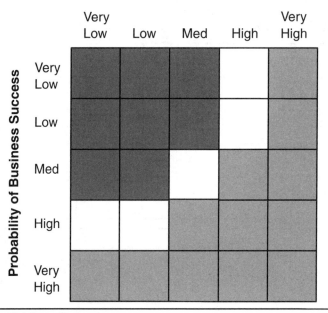

**Probability of Technical Success**

**Figure 4.6**   Risk/benefit matrix

simplify the calculation, the graph shows the results of the computation by placing a project in one of the following three shaded areas:

- **Light shading:** These projects should be a high priority.
- **No shading:** These projects should be considered.
- **Dark shading:** These projects should not be considered unless there is some compelling reason to fund them.

When you have a large number of projects, you need to prioritize those that fall in the lightly-shaded cells. A good way to do this would be to prioritize the cells starting in the lower-right corner and working toward the center of the matrix.

## Select the Project to be Proposed

Step 1 ends with the selection of a project to take into Step 2. Several prioritization lists may have been created for the potential projects identified in the affinity packages. The decision will be based on both quantitative and qualitative data. In the final analysis, these data are guidelines for a decision that is first a good business decision. It would be unusual if all prioritized lists have the same project as highest priority, but it has happened. It is in keeping with the ACPF Brainstorming Model if more than one project were proposed. Let the best project survive the approval StageGate.

## Use ACPF Brainstorming in the Project Execution Phase

Brainstorming is an essential part of the brainstorming operating rules because, at several points in the life of the project, the creativity of the group will be tested. Brainstorming is a technique that can focus creativity and help the group discover solutions or create new or improved products, processes, or services. In some situations, acceptable ideas and alternatives do not result from the normal team deliberations. In such cases, the project manager might suggest a brainstorming session. A brainstorming session is one in which the team contributes ideas in a stream-of-consciousness mode, as described in the Divergent Phase. Brainstorming sessions have been quite successful in uncovering solutions where none seemed possible. The team needs to know how the project manager will conduct such sessions and what will be done with the output. A simple and quick method for creating ideas to fuel the start of a complex project is given in Step 2.

# STEP 2: ELICIT REQUIREMENTS

Many would argue that complete requirements can only be elicited for very simple projects that have a long history of successful execution. The ACPF is based on that assumption.

## Definition of ACPF Requirements

First, we need the working definition of an ACPF requirement. This definition is consistent with the International Institute of Business Analysis (IIBA, 2009) definition, but takes a different perspective on requirements and their elicitations.

---

**ACPF Requirement**

An *ACPF requirement* is a specific end-state condition whose successful integration into the solution delivers specific, measurable, and incremental business value to the organization. The set of ACPF high-level requirements forms a necessary and sufficient set for the attainment of all project success criteria and the delivery of the expected business value.

---

Requirements define the properties and characteristics of the product, process, or service that is the deliverable of the project. These requirements are the basis for analyzing the effect of any changes to a current situation that your client is seeking. A requirement exists either because the product, process, or service demands certain functions or qualities not present in the current solution. Project requirements start with what the customer really needs, and end when those needs are satisfied. (Note that I am saying *needs*, not *wants*.) This often leads to nonessential or over-specified requirements, or some other anomaly. You are cautioned to be very careful about assuming who knows what and who understands what. Double check that the client understands every step of the way. The conditions of satisfaction (COS) (described below) is a client-facing tool I developed more than 20 years ago, and it has served me well for these purposes.

---

What your client *wants* may not be what your client *needs*. Your job is to make sure that what they want is what they need and that you will deliver what they need.

---

This definition of an ACPF requirement is quite different than the IIBA definition of a requirement, but in its simplicity and uniqueness, it puts the connection between requirements and the project in a much more intuitive light. ACPF requirements will be the causal factors that drive the attainment of the success criteria, as stated in the POS. Every ACPF requirement should be directly related to one or more project success criteria. This definition results in a small number (8-12) of requirements at the beginning of the project, whereas the IIBA definition generates hundreds of requirements, which can never be considered a complete set at the beginning of the project. The mind could not grasp completeness, anyway.

Subject to the learning and discovery that may uncover other requirements, the list generated using the ACPF requirements definition can be considered complete at the beginning of the project. The decomposition of those requirements is not fully known at the beginning of the project, however. An ACPF requirement is a more business value-oriented definition than the IIBA definition.

The learning and discovery derived from completed project cycles will clarify the ACPF requirements through decomposition to the function, sub-function, process, activity, and feature levels. The first level decomposition of an ACPF requirement is to the functional level, and can be considered equivalent to IIBA requirements. So, while you can identify all ACPF requirements at the beginning of the project, you cannot describe the details of the requirements at the functional, sub-functional, process, activity, and feature levels. This detail is learned and discovered in the context of the cycles that make up the project. This two-step process for Requirements Elicitation is consistent with the lean principles, too.

The ACPF definition of requirements should be preferred to the IIBA definition because it ties requirements directly to the project success criteria, which is not the case with the IIBA definition. That makes it possible to prioritize ACPF requirements, whereas no similar case can be made for prioritizing IIBA requirements. Under the IIBA definition, setting priorities is more of a technical assessment than a business assessment.

The choice of a single project to propose can be made based on the high-level requirements. Since the requirements describe an acceptable solution, the decision can be driven by the degree of fit between a proposed project and the effectiveness it will have in producing deliverables that satisfy the requirements. Reaching this decision is subjective—not objective.

## Stakeholder Participation in Requirements Elicitation

Those who affect or are affected by a project define the members of the stakeholder group. They interact with each other across the project life span. These interactions will be discussed in context. How stakeholders interact with one another through the Project Ideation Phase is shown in Figure 4.7. In general there are eight such stakeholders:

- **Sponsor**—The senior manager who "pays the bill." S/he may originate the idea for the project or may respond to a request from the client manager for the product, process, or service. It may be a new product, process, or service to take advantage of an untapped business opportunity or a project that improves an existing product, process, or service.
- **Client Manager**—The person or department that will own the deliverables from the project. They collaborate with the sponsor and the user regarding project deliverables, and represent both the sponsor and the

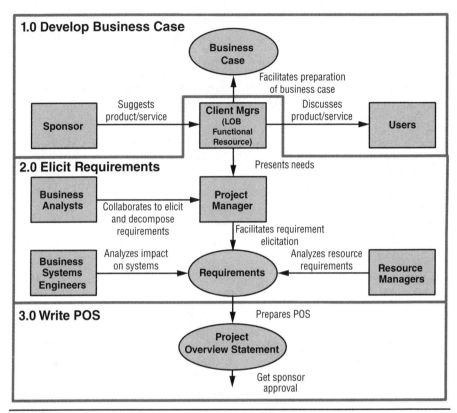

**Figure 4.7**   The stakeholder interaction model for the Ideation Phase

user in the requirements elicitation and decomposition exercises. They will often manage the implementation of the deliverables produced by the project. There will be situations where the deliverables are owned by more than one department, as will be the case with enterprise-wide applications. These situations present challenges to satisfying competing needs.

- Users—The person or department that will use the deliverables from the project. They may be internal or external to the enterprise. In many cases, a user may have proposed the original project idea.
- Line-of-Business (LOB) Managers or Directors—A collective manager type. There are no positions named "LOB Manager." An LOB is a manager or director of a business unit that directly produces business value, usually but not always financial. An LOB manager or director has responsibility for a product, process, or service that uses resources

to directly interact with customers, users, or clients to produce business value.

- **Functional Managers**—A collective manager type. There are no positions named "Functional Manager." Some functional managers are resource managers. The key differentiator is whether they manage resources directly or use resources to produce business value. So, for example, the Director of Marketing is a functional manager. S/he uses the data warehouse (a resource) to produce a marketing plan that generates business value through increasing sales. On the other hand, the Director of Human Resources is a resource because s/he directly manages human resources. One might argue that they could also be a functional manager if they manage a professional development program that produces a skill and competency inventory that is aligned with the project, program, and portfolio needs of the enterprise. If you think at the role level, the apparent conflict is easily resolved. In the role of managing a human resource, they are a resource manager. In the role of managing the professional development program, they are a functional manager.

- **Resource Managers**—A collective manager type. There are no positions named "Resource Manager." This is anyone in the organization who has total and direct stewardship responsibility over a resource that contributes directly to the creation of business value. It includes those functional managers with responsibility for resources that have business value, for example, Human Resource Managers (human assets); financial managers (financial assets); sales, marketing, and public relations managers (intangible assets); IT and engineering managers (intellectual property and knowledge assets); and plant or equipment managers, who have stewardship over and manage the physical assets of an organization. Depending on the specific circumstances, these people are often those who, in their role, function as project sponsors. They have decision-making authority over where the assets under their charge are deployed to create expected business value.

- **Business Systems Engineers**—The technical person(s) who has stewardship responsibilities for the design and implementation of the associated business processes and systems that are affected by or affect the deliverables. Many organizations still use the title Systems Analyst.

- **Project Managers**—These are the enablers. They are the facilitators of the requirements elicitation and decomposition process. They are responsible for managing the resources to produce the project deliverables. In the co-manager role, the project manager might manage the developer team. The other co-manager will manage the client-side team. These managers could be anyone from among the other managers cited above.

- **Business Analysts (BAs)**—These professionals are familiar with the customer processes, user practices, and the processes they will be using to apply the products or services delivered by the project. They will often act as support to the project manager and as an interface between the project manager and the client. Their primary responsibility is to help transform stated business needs into business requirements. Those in more senior business analysis positions may be appointed co-managers by the business unit of their specialty.

## Conditions of Satisfaction

Before any requirements can be gathered, every ACPF project should begin with a COS—put the COS in your ACPF/kit—where a client representative or client group meets face to face with a project manager or core project team to discuss their request. A BA often participates in the role of a hinge pin, linking the client and the project team. "Wants" are presented by the client, and deliverables proposed by the project manager.

At the first meeting of the client representative and the development representative, a seemingly unstructured conversation takes place, where both parties come to an understanding of the situation and how it will be approached. I call this conversation the COS. I've never been able to verify where it originated. All I know is that it works, and it should be in the toolkit of every project manager. I've been using COS for over 20 years and wouldn't consider starting a project without going through a COS session with my client.

The COS (Figure 4.8) is a purposed conversation between a development representative and the client representative. On one extreme, the COS may be a brief, one-on-one conversation between two people. In some cases, it might be a multiple day planned meeting with several participants. At the extreme, it might involve prototyping and even functional specification. The COS is a robust process and should be thought of as an approach to be adapted to the situation. Whatever approach you decide to use, it must be conversationally based. Conducting a COS by walking around to visit each affected party is not an alternative. Furthermore, I advocate that the conversations cannot be replaced with a stream of e-mails, so don't even think about accepting a stream of e-mails as a substitute for a face-to-face conversation. There is something foreboding about the written word (regardless of its intended message) in that it becomes set in stone once delivered. There is always a risk that what you said (or what was interpreted that you said) will

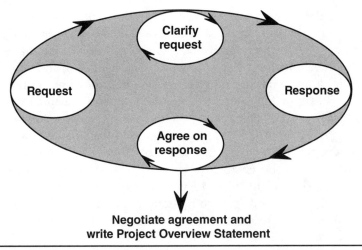

**Figure 4.8**   Conditions of satisfaction

be misinterpreted. That triggers another e-mail, and so an endless stream of e-mails follows—the so-called "e-mail war." Avoid that trap by face-to-face conversations where misunderstandings are far less likely to occur, and if they do, are easily cleared up. Pay the price and do it right!

## COS Benefits

Two important benefits accrue to the project from the COS:

1. **Through the COS, you and your client will establish a common language.** Having a common language is a critical success factor for effective complex project management. It amazes me, when I test the accuracy of communication between parties, how often the message sent is not the message received. We carelessly assume that the receiver of our communication has the same understanding of the terminology as we do. People are often embarrassed to admit that they do not understand something you have said or written. That does not excuse you from making sure that the message you send is the message received.

   Let me give you an example from one of my public training classes that will drive home the importance of a common language. I asked each attendee (all software developers) to write down their definition of the word *implementation*. They could do so by simply listing what is included or what is not included. Then, we would compare definitions. Would you be surprised to find out that there were about as many definitions of the word *implementation* as there were participants in the exercise? This was amazing to me because those of us in the information technology business can hardly speak a sentence without using the word *implementation*, and yet we really don't know what the other is saying when they use the term. What do you think the client understands about your meaning of the term *implementation*? Point made! With reference to your own projects, can you say that you and your client really understand one another? Maybe you both do, but probably not. The COS is a tool you can use to assure a good channel of communication between the development team and the client team. It is a great insurance policy against a failure to clearly and completely communicate. You can have a similar conversation about the project and know that each party understands the other. While this may sound trivial, it definitely is anything but trivial.

2. **You have a negotiated yet tentative agreement with your client, and you can both approach the project based on that agreement.** The negotiated agreement becomes the foundation on which the project proceeds. You will use it for problem solving, conflict resolution, and decision making. It will be used to bring others on board as the project proceeds. Most important of all, it is the basis on which ACPF planning is built and prioritization decisions can be made. If you do this right, you are well on your way to a successful ACPF project. If you do this wrong, there is a very high probability of significant problems or even project failure.

What has been accomplished by both parties at this point is an understanding of what has been requested and what can be provided. There may not be agreement at this point, but at least there is an understanding, and the differences can be negotiated until there is an acceptable agreement.

### *Expectation Setting*

Because of the uncertainty and complexity that surrounds an ACPF project, it is critical that you clearly set expectations with your client. A strong and forceful sponsor or client can often put you in the position of adding new deliverables within time and budget constraints that are not feasible. Meeting your client needs is uppermost in your mind, but don't compromise beyond what is realistic. In every agile project solution, scope is variable and not clearly definable at the beginning of the project. Scope is learned and discovered as part of the project work. The client must understand and accept the implications of this uncertainty and complexity, as well as the attendant risks. Clients might be locked in the traditional project world, which is focused on defining deliverables up front. That is not the complex project world, and you should consider educating them to the differences. Those differences are profound!

I have negotiated a number of contracts for complex projects and my biggest stumbling block has always been defining deliverables. The contract language roughly says something like the following:

---

**Conditions of satisfaction**

Neither you nor your client can define exactly what scope will be delivered at the end of the project, but you know that it will be the maximum business value that can be delivered given the time and budget constraints the sponsor has established.

---

In other words, this will be a partnership that will work to deliver the best solution possible. Having that partnership is a critical success factor for every ACPF project.

## The COS Is a Dynamic Process

The COS process is not a one-time event. It is a dynamic process. It occurs repeatedly throughout the project. At each client checkpoint or other project milestone, the COS is revisited but with the participation of the client team and the development team.

The initial COS might have included only you and the client representative. Because of the learning and discovery that has taken place, something will have surely changed that renders the previous agreement out of date and in need of revision. This revisiting of the COS is your guarantee of always staying in alignment with what the client needs. It is also the pathway to move the client from what they want to what they need. Remember, the ACPF embraces change, and here is the place where change enjoys the light of day.

## Wants vs. Needs—A Warning and a Suggestion

What the client wants may not be what the client needs! After more than 40 years of project management experience, I have come to the conclusion that many of the client's wants are not much more than their attempt at a solution to a problem they have, but whose definition neither of you are privy to. The client's solution landscape is limited to their area of expertise, which may not include the solution to their problem. Unless I have evidence to the contrary, my assumption is that *wants* do not reflect actual *needs*.

So, my advice to you is to make sure that the client's wants and actual needs are the same. I have done that quite successfully by applying root cause analysis—put it in your ACPF/kit—during the required COS session. For every want expressed by the client, I ask them, "Why do you want that?" By repeatedly asking *why* questions, I eventually get to the real reason for the want, and no further questions are asked about that particular want. You have found a need. There may be several wants for you and the client to explore. Eventually, you and the client together will have identified all of the needs. Through the collection of needs, you and the client will be able to define the problem, and through the project, eventually find a solution.

A further suggestion is to be careful in your questioning so that the client does not feel like they are on the defensive. *Why* questions can be softened by saying instead, "What do you expect that to do for you?" That might lead you to questions like, "Can we try to find something that works better?" or, "Here's an idea that might work. What do you think?" If you are going to build a meaningful relationship with your client, they need to feel like you are both on the same team and working toward the same goal.

The difference between wants and needs are often discovered as part of the COS exercise. This is critical to the success of the project. I have found that what the client says they want is their attempt at finding a solution to an unstated problem. Only by drilling down into the statement of wants can the project manager discover the true problem, and hence can begin to formulate a statement of what is actually needed to solve the now de-fined problem. This process becomes the basis of a requirements gathering process. The requirements gathering process can take place as input to the project proposal, or take place as part of project planning once the project proposal has been approved. Through discussion, both parties will come to understand each other and form an agreement of what is needed, and then document that agreement in a one-page POS. The POS is described in Step 3. The POS should be written in the language of the business so that anyone who has occasion to read it will understand it. You do not have the benefit of accompanying the POS to answer questions from the reader about what you really meant.

Once the wants versus needs conversations are complete, the needs will have been established. For the simplest of projects, that may be sufficient for project definition and the POS can be written. When not, more analysis is needed, and requirements elicitation and gathering will be needed.

## Requirements Breakdown Structure

Requirements have always been a sticking point in the process of deciding how to manage a project. There will be those situations where the project has been done several times, and there is a dependable history of those efforts. For example, the project involves installing a computer network in a field sales office. This project has been done several times before in other field offices. There are no surprises and all requirements should be known. There may even be a template work breakdown structure (WBS) and a complete parts list with approved vendors as well.

At the other extreme are projects that have never been done before, and there is little history of similar efforts for even parts of the project. These will be high-risk projects and most likely complex projects, too.

In order to handle both situations, I developed a two-step requirements elicitation process. The first step is to generate a set of high-level requirements that form a necessary and sufficient set of requirements in which inclusion in the solution will assure project deliverables that meet expected business value. Regardless of the complexity of the project, this high-level identification of requirements will be complete. These requirements capture what will be in the acceptable solution, but not how they will be developed or even if they can be developed. These high-level requirements are considered a complete description of what a solution must deliver from a performance perspective.

The second step is to decompose the high-level requirements for further description of what each requirement includes. The results of the second step inform the team as to how they might manage the project. At this point, however, the decomposed requirements definition is limited to what needs to be part of the acceptable solution, but not how those decomposed requirements will be built and integrated into the acceptable solution. The *how* it will be built is answered with the WBS (see Chapter 6).

---

**Requirements Breakdown Structure**

The *requirements breakdown structure* (RBS) is a hierarchical description of all of the ACPF requirements that must be present in the solution in order to deliver the business value expected. The RBS hierarchical structure may include any or all of the following:

- Functions
- Sub-functions
- Processes
- Activities
- Features

## Elicitation and Decomposition of ACPF Requirements

In the ACPF world, the elicitation of requirements is a two-stage process: ACPF requirements elicitation and ACPF requirements decomposition.

### First Stage, ACPF Requirements Elicitation

The first stage of ACPF requirements elicitation is business focused. In this stage, only the highest-level requirements are identified. These requirements form a necessary and sufficient set of requirements of which successful integration into the solution will define project success. Whether or not the expected business value is achieved will follow from the sponsor and client business model, and the suitability of the solution to complement that model. These highest-level requirements can often be used as success criteria for the POS of the proposed project. In this case, the metric is a simple *yes* or *no* if the requirement is met. The first stage is completed during Step 2 of the Project Set-up Phase.

### Second Stage, ACPF Requirements Decomposition

The second stage, ACPF requirements decomposition, is technically focused. Here, the highest-level set of requirements developed in the first stage are decomposed for further identification at a lower level (functions, processes, features). These are good scoping descriptions of the solution. There are several approaches available for performing this decomposition, described later in this chapter. For simple projects, the second stage is usually completed during Step 2 of the Project Set-up Phase. For complex projects, the second stage is usually initiated during Step 2 of Project Set-up, but cannot be completed until the Project Execution Phase.

## Representing Requirements: The Requirements Breakdown Structure

So far, requirements were defined from the perspective of what those requirements have to do. Functions, processes, and activities offer us the details of that definition. Given that understanding, our requirements admit a structure like that shown in Figure 4.9. For those of you familiar with the WBS, you will see that this is quite similar to a functional-based WBS. And it is, so nothing is new there. However, what is new is what we are going to do with the RBS. The RBS will be the basis on which you decide how to structure the project management approach you will use for a project with this type of RBS (the reference here is for the complexity, completeness, and uncertainty of the RBS for the project at hand).

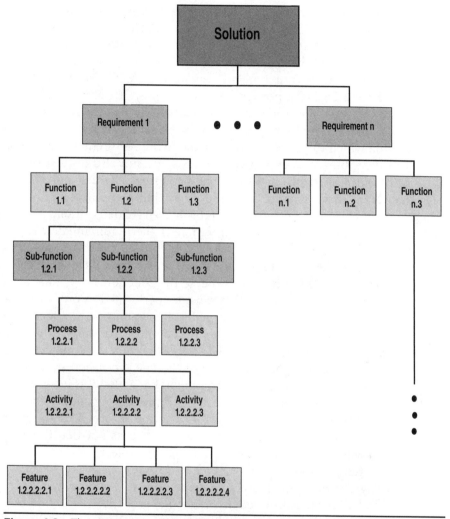

**Figure 4.9**   The requirements breakdown structure

As you gather and document requirements by whatever method you choose, place them in their appropriate level in the RBS. The graphical format shown in Figure 4.9 works well. Alternatively, you could present the RBS in an indented outline format. It's all a matter of preference.

Here is a brief description of each level in the decomposition:

- **Solution**—The solution is the output from Step 1: Develop the Business Case.

- **Requirement**—Requirements 1 through $n$ form the necessary and sufficient set that describes an acceptable solution. Usually, this set will contain 6-12 requirements. The "necessary and sufficient conditions" statement means that all ACPF requirements are needed in order to achieve the success criteria, and none of the ACPF requirements are superfluous. This is important because the project was justified based on the expected business value, as described through the success criteria. Linking the ACPF requirements to the success criteria provides a basis on which to prioritize not only the ACPF requirements, based on their contribution to expected business value, but also to the prioritization of the functions, sub-functions, processes, activities, and features that define requirements decomposition. Unlike the IIBA definition, *requirements* is a term restricted to this high-level description.
- **Decomposition Levels**—Decomposition of the requirements can occur on different levels:
  + **Function**—At the discretion of the project manager, the highest level of decomposition may be at the function level. This level comprises the functions that must be performed in order for the parent requirement to be acceptable. It is important to understand that the RBS reflects what is known about the solution at the time the RBS is first defined. This initial list of functions may or may not be complete. Neither you nor the client can be expected to know if that list is complete. You might know that it is incomplete, but you would not know that it is complete. How could you? For the sake of generating the RBS, you have to proceed on the basis that the initial list will be complete. If it turns out that it is not, you will discover that as part of doing the project.
  + **Sub-function**—At the next level of decomposition are sub-functions. For more expansive functions, you may not have any idea of what those sub-functions might be, and that is okay. In any case, the project team should make every effort to identify the sub-functions that further define a function. Once these sub-functions have been developed, the function they define will now be complete. This is the same as the premise underlying the WBS architecture and is very intuitive. For many adaptive projects, additional sub-functions will be discovered as part of doing the project.
  + **Process**—Complex functions and sub-functions can be further described with the business processes that comprise them. These are the business processes that are commonly used in today's organizations. To make them more understandable, the functions might

be decomposed into sub-functions and the business processes that comprise the sub-functions then decomposed to processes.

+ **Activity**—Activities are otherwise known as "process steps."
+ **Feature**—At the lowest level of decomposition are features. These are the visible enhancements and characteristics of the entity that they describe. Think of them as cosmetic (i.e., authentication screen background design) and you won't be far off.

Note that not all decomposition levels are necessary for every requirement. Some requirements will be more comprehensive than others, and utilize all levels. The simplest requirement might be best described using only a features list. The decomposition is subjective. In the final analysis, all that is needed is a decomposition that clearly describes each requirement.

The RBS will be useful as an aid in helping decide which strategy is best for the project management process to be followed, in other words, the nature of the project as viewed through its RBS. It is the best guide you will have for choosing the best strategy for managing the project.

If you get the RBS right, you are halfway home. That means we should pay particular attention to what is put into the RBS, and make sure you are not victims of scope creep. We will have enough outside influences to add to scope. We do not need to be a party to that now.

## Approaches to Requirements Elicitation and Decomposition

Requirements have to be gathered through a carefully planned engagement with the client. Of all the requirement gathering approaches, I recommend six that work particularly well within the ACPF world. These are widely used methods for generating requirements. It is usually the case where more than one method is chosen to generate the requirements on a project. Selection of the best methods to generate potential requirements for the project is the responsibility of the project manager, who must evaluate each method for costs, ease of implementation, reliability, client comfort level with the chosen process, and risks. Further, selection of a particular method should be based on specific product and project needs, as well as proven effectiveness. Certain methods have been proven effective for specific industries and products. An example of this would be using physical, three-dimensional wireframe models in product design or solid models in bridge construction.

Requirements elicitation is the first and challenging task that the project manager and client will face in the life of a complex project. To do this effectively is as much an art as it is a science. On the art side of the equation, the project manager will have to prepare the client to engage in the elicitation, decomposition, and documentation process. The attitude, commitment, willingness of the client to be meaningfully involved, and preparation of the client are major determinants in the choice of approach. This preparation will include the choice of approach to be used and perhaps some preliminary training of the client and the core team. Some clients will be open and proactive in participating; others will not. Some will be sure of their needs; others will not. Some will be expressing their wants, which may be very different from their needs.

On the scientific side are the many techniques that have been used successfully to decompose and document requirements. I have had good success using brainstorming, user stories, interviews, facilitated group sessions, prototyping, and requirements workshops. All of these should be in your ACPF/kit.

It is important to realize that requirements identification and decomposition are critical to understanding the direction of the project. It is now that the framework for the project begins to take shape.

The steps to generate requirements begin by looking at the business function as a whole. This is followed by the selection of a method or methods for gathering requirements. This effort must be planned. A few of the several approaches to requirements elicitation are shown in Table 4.3. These are ordered from least formal to most formal. These are usually understood or easily adopted in less sophisticated environments. (A good reference on methods for gathering requirements is Robertson and Robertson, 2012.)

I single out these six methods because they work best when trying to translate business requirements into business deliverables. Across the entire history of the ACPF, I have had the most experience and success with these methods.

These methods can also be used to decompose requirements and generate the RBS. Regardless of the method you use to generate the RBS, I strongly advise creating an RBS for every project for the following reasons:

- Most meaningful to the client.
- Is a deliverables-based approach.
- Is consistent with the PMBOK.
- Remains client-facing as long as possible.
- Is the higher order part of the WBS.

### Brainstorming

The ACPF Brainstorming Process is an adaptation and extension of the standard brainstorming process and was discussed earlier in this chapter.

Table 4.3    Selected methods for eliciting requirements from business needs

| Method | Strengths | Risks |
|---|---|---|
| Brainstorming | Can identify ideas from others' ideas | Must control to avoid criticizing ideas |
| User Stories | State of system described before entering system<br>Completed scenarios used to describe state of system<br>Normal flow of event and exceptions revealed | Newness has resulted in some inconsistencies<br>Information may still be missing from scenario description<br>Long interaction required<br>Training expensive |
| Interviews | End user participation<br>High-level descriptions of functions and processes are provided | Descriptions may differ from actual detailed activities<br>Without structure, stakeholders may not know what information to provide<br>Real needs may be ignored if the analyst is predjudiced |
| Facilitated Group Sessions | Excellent for cross-functional processes<br>Detailed requirements can be documented and verified immediately<br>Resolves issues with an impartial facilitator | Use of untrained facilitators can lead to a negative response from users<br>The time and cost of the planning and/or executing the session can be high |
| Prototyping | Innovative ideas can be generated<br>Users clarify what they want<br>Users identify requirements that may be missed<br>Client-focused<br>Early proof of concept<br>Stimulates thought processes | Client may want to implement the prototype<br>Difficult to know when to stop<br>Specialized skills are required<br>Absence of documentation |
| Requirements Workshop | Good way for first time use | May overwhelm client |

## *User Stories*

I use user stories on occasion, but very informally. Basically, a user story is just that. Pick some piece of a business process and have the user tell you how it operates—who does what and when. I use the story as the jumping-off point for a discussion of what does not work well, and why, as a prelude to process improvement. This keeps the user well within their comfort zone and does not require them to have any special knowledge about user stories and how to document them.

## Interviews

Interviews are one-on-one sessions with operational level managers and users who can provide guidance on requirements. These interviews can be biased because they are one-on-one. I only use them when scheduling of the appropriate groups is not possible (geographically dispersed, for example). If interviews are used, some type of review of the resulting requirements by all affected managers and users is necessary.

---

**Warning**

I have tried separate group interview sessions for well-defined groups. Do not confuse a group interview with the facilitated group session. Including the manager of the group is not a good idea. There is a risk that it will stifle open input. That would render the group interview as biased and misleading. You might not even be aware that it is happening. My advice is to interview the manager separately from the others. If there are conflicting results, you will have to reconcile them.

---

## Facilitated Group Sessions

A facilitated group session is probably the approach used in every requirements decomposition session, and it often integrates one or more of the other approaches. There are a number of ways to structure these sessions that I want you to be aware of. You will need a trained facilitator and a little planning to decide how best to approach the facilitated group session:

- **One single group session**—This type of session works well for smaller projects and for projects that involve only one business group. I prefer this approach whenever possible. All involved parties hear the same discussion and conclusions in real time.
- **Separated group sessions**—As the project gets larger, you might consider breaking the project into subprojects for the purposes of requirements decomposition. Subprojects would allow you to invite those business groups with specific expertise or interest in a particular subproject. This approach has the added step of combining the results of the multiple sessions. Resolving differences can become an issue, and some type of shuttle diplomacy may be required. Compromises are often needed to come to closure.

## *Prototyping*

Many clients cannot relate to a narrative description of a system, but they can relate to a visual representation of a system. For requirements decomposition purposes, the idea of a prototype was conceived several decades ago. Its original purpose was to help clients define what they wanted. By showing them a mock-up of a solution, they could comment on it and give the developers more insight into what constitutes an acceptable solution. Originally these prototypes were storyboard versions, not production versions. Later prototypes did become production versions of the solution when used in complex projects. For details on prototyping, see Chapter 6.

## *Requirements Decomposition Workshop*

You always have to be prepared to work with a client who has not previously experienced requirements elicitation sessions. I have had my best results when I offered the training concurrently with the practice of that training. It puts the training in the context of an actual application. Clients tend to remain motivated throughout the workshop because they have an immediate need to be satisfied, and the quality of the results tends to improve over other approaches with first timers. A typical requirements decomposition workshop is a structured event with an agenda.

## Choosing a Requirements Elicitation Approach

There are several things to take into consideration when deciding which approach to take:

- **The experience of the client team**—If the client team has a memorable and effective experience with any of the requirements gathering approaches, try to select from among them. To the most extent possible, you should put the client in their comfort zone so that they can focus on the work of defining requirements.
- **The experience of the development team**—If the development team has a memorable and effective experience with any of the requirements gathering approaches, try to select from among them. Given the choice of two or more approaches, choose the one that favors the client.
- **The complexity and nature of the project**—The more complex the project, the more you would want to use approaches that give detailed information and are less likely to overlook anything. A formal process should be preferred to an informal process.

- **The experience of the session facilitator**—First of all, the session facilitator should not be a member of the client team or the development team. This may come as a surprise, but there are good reasons to back it up. The facilitator's job is so critical that you need someone with experience and with no bias toward the project. Their job is to facilitate, not politic. The client team leader and the development team leader need to focus their attention on the deliverables from the requirements gathering exercise, not on the process of getting them, and so they are not good choices. If there is no one internal to the organization that meets the criteria, hire an outside consultant. This is no place to cut expenses. The more critical and complex the project, the more you should favor the use of an outside facilitator.

## Elicit and Document Requirements

Complete and clear document requirements at the beginning of a project have never really happened. It just isn't possible, except in the simplest of projects. (Infrastructure projects are an example because they tend to be isolated from the outside world.) A few "cowboys" would claim to have done so, and launched into project planning under the assumption of having a complete requirements document. Later, to their dismay, they are deluged with scope change requests from the client: "What happened? I thought we had all of this nailed. You told us you were satisfied and that we had done an exemplary job of gathering and documenting your requirements." The problem is not with the process. The problem is not with the initial documentation. The problem is that the world is not a static place. It never has been and never will be. So, why should you expect your requirements document to stand still while you do the project? Change is inevitable, regardless of how well we did at the outset. There must be better ways. And there are!

In Chapter 6, the RBS is established as the foundation of all great project management. The RBS is the major input to help you make the decision as to which category of project you have, and which Project Management Life Cycle (PMLC) model would be most appropriate for managing the project. I will show how the RBS can be used to help the project team decide which strategy, among the five major project management categories, should be chosen and under what circumstances you should use each one. The strategy that you choose then becomes the infrastructure on which you will choose a project management model and build your project plan. The status of the RBS relative to its completeness can be used as the measure of progress towards the solution.

The completeness and clarity of the RBS present you with two critical decisions as to which of five major directions to go (Linear, Incremental, Iterative, Adaptive, or Extreme). Within that choice is which specific PMLC model will be used. In this book, the chosen direction is down the adaptive road, the ACPF road. As you will see, these decisions are not obvious. While there is some objectivity involved, the decision process leans heavily towards the subjective side.

I advise creating an RBS for every project because it:

- Is most meaningful to the customer.
- Promotes customer ownership and eventual buy-in of the solution.
- Is a deliverables-based approach and in the customer's comfort zone.
- Can be used to measure progress towards solution definition.
- Can be used to measure project status.
- Is consistent with the Program Management Institute's PMBOK.
- Remains customer-facing as long as possible into the planning exercise.

The situation depicted in Figure 4.9 is all well and good, if you happen to know the complete RBS. If you don't, you have a problem. In complex projects, an incomplete RBS is the rule rather than the exception. It would be unusual to have a complete RBS at the start of a complex project. Some functions and features may not be known, and their absence may not be known at this early stage, either. Being able to say that the RBS is complete is based more on a feeling than on hard fact. The ACPF is designed to learn and discover the complete RBS, and hence the solution, through iteration.

> Conventional wisdom says that a complete RBS is not possible at the start of a complex project, but can only be defined through an iterative process. There may be exceptions for projects that are often repeated.

So far, we have defined requirements from the perspective of what those requirements have to do. Functions and features offer us the details of that definition. Given that understanding, our requirements admit a structure much like that shown in Figure 4.8. For those of you familiar with the WBS, you will see that this is quite similar to a functional-based WBS. It will be the basis on which you decide how to structure the project management approach you will use for a project with this type of RBS (the reference here is to complexity, completeness, and uncertainty of the RBS for the project at hand).

The RBS is the input to creating the WBS, or at least as much as is known from the incomplete RBS. Figure 4.10 illustrates how we can start with the current RBS and build as much of the WBS as needed.

Beginning with the list of requirements generated from any one of the methods identified in Table 4.3, you have to create a deliverables-based WBS. For example, assume Figure 4.10 is the known RBS. Function #1.1 is the lowest level in this part of the RBS. No further detail is known or needed in order to define how this function will be built and so the WBS for this function could be built. However, if nothing is known about Function #1.1 without that information, its WBS cannot be built.

There are two ways to collect what the client knows about the requirements of an acceptable solution:

- **Conduct Conditions of Satisfaction**—The recommended choice for smaller, less complex projects when the characteristics of an acceptable solution are either completely known or mostly known.

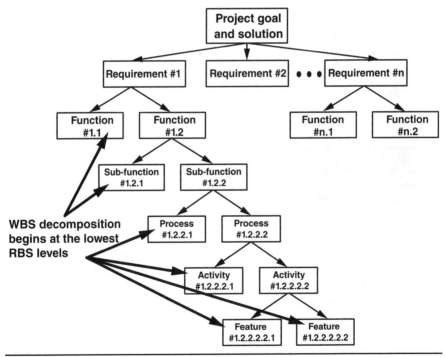

**Figure 4.10**   Creating the WBS from the RBS

- **Elicit Requirements**—The recommended choice for larger, more complex projects, or where very little of the acceptable solution is known.

## STEP 3: WRITE A PROJECT OVERVIEW STATEMENT

A POS is the first formal document that describes the project idea at a high level and is used for general distribution. It is written in the language of the business so that anyone who has the occasion to read it, will understand it. No "techie talk" allowed. It is only one page, so there isn't an opportunity to say much, other than a few basic pieces of information.

### Definition of the Project Overview Statement

The deliverable from the COS is a negotiated agreement. The POS is the documented and approved statement of that agreement. The POS is brief—one page is always sufficient. A POS basically summarizes the COS and RBS, regardless of which is available. A POS template with an example is shown in Figure 4.11. The POS contains the following five sections, which are discussed next:

- A statement of the problem or opportunity (reason for doing the project).
- A goal statement (what will generally be done).
- A statement of the objectives (general statements of how it might be done).
- The quantifiable business outcomes (what business value will be obtained).
- General comments on risks, assumptions, and obstacles to success.

After more than 40 years of managing projects, I can honestly say that I have always been able to write a one-page POS regardless of the scope of the project. Being able to write a one-page POS means that you really understand the project and can communicate it intelligently to senior management. Think of it as though it was the two-minute elevator speech and you won't go far astray. I've seen project initiation documents as large as 70 pages. I'm not sure who reads these, if anyone. If they do, do they really understand the project at the level of detail needed for granting approval to create the project plan? I doubt it! A document of that length may be of value to the development team but not to the sponsor and certainly not to the executive who will be approving it.

| PROJECT OVERVIEW STATEMENT | Project Name **Common Cold Prevention Project** | Project No. **14 - 21** | Project Manager **Carrie deCure** |
|---|---|---|---|

**Problem/Opportunity**

There does not exist a preventative for the common cold.

**Goal**

Find a way to prevent the occurrence of the common cold.

**Objectives**

1. Find a food additive that will prevent the occurrence of the common cold.
2. Alter the immune system to prevent the occurrence of the common cold.
3. Define a program of diet and exercise that will prevent the occurrence of the common cold.

**Success Criteria**

The solution must be effective for at least 90% of persons of any age.
The solution must not introduce any harmful side effects.
The solution must cost the consumer less than $20.00 per dose.
The solution must be accepted by the FDA.
The solution must be obtained over the counter at any pharmacy.
The solution must return at least 20% gross profit.

**Assumptions, Risks, Obstacles**

Assumption: The common cold can be prevented.
Risk: The solution will have harmful side effects.
Obstacle: Drug manufacturers will hinder the search for a cure.

| Prepared By **Earnest Effort** **VP Project Management** | Date **6-14-2014** | Approved By **Hy Podermick** **VP Research & Development** | Date **6-16-2014** |
|---|---|---|---|

**Figure 4.11**  A typical POS template with example data

## Problem/Opportunity Statement

A well-defined need, and a clear solution pathway to meet that need, define a project that the traditionalist expects. A rather vague idea of a want, coupled with a vague idea of how it will be satisfied, define a project that the complex project manager expects. The problem or opportunity that our project is going to respond to must already be recognized by the organization as a legitimate problem or opportunity that must be attended to. If anyone in the organization were asked about it, s/he would surely answer, "You bet it is, and we need to do something about it." In other words, it is not something that needs a defense. It stands on its own merits. Furthermore, the problem or opportunity statement must be couched in terms that anyone in the organization who would have a reason to read the statement could understand without the need for further explanation.

## Defining the Goal of This Version of the Solution

The goal will be a simple yet definitive statement about what this project intends to do to address the problem or opportunity. It might be a total solution, but to be more realistic, it would be a solution that addresses a major segment of the problem or opportunity. I say this because all too often we define projects that are far too large in scope. Sure, you would like to cure all cancers, but be realistic. Maybe curing one form of cancer would be a lofty enough goal.

Having a goal that is too ambitious will open the project to scope reduction as the project becomes framed in a more attainable way. Furthermore, there can be changes in the environment that renders a too ambitious goal ineffective or unattainable. So, a project with a long delivery time is exposed to cancellation before it can deliver any business value. By defining the goal of this version to be a reachable target, rather than a lofty or unattainable ambition, we protect the client and the team from scope reduction and significantly increase their chances of delivering business value. We are sure that this has a lot to do with the high incidence of project failure. It may sound pedestrian to some of you, but I believe that you will be far more successful in the long run by biting off less than you think you can chew.

> Management did not appoint you project manager due to expecting heroic efforts, just successful ones.

## Writing the Objectives of This Version

By way of analogy, I think of the goal statement as a pie and the objectives statements as slices of the pie. All of the slices that make up the pie are the objectives statements. If you would rather have a mathematical interpretation, think of the objectives as necessary and sufficient conditions for the attainment of the goal. In either case, the objectives statements give a little more detail on how the goal will be achieved. They are the boundary conditions, if you will. I would expect to see you write six to eight objectives statements to clarify your goal statement. Together, the project statement and the objectives statements define the goal of the project. They will be either a clear or not clear statement of the goal of the project.

I have also used the set of necessary and sufficient high-level requirements as objectives statements. This works quite well when you can translate these requirements into quantitative success criteria.

## Defining the Success Criteria

The success criteria (or explicit business outcomes) are quantitative statements of the results that will be realized from having successfully completed this project. They are formulated in such a way that they either happened, or they did not happen. There will be no debate over attainment of success criteria. Statements like "Pretax profit margins will increase from their current average of 23 percent per month to an average of at least 34 percent per month by the end of the second quarter of operations using the new system" are acceptable. Statements like "Increase customer satisfaction" are not. We would expect to see two or perhaps three success criteria for your project. Success criteria generally fall into one of three categories:

- A quantitative metric related to increased revenues (IR)
- A quantitative metric related to avoidance of cost (AC)
- A quantitative metric related to increased service levels (IS)

This list is identified with the acronym IRACIS.

## Listing the Major Assumptions/Risks/Obstacles

Put yourself in the shoes of the financial analyst who might ask, "I am being asked to invest $10 million in a new process that is supposed to cut operating expenses by 5 percent per month for the next five years. What risks are we exposed to that might prevent us from achieving that ROI?" What would you tell the analyst? That is what you would list as major risks or obstacles. As another example, you might make senior managers aware of the fact that certain staff skill shortages are going to be a problem or that the ongoing reorganization of sales and marketing will have to be complete or there will be serious consequences during system implementation.

## Seek StageGate #1 Approval

StageGate #1 is the senior management approval to proceed to the Project Set-up Phase. Along with this approval is the release of the resources that will be needed for that phase. Since requirements gathering is a labor intensive version-defining activity, it is not done until StageGate #1 approval is granted. There is still a lot about this project that has to be defined before any version planning work can be done and one more approval step (Stage-Gate #2) before the actual work of the project is authorized and budgeted by senior management.

There will be occasions when the POS is not approved. This usually means that the sponsor has not made a compelling argument for the business viability of their intended approach to the problem or opportunity. Despite the fact that the business need may be critical, the risk of failure is weighed against the expected business value of the solution. Expected business value may not justify the cost of the project. It does not mean that the project is not important to the executives, just that the approach chosen does not make good business sense. Some other approach is needed. The sponsoring business unit is invited to revise and resubmit the POS. Alternatively, the POS may be rejected without further consideration.

## PUTTING IT ALL TOGETHER

In the Ideation Phase we have brought an idea from a very informal statement of need or opportunity to an initial definition of one or more prioritized projects, and finally to a choice of the initial project to be pursued. The Ideation Phase concludes with a one-page statement of that project that is forwarded for management approval. The Ideation Phase is an essential first step to defining a project and seeking the resources and authorization to proceed to the Project Set-up Phase.

# 5

---

# ADAPTIVE COMPLEX PROJECT FRAMEWORK: SET-UP PHASE

---

*Let all things be done correctly and in order.*
1 Corinthians 14:40

## CHAPTER LEARNING OBJECTIVES

This chapter will provide readers the knowledge or ability to:

- Classify a project into the four-quadrant landscape; categorize the project as Linear, Incremental, Iterative, Adaptive, or Extreme; and choose a specific Project Management Life Cycle (PMLC) model for project execution.
- Know how project characteristics, and internal and external environmental conditions, will alter the chosen PMLC model for a better fit to improve the likelihood of generating the expected business value.

The Project Set-up Phase of the Adaptive Complex Project Framework (ACPF) is unique. That uniqueness gives the ACPF a powerful and effective process for successfully managing any type of project from ideation to the end of its useful life. First, few project management books discuss the decision processes and practices over the entire project life span. Second, and most important but often overlooked, the ACPF is based on the fact that every project is unique and to a certain extent the best approach to managing it will also be unique. Finally, a project is a dynamic entity that changes for all sorts of reasons, both predictable and unpredictable, and for that reason the best management approach will also be dynamic and change along with the changing project conditions that arise during the Project Execution Phase. These three reasons place several challenges on the project manager, the client manager, the client team, and the development team. They must be constantly vigilant, work as a unified team, and be always ready to accommodate change.

The Set-up Phase contains the analytic tools and decision models the team will need to build and maintain for the success of their complex projects.

## COMPLEX PROJECT SET-UP PHASE

Project Set-up begins with a definition of the business problem or untapped business opportunity, and a high-level definition of solution requirements as described in the Project Overview Statement (POS), and proceeds to choosing and adapting the best fit management model(s) to effectively discover, develop, and deploy a solution to the specific business problem and/ or untapped business opportunity. These management models include project management, and may also include systems development, business process design, and process improvement. Figure 5.1 illustrates the steps that are executed during the Project Set-up Phase.

The ACPF leads the sponsor and co-project managers through a decision model to define that management process and implement any adaptations to better align with the project situation. Project Set-Up consists of Steps 4-7 of the twelve-step ACPF, shown in the shaded Set-up Phase boxes in Figure 5.2.

Let us begin by taking stock of what we have accomplished at this point in the ACPF project life span:

- We have defined the problem or business opportunity.
- We have proposed and justified the business value of an acceptable solution.
- We have elicited the high-level solution requirements.
- We have submitted the POS and obtained sponsor approval to proceed with Project Set-up.
- StageGate #1 has been satisfied.

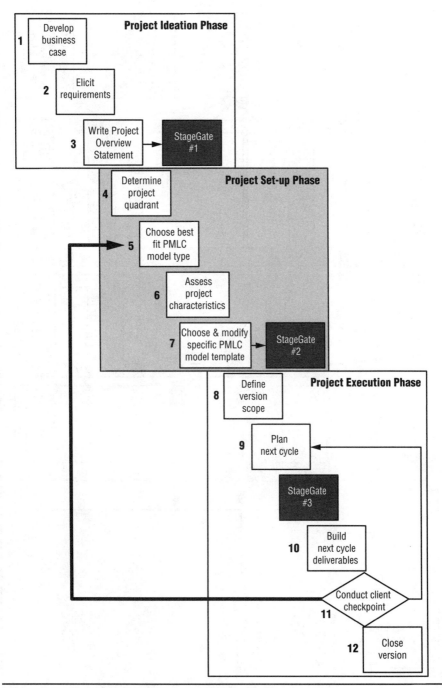

**Figure 5.1**   Complex Project Set-up Phase

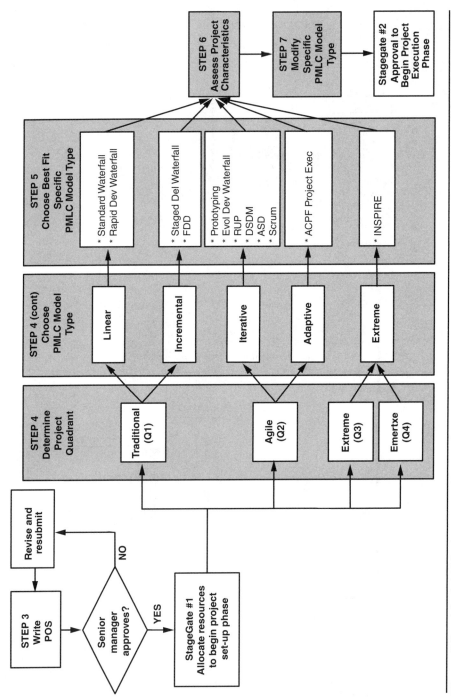

**Figure 5.2**   A look inside the Project Set-up Phase

There are still several questions to be answered before we can request approval to execute the project:

- What type of project is this?
- What is the best fit PMLC model type from among the five choices?
- What specific PMLC model should we use?
- What modifications will be needed to align with the project characteristics and its total environment?
- StageGate #2 has not yet been satisfied.

These questions will be answered in Steps 4 through 7 (the shaded portions of Figure 5.2).

## STEP 4: DETERMINE PROJECT QUADRANT

Recall from Chapter 2 that the project landscape was a four-quadrant landscape, as shown in Figure 5.3.

- **Traditional Project (Quadrant 1):** Traditional projects are the familiar ground when one thinks of projects. A goal is defined and the solution to deliver the requirements to achieve that goal is also defined. Both

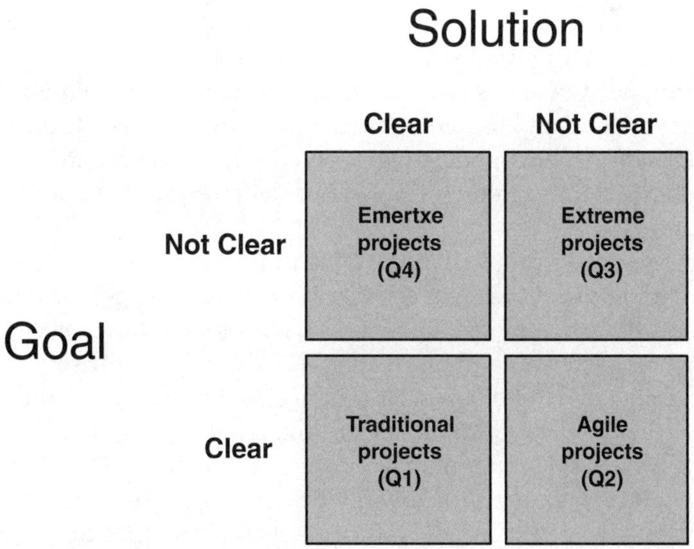

**Figure 5.3** The ACPF project landscape

goal and solution are clear. A plan is developed, the budget approved, resources are acquired and scheduled, and everyone is satisfied. The project is executed, some changes are approved, and the delivered value is anticipated—a nice, neat package. While most contemporary projects are not of this type, traditional projects still exist. Construction projects are examples of Quadrant 1 (Q1) projects.

- **Agile Project (Quadrant 2):** Agile projects present a major variation that sets them clearly apart from the traditional project. A goal is still defined, but the solution and its detailed requirements are not completely known at the outset. The complete requirements of a satisfactory solution can only be learned and discovered by doing the agile project. The management approaches that are used for agile projects are different than those used for traditional projects. The major variation is that scope is variable in an agile project.

- **Extreme Project (Quadrant 3):** "Extreme projects" are just that—extreme. The goal may be nothing more than a desired end state, a dream. A solution to achieving that end state may or may not be found. In many cases, the goal is variable and so is the solution. The management approaches used for extreme projects are different than those used for either traditional projects or agile projects.

- **Emertxe Project (Quadrant 4):** At first brush, emertxe (pronounced ee-MURT-see) projects look like solutions looking for problems to solve. But the reality is quite different. The solution may be a product, the juice from a remote tree grown only in Borneo, or a technology, and the question is whether or not it has business value. In other words, what business goal can be achieved using the solution, and does it have sufficient business value to justify its adoption? It turns out that the management models used for emertxe projects are the same as those used for extreme projects, but the interpretations are different.

The purpose of the project landscape is to provide a simple structure that the client and project manager can use as the beginning point as they search for the best fit PMLC model. Once they have assigned the project to a quadrant, they can determine the best fit PMLC model type within that quadrant. That choice will be based on a subjective assessment of the degree to which the high-level requirements and the requirements breakdown structure (RBS) have been completely and clearly documented. Most thought leaders would argue that this can only be done in the simplest of situations. Once the best fit PMLC model has been chosen, the specific model choice and its modification will be a function of the project's characteristics.

The choice of quadrant should follow directly from Step 2: Elicit Requirements. In that step, the necessary and sufficient set of high-level requirements will have been defined. As part of the elicitation process, there will be some visibility into the level of detail associated with each of those requirements and how they might be delivered. The biggest decision to be made here is whether or not the project belongs in Q1. If you aren't sure, don't guess. Place the project in Q2. That is perfectly acceptable, and will not negatively affect the outcome. That is the best information available at this early stage and is used to choose the project quadrant. Five types of models populate the project landscape as defined in Figure 5.4.

Note that the only substantive graphical differences between the five PMLC models are the feedback loops. In the Linear case, there is no feedback. In the Incremental case, the feedback loop is to the next increment with the scope and plan remaining intact. In the Agile case, both feedback loops are to the next just-in-time plan. However, at the detailed level the purposes and interpretations are quite different. For the Extreme case, the feedback loop is to the scoping phase, where both the goal and solution can be reset.

## Traditional Project Management

The traditional project management (TPM) quadrant contains the simplest of all project types, but the least likely to occur in today's challenging and constantly changing business climate. TPM projects are familiar to the organization and routinely done. Many of these projects will be repeated on a scheduled basis. The client has clearly scoped the problem, often with the participation of a business analyst (BA), and the project team has defined how they will solve the problem (the solution and its requirements). Such projects also put the team on familiar technology grounds. These are usually low-risk projects.

A complete plan is generated. The limiting factor, in plan-driven approaches like this, is that they are change-intolerant. They are focused on delivering according to time and budget constraints, and rely more on compliance to plan than on delivering business value. The plan is *sacred* and conformance to it is the hallmark of a successful project. Any changes to that plan are disruptive and the cause of additional non-value-added work. The BA can play a pivotal role here by screening, documenting, prioritizing, and scheduling the submission of client scope change requests.

Few changes are expected in TPMs and not planned for in the schedule, either. This is where many TPM PMLC models get into trouble. The

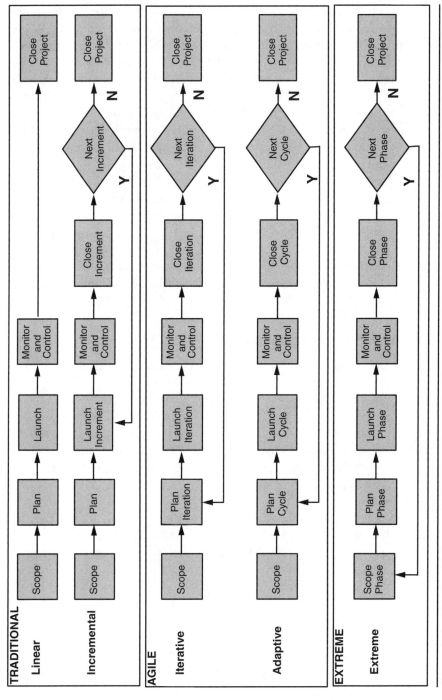

**Figure 5.4**   PMLC model types

assumption underlying all TPM projects is that the RBS is complete and there will be few, if any, change requests. Change requests can be very descriptive and may be very important to the business value of the final solution, but their implementation can be very disruptive. In addition to the time spent by one or more team members, there can be a significant impact on the project schedule, not to mention changes to resource requirements and staff availability.

Every change request requires that the following actions be taken:

- Someone (a BA, project manager (PM), or change control board) needs to decide if the requirements change request warrants an analysis and disposition by a project team member.
- The PM must assign the request to the appropriate team member.
- The assigned team member conducts the analysis and writes the Project Impact Statement.
- The PM informs the BA and/or the client of the analysis and recommended actions.
- The PM, the BA, the client, and the change control board must make a decision as to whether the change will be approved, and if so, how it will be incorporated into the project plan and schedule. If the change request is approved, the project scope, cost, schedule, resource requirements, and client acceptance criteria are updated.

All of this takes time away from the team member's scheduled project commitments. If there are too many requirements change requests, you can begin to appreciate the effects on the team members' productivity, and ultimately, the project schedule. Furthermore, much of the time spent planning the project before the request was made becomes non-value-added time because the project plan must be revised to incorporate the approved change.

There are two variations of TPM to consider: Linear and Incremental, and the challenges of managing scope change requests are different for each variation.

## Linear PMLC Models

Linear PMLC models are the ones that most business managers have in mind when they think about project management. Indeed, they are the simplest models and have been in use longer than any other project management model. Linear TPM PMLC models are a good place to start the journey of learning to become a complex project manager. For software development projects, the Standard Waterfall model is the simplest and most familiar example of a Linear TPM PMLC model. The Rapid Development Waterfall model is another type of Linear TPM. Variations of the Feature-Driven Development model are also classified as Linear. For all of these examples, the goal and solution are clearly defined. That means a complete work breakdown structure (WBS) can be built and a complete project plan developed with all resource requirements known and scheduled.

As described in the previous section, change requests require project team resources to process and if approved, can have a major impact on schedules and resource requirements. Here is where the support of the BA can be invaluable. The BA can be the filter between the client and the project team by prioritizing change requests, documenting the requests, and submitting them at the appropriate time. The BA's working knowledge of the TPM PMLC will be a big assist to the PM and the project team.

## Incremental PMLC Models

These projects have exactly the same characteristics as projects that use a Linear TPM PMLC model. That is, the goal and solution are both clearly defined. The only difference in project management approach for these projects is that the client chooses to release the deliverables in stages or increments. In a Linear TPM PMLC model, all deliverables are released at the end of the project in one release. In an Incremental TPM PMLC model, the deliverables are released over time. These releases can be scheduled as needed, or in line with the established enterprise release strategy. Incremental PMLC models are used to create marketing advantages that accrue from early entry. The Staged Delivery Waterfall and variations of the Feature-Driven Development models fall into this classification.

Decomposing the complete solution into increments is a challenge to the effective management of these projects. The role of the BA in these projects is more challenging than in the Linear TPM PMLC models. The BA is the critical component, and must collaborate with the PM in decomposing the deliverables because they are all related to the requirements. Decomposing the deliverables requires knowledge of the product/ process because the grouping of deliverables across several increments has to produce marketable partial solutions and adhere to the dependencies that exist between groups of deliverables. Incremental TPM projects are best staffed by both a PM and a BA, working together to decide what will be included in each increment. To do this effectively, the PM only needs minimal skills in business analysis and the BA only needs minimal skills in project management. The interaction between the PM and the BA is constant throughout the project.

The major drawback to Incremental TPM PMLC models is that they encourage requirements change requests. By giving the client a partial solution, they are encouraged to want to make changes and that is not your intent. So, be careful when you agree to this approach. Having a BA as your partner will facilitate these unexpected change requests, much like in the TPM PMLC. It might be a good idea to set some management reserve time aside in anticipation of those requests.

## Agile Project Management

A project that has a clear goal, without knowing how to achieve the goal (the solution), falls in the Agile Project Management (APM) quadrant. Agile projects dominate the landscape. Testimonial data that I have gathered from all over the world suggests that fully 70 percent of all projects are APM projects. APM projects have their own project management models that are quite different from TPM project management models.

The range of complexity and uncertainty that characterizes APM projects is wide and deep. APM projects dwarf TPM projects with their challenges to both the PM and the BA. The least complex and uncertain APM projects will require one agile approach (Iterative PMLC models), while those projects at the highest levels of complexity and uncertainty will require a different agile approach (Adaptive PMLC models). Both variations are structured to handle frequent change, and this process must be managed. Iterative PMLC models require the PM and BA to have a *working knowledge* of the other's discipline. Adaptive PMLC models require the PM and the BA to have *mastery* of the other's discipline. From a project management and business analysis perspective, the PM and their BA partner need to have skill profiles that are the mirror images of one another. Both the PM and the BA can function in both roles. Meaningfully involving the PM and BA as partners can go a long way to mitigating much of the risk associated with the unknown.

You should have guessed by now that an APM project can be very high risk. If previous attempts to solve the problem have failed, it means the problem is complex and there may not be an acceptable solution. The organization will just have to live with that reality and make the best of it. Projects to find that elusive solution might work better if they are focused on parts of the problem, or if approached as process-improvement projects. Much of that risk can be mitigated if the PM and the BA function as co-project managers on the project.

There are two variations of APM to consider: Iterative and Adaptive.

### Iterative PMLC Models

Iterative APM PMLC models are used in the simpler of the two types of APM projects. Iterative APM PMLC models are appropriate for projects in which the solution is nearly complete. There may be several known alternatives for the few missing pieces of the solution. The project will have to determine which alternatives best meets client requirements. This will be done through a number of iterations until the complete solution comes into focus. The Evolutionary Development Waterfall model and Prototyping are popular examples of Iterative APM PMLC models. As long as there is some reasonable idea as to what the solution will look like, the developer can build on it, and eventually get a complete picture of the solution. Presently, there are a number of Iterative PMLC models. In this book, six Iterative PMLC models are discussed.

### Adaptive PMLC Models

At the other end of the APM Quadrant, are projects in which the solution is almost totally unknown. These projects are the most complex and uncertain of the APM projects. Solutions may have been attempted several times before, with little or no success. These projects will typically be very challenging and high risk because the search for an acceptable solution is striking out into the great unknown and no one can predict the outcome. Perhaps there is no solution that meets the goal, and that is the reason all previous attempts have failed. Or, maybe there is a solution, but it only partially meets the goal, and it didn't make sense to implement it. Finally, a solution may have been found, but it did not meet expected business value and so was never implemented. Obviously, these projects will be critical mission projects and some solution must be found.

No approach other than an Adaptive PMLC model will work on these projects. If these projects are successful in finding a solution that meets the goal, there will be a high business value return to the organization. If that were not the case, such a project would not be a high priority project. But the risk is high and stacked against success. From a management perspective, the best risk mitigation strategy is to have co-project managers whose skills in project management and business analysis are at the expert level. Presently, there is only one adaptive PMLC model—ACPF.

## Extreme and Emertxe Project Management

Projects in the extreme project management (xPM) quadrant do not have a clear goal or solution. The only projects that occupy this part of the project landscape are research and development projects. xPM PMLC models are used in xPM projects. xPM extends to the remotest boundaries of the project landscape and are those projects whose goals and solutions cannot be clearly defined. For example, research and development (R&D) projects are xPM projects. What little planning is done, is done just in time, and the project proceeds through several phases until it converges on an acceptable goal and solution, if at all. Clearly, the PMLC model for an xPM project requires maximum flexibility for the project team, in contrast to the PMLC model for a TPM project, which requires adherence to a defined process.

The goal is often not much more than a guess at a desired end state with the hope that a solution to achieve it can be found. In most cases, some modified version of the goal statement is achieved. In other words, the goal and the solution converge on something that hopefully has business value.

Projects in the emertxe project management (MPx) quadrant have a clear solution, but the goal is not clear. This sounds like a solution looking for a problem, and may seem like nonsense at first, but that is not the case. Like xPM projects, these are also R&D projects, but with a twist.

If you haven't already noticed, emertxe is "extreme" spelled backwards. I chose that name because MPx projects will use the same management approach as xPM projects, except the time scale is reversed. Let me explain. In an xPM project, there is a fuzzy goal that will only be clarified when a best fit solution is found. That best fit solution will meet some goal that is a special case of, and probably a more limited version of, the original goal. In an MPx project, you have a solution and are asked to define the goal that it meets. There was no goal statement at the outset, but the solution will define the goal. Just as in an xPM project, the question becomes: Does the goal and solution converge to a deliverable with acceptable business value? If it does, you have succeeded! Both xPM and MPx projects can follow an ACPF approach.

For both xPM and MPx project types, I have had more success using a BA with sufficient project management skills to co-manage such projects. The creative process is more important than compliance to a rigid project management process. The more intimate the subject matter expertise of the project manager, the more likely the project will succeed. Figure 5.5 looks at the similarities and differences across the project landscape.

Figure 5.6 classifies the PMLC models across the 4 quadrants and 5 PMLC model types.

| TPM | APM | xPM |
|-----|-----|-----|
| One cycle | Fixed # of cycles | Unknown # of cycles |
| Fixed budget & time | Fixed budget & time | Variable budget & time |
| Fixed scope | Variable scope | Unknown scope |
| Complete WBS | Level WBS | No WBS |
| Plan driven | Just-in-time planning | Just-in-time planning |
| Change intolerant | Change expected | Change necessary |

**Figure 5.5**   Project management landscape comparisons

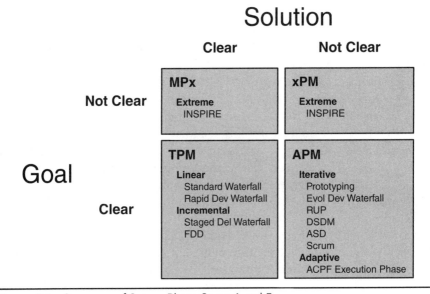

**Figure 5.6**   Summary of Set-up Phase Steps 4 and 5

## STEP 5: CHOOSE THE BEST FIT PMLC MODEL

At this point, the project has been classified into one of the four quadrants of the project landscape. Within the quadrant, we now have to choose a PMLC model type from among Linear, Incremental, Iterative, Adaptive, and

Extreme to manage the project. The next step is to choose a specific PMLC model as the best fit.

Within the chosen PMLC model type, the portfolio of PMLC models are in the organization's ACPF/kit. Using Figure 5.6 as an example, there are 12 PMLC models in the recommended ACPF/kit. I have had experience in using all twelve of these PMLC models. These models form my portfolio. Your portfolio will probably be different. Some subset of these models will be chosen for an organization's ACPF/kit, which will cover the types of projects in their landscape.

The portfolio of specific PMLC models will be different for each enterprise. The contents of your portfolio will be a matter of the industry in which you practice project management; the history of project management in the enterprise; the types of projects encountered; and, the human resource base modified by its experiences and preferences.

## Traditional Project Management Models

As already discussed, TPM PMLC models require a complete and clearly defined solution. That definition extends to the set of high-level requirements. The reason is that all of the TPM variations require complete requirements so that the complete WBS can be generated and the complete project plan created. A complete RBS will define what the solution must do, and a complete WBS will identify all of the work that has to be done to meet the RBS definition.

There are reasons why one would want a complete plan:

- To be able to document exactly what will be delivered
- To estimate the human resource requirements needed
- To develop the project budget
- To build a complete project work schedule so resources can be committed.

This is a nice, comforting list to have at the beginning of a project. However, it rarely occurs. What happens more often than not, is that changes are requested, and if approved, then the resource requirements may have to change, and the project plan changes, as well. Do you begin to see all of the labor and time wasted putting together the original resource requirements and project plan? The ACPF saves all of that wasted time by using a just-in-time planning process!

Among the TPM approaches, there are two PMLC model types: Linear and Incremental. All other TPM approaches are specific examples of one of them. These general models are defined below with at least one specific model of each type given.

### Linear PMLC Model Types

These models have a number of phases that operate in sequential order with no feedback loops. Figures 5.7 and 5.8 show two popular TPM models. Note that both models are Linear; there are no feedback loops. The Standard Waterfall model has been around for more than 50 years and is discussed in any book on systems development life cycles. While the Standard Waterfall model was originally meant for software development projects, it has also found favor in non-software development projects. The Rapid Development Waterfall model is more recent and is frequently used to get a product to market faster by grouping development into parallel and nearly independent "swim lanes." Grouping for effective and speedy development is challenging. It requires swim lanes that are as independent of one another as possible. The linearity of the process is still maintained with these parallel swim lanes. Figure 5.8 illustrates three parallel swim lanes. That number is variable, of course.

There are several things to consider in creating such a development schedule. The biggest will be the risk that you have added by using aggressive parallel swim lanes. By squeezing the work into a shorter time frame,

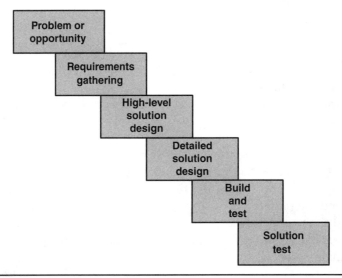

**Figure 5.7**   The Standard Waterfall model

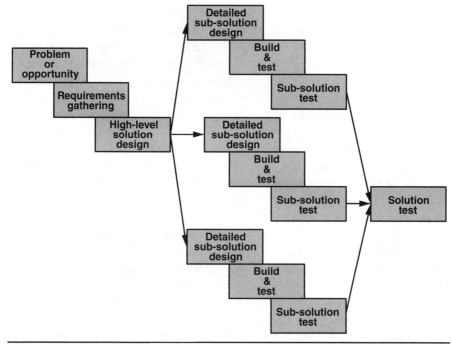

**Figure 5.8**  The Rapid Development Waterfall model

the incidence of errors and staff scheduling conflicts increases. For example, what if a scarce skill is needed in several swim lanes. That means you will have a resource dependency across multiple swim lanes. Resource contention becomes a real problem. The amount of work has not decreased; it just must be completed in a shorter time frame. Allocating the work to concurrent swim lanes shortens the project duration, but increases the risk of completing the project on schedule. The last parallel swim lane that is complete determines the completion date of the development project. It is clear that the risk from a Rapid Development Waterfall model is greater than that of the Standard Waterfall model.

## Incremental PMLC Model Types

Incremental PMLC models are a variant of Linear PMLC models, but deserve separate discussion. Just as the Linear models require a clearly defined and documented goal and solution, so also do the Incremental models. Whereas Linear PMLC models build and release deliverables all at one time, Incremental PMLC models build and release deliverables in stages over time.

Think of taking the Rapid Development Waterfall model and stretching the swim lanes out in sequence with releases at the completion of each swim lane. You would have an Incremental PMLC model without the added risk of a compressed schedule. You don't get off scot-free, though. You will have incurred other risks. For marketing and early sales reasons, these models are often chosen. For example, to release a product in stages to test market acceptance and other variables, an Incremental PMLC model is often used.

The downside of Incremental PMLC models is that the client is tempted to introduce scope change requests between increments. That's OK, but the original project time box will have to allow time for those scope change requests to come forward from the client, be evaluated, and be acted upon. Management reserve is a time contingency added as a task to the end of the project schedule to accommodate the time needed to process and incorporate changes. That is an often overlooked detail in Incremental PMLC models. Also, having downtime for the development team between increments is a temptation for their resource managers to temporarily reassign those team members elsewhere. There is always the promise that they will return to the team when the next increment is ready to start, but that rarely happens. As a form of insurance to protect against the loss of a team member, hand-off documentation is usually prepared. That adds work not found in Linear PMLC models.

When considering using an Incremental PMLC model, you need to give some thought to the added risk. Figure 5.9 is an example of a Staged Delivery

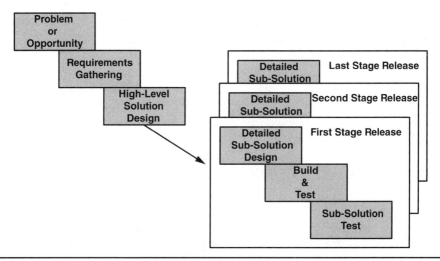

**Figure 5.9**   Staged Delivery Waterfall model

Waterfall model, which suffers the same risks as any other Incremental PMLC model. A constraint of the model is the content of each increment. The deliverables from Increment "N" must have all predecessor deliverables built in the previous "N-1" increments. This is likely to compromise or delay increments having business value sufficient to warrant release to the end user or the market. At best, the process is cumulative. That is, not every increment will contain sufficient business value. Several successive increments might be needed in order to offer sufficient business value to be released.

The Feature-Driven Development (FDD) model (Figure 5.10) is similar to the Staged Delivery Waterfall model, except swim lanes are defined around the technical dependencies among the functions and features assigned to the swim lane. As a result, FDD is not client or business value focused. FDD first appeared in *Java Modeling in Color with UML* (Coad, De Luca, and Lefrebvre, 1999). A more comprehensive treatment of FDD can be found in *A Practical Guide to Feature-Driven Development* (Palmer and Felsing, 2000).

Note that the solution must be known in order to use FDD effectively. A model of the solution is developed and used to create the functional WBS. The functional WBS contains a detailed list of features. The features list is grouped into similar features, based on technical dependencies, and prioritized for development. FDD iterates on the design and building of the groups of features.

Much like the Rapid Development model, FDD prioritizes parts of the solution. But this time, it is prioritization based on technical dependencies. With the addition of functions and features to the solution, the solution grows in terms of business value. Intermediate production solutions can be released as part of this approach. Just as in the Rapid Development model, there can be multiple design/build swim lanes running concurrently in the Feature Driven Development model.

FDD provides for the early release of chunks of functions and features so that the customer can begin to realize business value without having to wait for the single release of the complete solution. There may be several cycles of development before the client is satisfied that the cumulative features list has enough business value to be released, as in the sense of the Staged Delivery Waterfall model. FDD models may use concurrent swim lanes, sequential phases, or a combination of the two.

## Agile Project Management Models

For TPM projects, change is the exception. For APM projects, change is the norm. This difference is significant and results in completely different

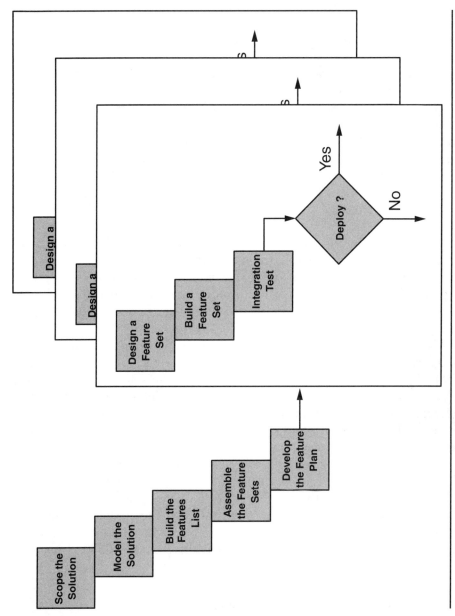

**Figure 5.10**    Feature-Driven Development model

approaches to managing projects. While the TPM project will use some form of a Linear or Incremental PMLC model as discussed previously, the APM Project will use some form of an Iterative or Adaptive PMLC model, as discussed below. When the solution is not clearly and completely defined, you will have to approach the project as some type of agile project and use the appropriate Agile PMLC model. Agile projects come in two flavors:

- **Most of the solution is known:** Projects in which the goal is clearly defined and documented, and whose solution is complete up to the point of specifying the final rendering of one or more features. These projects are what I would call "minimalist agile" projects. These projects should use Iterative PMLC model types, but could also use an Adaptive PMLC model type, as discussed.
- **Most of the solution is unknown:** Projects in which the goal is clearly defined and documented, but whose solution features and functions are not clearly defined and documented. In other words, much of the solution has not been identified. These projects are what I would call "maximalist agile" projects. These projects should use an Adaptive PMLC model type, as discussed.

## *Iterative PMLC Model Types*

Iterative PMLC models types are minimalist agile approaches. The Iterative PMLC model types are most effective where we still know all of the functions, but some of the features are not known as definitively as the client would like. A good example of this model is the Prototyping model shown in Figure 5.11.

### Evolutionary Development Waterfall Model

In the Evolutionary Development Waterfall model, the project begins much like a Standard Waterfall model. The known parts of the solution are developed based on current requirements. Through the Evolutionary Development Waterfall model (Figure 5.12), iterations on the further details of the solution will be undertaken. As the features and functions needed to deliver the requirements are developed, the requirements may well change, but few additions or deletions to the original requirements are expected. The WBS for the current version is created along with duration, cost, and resource requirements. This model closely resembles the production prototype approach that has been popular for many years.

Unlike the traditional models, it should be obvious that the meaningful involvement of the client is critical to the success of an APM project. The

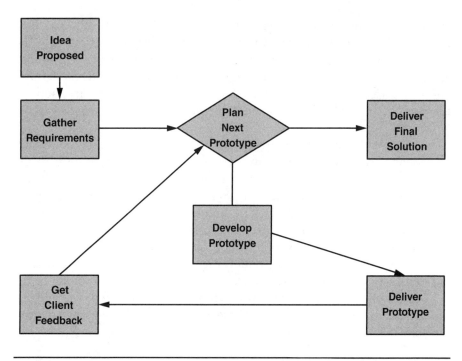

**Figure 5.11**    Prototyping

client works with a version of the solution, and provides feedback to the project team for further enhancements and changes to features and functions. This process continues as version after version is put in place. At some point in time, the client is satisfied that all requirements have been met. Note that this model always presents the client with a production-ready version of the solution.

In the Evolutionary Development Waterfall model, the learning and discovering experience is obvious. With each iteration, more and more of the depth of the solution is revealed. That revelation follows from the client and developers having an opportunity to play with the current solution. For simple and obvious enhancements, this approach works just fine.

There is one variation worth mentioning here. There may be cases where iteration on solution design might precede iteration on version. While these tend to be the early efforts for an adaptive model, they can be used here with good effect. Iteration on design helps the client move up the learning curve of understanding the solution concept. Armed with that understanding, the client is better prepared to participate in iterations on the version.

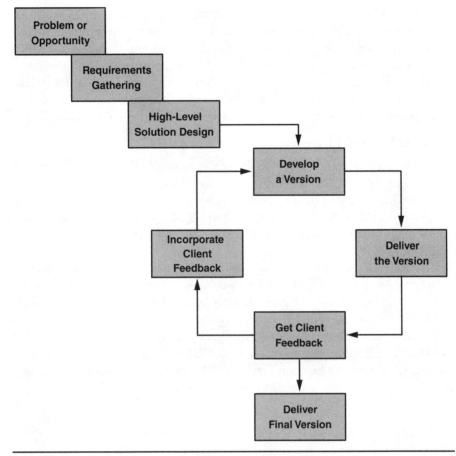

**Figure 5.12**  Evolutionary Development Waterfall model

Design iteration is done quickly. If you have the right design tools, in my experience, design iteration can be done in a matter of days, not weeks or months.

The discovery of additional features is a process that fully engages the client in meaningful exchanges with the developers. Both client and developers work with the prototypes, sometimes independently and sometimes in collaboration. The collaboration would be done in an effort to decide how to go forward with new or redefined features in the next and subsequent iterations.

The Evolutionary Development Waterfall model works fine for those situations where only a small part of the solution has not been clearly defined.

How to represent a feature in the solution, for example, would be a case where a small part of the solution is not clear. The development team merely presents the client with renditions of the alternatives and asks for a decision as to which alternative is preferred, and then implements it in the solution. However, when the missing parts of the solution are more significant, like how to make a particular decision, then a more powerful approach is needed. This more powerful approach would be some form of an Adaptive PMLC model.

### Rational Unified Process

The Rational Unified Process (RUP) is a completely documented software engineering process for building a solution in an iterative fashion. There is an extensive library of books and Internet resources available. A good starting point would be the book by Krutchen (2000). The RUP consists of four concepts: Inception, Elaboration, Construction, and Transition, as shown in Figure 5.13.

The RUP is probably the most well-known iterative software development process. It adapts quite well to a process approach that is documentation-heavy to one that is documentation-light. The foundation of the RUP lies in the library of reusable code, requirements, designs, etc. That library will have been built from previous project experiences, which means that the RUP can have a long payback period. The library must be sufficiently populated in order to be useful from an ROI perspective. Four to five completed projects may be enough to begin to see some payback.

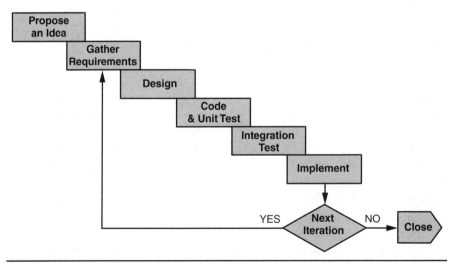

**Figure 5.13**    Rational Unified Process model

The RUP ranges widely over the project landscape. When complexity and uncertainty are low, but the solution is not fully defined, the RUP is a heavy process. It requires considerable documentation, especially for code reuse.

Note that each iteration begins with a requirements gathering session. The presumption is that the previous iteration will have clarified future directions for the project to take, and those would be fleshed out in the next requirements gathering exercise. The direction that an RUP project takes tends to be reactive to the requirements gathering activity. The ACPF, on the other hand, is a proactive model that seeks out missing solution parts through Probative Swim Lanes. The ACPF does not depend totally on discovery of the solution, which is passive, but also depends on proactive initiatives, which are activities designed to learn about the solution. It is this property that sets the ACPF apart from all other Agile PMLC models. The RUP consists of four concepts that run concurrently through all iterations:

- **Inception**—Through a series of requirements gathering sessions in each iteration, an understanding of the scope of the development effort is agreed to and a cumulative solution as to how the scope will be developed can begin. Whatever parts of the solution have not been implemented, it is expected that the requirements gathering sessions at the start of an iteration will uncover those missing parts.
- **Elaboration**—Where Inception focuses on *what* is to be done, Elaboration focuses on *how* it will be done. This is a technical design activity with the appropriate technical specification and plan as deliverables. The RUP is an architecture-centric process, and so these technical specifications must technically integrate with the deliverables from all previous iterations. The RUP is not a client-centric process like the ACPF. In the ACPF world, these first two RUP concepts are the equivalent of the Version Scoping Phase and Cycle Planning Phase.
- **Construction**—This is the build phase of an RUP iteration. It is equivalent to the Cycle Build Phase of an ACPF project.
- **Transition**—The solution may be released into production if the client is satisfied that such a release has business value and can be supported by the organization. This is the same as the release decision in an ACPF project.

## Adaptive Software Development

Adaptive Software Development (ASD) is fully described in a book by Highsmith (2000). ASD has three phases: Speculate, Collaborate, and Learn. These three overlapping phases are shown in Figure 5.14.

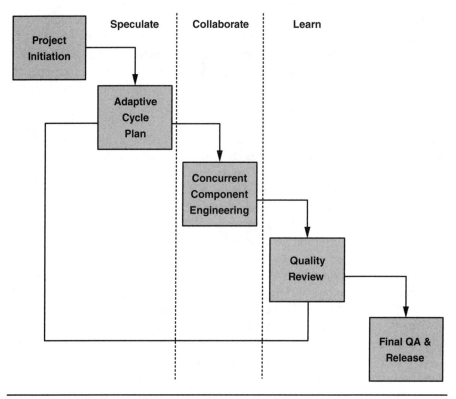

**Figure 5.14** Adaptive Software Development model

- **Speculate**—The Speculate Phase is nothing more than a guess at what the final goal and solution might look like. It may be correct or it may be far from the mark. It really doesn't make much difference in the final analysis because the self-correcting nature of ASD will eventually lead the team to the right solution. "Get it right the last time" is all that matters.
- **Collaborate**—A Speculate Phase has been completed and it is time to take stock of where the team and client are with respect to a final solution. The client team and the development team must collaborate on their journey to discover that solution. What great "aha's!" did the entire project team discover? What direction should the project take in the next and succeeding iterations?
- **Learn**—What was learned from the just completed phase, and how might that redirect the team for the next phase?

**The ASD Life Cycle Model**

Figure 5.14 also shows the detailed phases of ASD:

- **Project Initiation**—The objective of the Project Initiation Phase is to clearly establish project expectations among the sponsor, the client, the core project team, and any other project stakeholders. This would be a good place to discuss, agree upon, and approve the POS. For a project of some size (more than six months), it might be a good idea to hold a kick-off meeting, which might last 2-3 days. During that time, requirements can be gathered and documented, and the POS written. As part of project initiation, a brief statement of objectives for each iteration is prepared. These are expected to change as the solution detail develops, but at least the sponsor, client, and development team have a sense of direction for their efforts.
- **Adaptive Cycle Plan**—Other deliverables from the kick-off meeting might include the project time-box, the optimal number of cycles and the time-box for each, and objective statements for the coming cycle. Every cycle begins with a plan for what will be done in the coming cycle. These plans are high-level. Functionality is assigned to sub-teams and the details are left for them to establish. This is at odds with TPM, which requires organized management oversight against a detailed plan. ASD is light when it comes to management processes.
- **Concurrent Component Engineering**—Several concurrent swim lanes are established for each functionality component. Each sub-team is responsible for some part of the functionality planned for the present cycle.
- **Quality Review**—This is the time for the client to review what has been completed to date, and revise accordingly. New functionality may emerge; functionality is reprioritized for consideration in later cycles.
- **Final QA and Release**—At some point the client will declare the requirements met, and there will be a final acceptance test procedure and release of the product.

**Dynamic Systems Development Method**

The Dynamic Systems Development Method (DSDM) (Stapleton, 2003) is what the Standard Waterfall model would look like in a zero gravity world. Feedback loops are the defining features that separate the DSDM from the Standard Waterfall model. DSDM advocates would claim that a DSDM approach will deliver results quicker, with higher quality and less cost, than any TPM PMLC model. The DSDM is an agile model. The feedback loops help guide the client and the project team to a complete solution. The business case is included as a feedback loop so that even the fundamental basis and justification of the project can be revisited.

The list below contains the nine key principles of the DSDM as enumerated in Stapleton (2003). Note that these principles are similar to those that we have previously identified as good practices:

1. Active user involvement is imperative.
2. DSDM teams must be empowered to make decisions.
3. The focus is on frequent delivery of products.
4. Fitness for business purpose is the essential criterion for acceptance of deliverables.
5. Iterative and incremental development is necessary to converge on an accurate business solution.
6. All changes during development are reversible.
7. Requirements are base-lined at a high level.
8. Testing is integrated throughout the life cycle.
9. A collaborative and cooperative approach between all stakeholders is essential.

Most Agile PMLC models can subscribe to the same principles. With minor variation, these principles are common to the ACPF PMLC model, too, and will be further commented on in the context of the ACPF later in this chapter. Figure 5.15 highlights the DSDM method.

The distinguishing feature of the DSDM is the incremental release and implementation of a production system at the end of each cycle. Note that "Functional Model" and "Design and Build" iterations all follow with an implementation phase. The DSDM delivers business value to the client as part of its overall process design. Other approaches may do the same as a variation, but the DSDM does it as part of the design of the approach itself:

- **Pre-project**—This DSDM Phase includes some type of project overview, charter, or high-level business case designed to support the decision that the project should be undertaken. Once the decision to approve the project is made, the project is funded and the feasibility study can begin.
- **Feasibility**—A decision must be made as to whether or not to use the DSDM on this project. The typical feasibility study is done, but with the addition of the question about the appropriateness of the DSDM. As part of answering that question, consideration is given to the support of the DSDM that can be expected from the organization and the

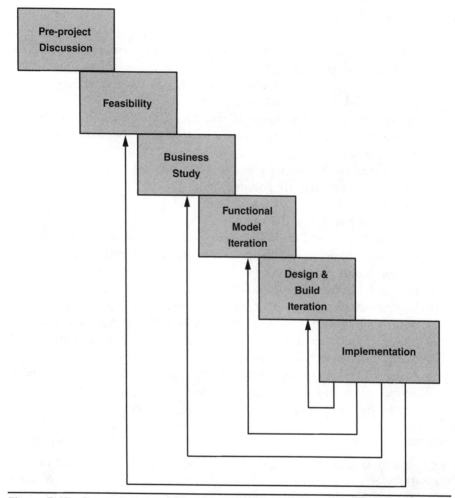

**Figure 5.15**   Dynamic Systems Development Method

capabilities of the available project team members. The DSDM feasibility study is not an exhaustive treatise, but is quite high level. Two weeks at most should be allocated to this phase. Remember you only want a decision to use the DSDM or not.

- **Business Study**—The client team, in collaboration with the developer team, will do a high-level investigation of the business processes affected by the project and identify information needs. The investigation is best conducted in a workshop environment with the appropriate subject matter experts involved. High-level process and data flow diagrams are often produced. Requirements are documented. System architecture is defined, but with the proviso that it will probably change as the project progresses. Finally, a high-level plan is developed. It will identify expected prototyping (if any) during functional model iteration, and design and build iteration phases.

- **Functional Model Iteration**—In this phase, the functional model and information requirements are refined through repeated cycles of the following tasks:
  - ✦ Identify what you are going to do in this next cycle.
  - ✦ Decide how you are going to do it.
  - ✦ Do it.
  - ✦ Check that you did it right.
- **Systems Design and Build Iterations**—These iterations will select prioritized requirements, and design and build them. Production prototypes are commonly developed, as well. A partial solution is delivered at each iteration, and the complete solution as a deliverable from this phase.
- **Implementation**—This is the hand-off from development to production. All of the typical implementation activities take place in this phase. These activities include installation, training, documentation, operations support, and user support.
- **Post-project**—A post-implementation audit will follow after a suitable period of use has passed. Revisions and other system changes are accepted and built into the system through new releases.

## Scrum

*Scrum* is a term taken from rugby. Scrum involves the team as a unit moving the ball downfield, in what would appear to be an *ad hoc* or chaotic manner. Of all the iterative approaches, Scrum would seem to define a chaotic development environment. The Scrum software development team is self-directed, operates in successive one-month iterations, holds daily team meetings, continuously offers the client demos of the current solution, and adapts its development plan at the end of each iteration. For a complete discussion on Scrum and software development refer to Schwaber and Beedle (2001).

---

**Scrum vs. the ACPF**

Scrum is empirical.
The ACPF is empirical *and* experimental.

Of all the development models discussed in this book, Scrum is clearly a customer-driven approach. It is the customer who defines and prioritizes the functions and features that the team prioritizes into phases, and builds one phase at a time. The Scrum process allows the customer to change functions and features as more of the solution depth is uncovered through the previous iterations. Depending on the working definition you are using, Scrum may be a strict application of the iterative class as defined herein, or it may border on the adaptive class discussed in the Adaptive PMLC model type section below. The Scrum process flow is shown in Figure 5.16.

The Scrum process flow is defined by the following five steps:

- **An Idea Is Proposed**—The original idea for the system may be vague. It may be expressed in the form of business terms. A function level description can be developed as part of the scoping phase, but not to the depth of detail that the client requires. It is not likely to be expressed in system terms.
- **Develop and Prioritize a List of Functionality**—The Product Owner is responsible for developing a list of functionality, which is called the Product Backlog. The list will help the team understand more detail

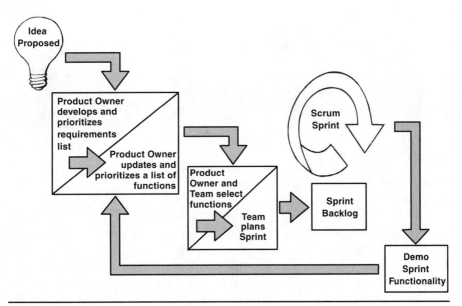

**Figure 5.16**   The Scrum process flow

about the idea and help them form some ideas about how to approach the project.

- **Sprint Planning Meeting**—This is an 8-hour meeting with two distinct, 4-hour parts. In the first part, the Product Owner presents the prioritized Product Backlog to the development team. This is the opportunity for the team to ask questions to clarify each piece of functionality. In this first part of the meeting, the team commits to the Product Owner the functionality it will deliver in the first 30-day Sprint. The Team then spends the remaining 4 hours developing the high-level plan as to how it will accomplish the Sprint. The work to be done is captured in the Sprint Backlog. The Sprint Backlog is the list of functionality that is not yet completed for the current Sprint.
- **Sprint Backlog**—This is the running current Sprint list of undone functionality for this one, 30-day Sprint.
- **Demo Sprint Functionality**—At the end of the Sprint, the team demos the solution to the client; functionality is added or changed, and the Product Backlog is updated and reprioritized for the next Sprint. This entire process continues until the Product Backlog is empty, or the client is otherwise satisfied that the current Sprint Version is the final solution.

---

**Note**

Scrum has often been characterized as a methodology that does not require a project manager. In fact, the position of project manager does not exist, but the role does. It is subsumed primarily by the team of senior developers, which operates as a self-managed and self-directed team. Co-location of the Scrum team is critical. Scrum teams of more than 10 members tend to be dysfunctional, although there have been some results to the contrary (Eckstein, 2004).

---

## Scrum Team Roles

There are three roles on every Scrum team:

- **Product Owner:** The Product Owner is the client representative. They are the primary interface between the client business unit and the developers.
- **Developers:** This is a small and usually co-located, self-directed, and self-managed team. They are otherwise assuming the role and responsibilities of the project manager.

- **Scrum Master:** This person is basically a compliance officer and coach. They assure that the Scrum project proceeds as expected.

For more details about Scrum team roles, see Schwaber and Beedle (2001).

### An Interesting Application of Scrum

One of my clients reported an interesting application of Scrum. All of their software maintenance projects are allocated to a Product Maintenance Backlog file and prioritized by the Product Maintenance Backlog Manager, who is also responsible for estimating the effort and resource requirements for each maintenance project. This is a project management consultant assigned to their Project Support Office. Not all developers are fully assigned or have delays in their project assignments, and they are responsible for periodically checking the Product Maintenance Backlog and work on maintenance projects found there. The objective is to empty the backlog. Periodic reports of the backlog size and dates measure objective attainment.

## *Iterative PMLC Model Recap*

The ACPF/kit that I am recommending for each enterprise includes six specific models, as shown in Figure 5.17.

In my experience, I tended to choose a specific Iterative model based on the degree of solution completeness. For the most complete solution, I often used Prototyping or Evolutionary Development Waterfall. For the least complete solution, Scrum was my preferred choice. If the conditions needed to use Scrum were not present, the DSDM would often suffice. These are not hard and fast rules, but have seemed to work in practice.

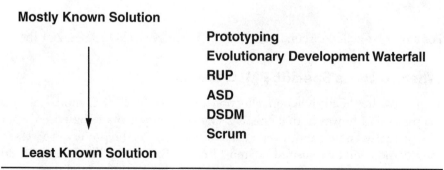

**Figure 5.17**   Six Iterative PMLC models ranked from most-known to least-known solution

## Adaptive PMLC Model Types

As defined in this book, an Adaptive PMLC model can change not only the stages in a chosen model, but also change to a different model. No other model does this in an organized and deliberative manner. Whereas Iterative PMLC models work well in situations where only minor parts of the solution (typically, features) have not been implemented in the solution, Adaptive PMLC models are most appropriate for situations where sizable parts of the solution have not yet been identified. In the most complex situations, incompleteness could even extend to requirements. Adaptive goes beyond adjusting a chosen PMLC model to the choice of the PMLC model itself. Any PMLC model that claims to be adaptive must be robust to the extent that model choice is within its scope. Given this understanding of "adaptive," the ACPF is the only adaptive PMLC model on the market today.

Figure 5.18 is the Project Execution Phase from the ACPF process flow. It shows the feedback loop that is unique to the ACPF PMLC model.

## Extreme PMLC Model Types

De Carlo was the first to offer any meaningful approach to the management of extreme projects (De Carlo, 2004). His work was the primary motivator for the later work that I did for the ACPF version of extreme project management, which I call "INSPIRE" (see Figure 5.19):

- INspire.
- SPeculate.
- Incubate.
- REview.

For a more detailed discussion of INSPIRE, see Wysocki (2010a, 2014b).

## When to Use a Specific PMLC Model

Step 5 of the ACPF is when selection of a specific PMLC model occurs. Keep in mind however that this is a choice that was made based on what was currently known about the goal and solution. As the project progresses, this decision will be revisited in Step 11 of the Execution Phase. Figure 5.20 summarizes the above discussions of each specific PMLC model type.

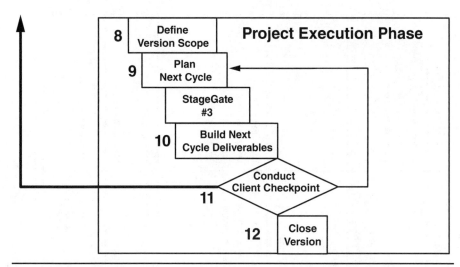

**Figure 5.18**   The ACPF Project Execution Phase PMLC model

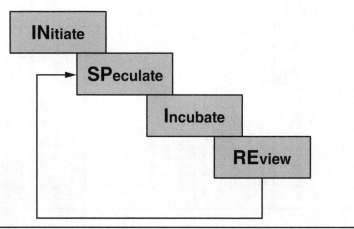

**Figure 5.19**   The ACPF INSPIRE PMLC model

| PMLC Model | Strengths | Weaknesses | When to use |
|---|---|---|---|
| **Linear**<br>–Standard Waterfall<br>–Rapid Development Waterfall | Entire project scheduled at the start<br>Resource requirements known<br>Does not require co-locations<br>Does not require most skilled team | Resistant to change<br>Costs too much<br>Too long to produce results<br>Requires complete plans<br>Not focused on business value | Simple projects<br>Repeatable projects<br>Owns all resources |
| **Incremental**<br>–Staged Delivery Waterfall<br>–Feature Driven Development | Produces business value early<br>Better scheduling of resources<br>Accommodates minor change<br>Offers product improvement<br>More focused on business value | Team may not remain intact<br>Requires hand-off documents<br>Increased client involvement<br>Takes longer<br>Partitioning may be problematic | Get to market faster |
| **Iterative**<br>–Prototyping<br>–Evolutionary Development Waterfall<br>–Rational Unified Process<br>–Dynamic Systems Development Method<br>–Adaptive Systems Development<br>–Scrum | Client reviews for improvements<br>Scope changes can be processed<br>Adapts to changing conditions | Requires active client involvement<br>Works best with co-located teams<br>Don't know deliverables till the end<br>High risk | Clear goal<br>Unclear solution |
| **Adaptive**<br>–ACPF Execution Phase | Same as iterative<br>Can change PMLC Model anytime<br>Based on lean principles | Heavy client involvement required<br>Very high risk | Unclear goal<br>Unknown solution<br>Most complex projects |
| **Extreme**<br>–INSPIRE | Keep options open as long as possible<br>Offers an early look at possible solutions | May be looking for solutions in all the wrong places<br>No guarantee of any business value<br>Very high risk | When the goal and/or solution are a desired end state |

**Figure 5.20** Comparison of the specific PMLC models

# STEP 6: ASSESS PROJECT CHARACTERISTICS

Virtually every PMLC model is adopted right out of the box. They are presented to the project manager as a predefined recipe to be followed. In some organizations, deviations are not allowed. This "one-size-fits-all" approach will frequently fail, especially in the complex project world. The data bears this out.

One of the first projects that started me on the road to ACPF design was a 1994 implementation of the Effective Project Management model (Wysocki and McGary, 2004), but with a twist. Beginning with this model as the starting point, the client defined 42 processes for their version of the implementation. Of the 42 processes, only 11 were required for every project. The others were optional, and could be used or modified at the discretion of the co-project managers. As we began sharing these processes with the project managers, they pointed out projects they had managed where they felt that exceptions to the 11 required processes should be allowed. In some cases, those exceptions would involve varying how the defined process was designed; in other cases, the exceptions would be to not do the process at all. The final version of the client's methodology included the required 11 processes, and allowed the project managers to deviate, but only with an accompanying justification and rationale for their actions. Almost immediately, team morale increased and the project managers were thankful for their new authority. In time, project failure percentages began to decrease. I took that result to the next level, deciding that no project management methodology could possibly account for all contingencies and that flexibility and adaptability would be a critical success factor in the ACPF.

My approach to developing the ACPF was first to describe a simple and intuitive classification scheme for projects, and to use that classification as the taxonomy for the five PMLC model types. Further analysis will help the project manager, client, and team reach a conclusion about the best fit project management methodology (such as Waterfall, Scrum, RUP, DSDM, or others). Even having reached that decision, the job is not done. Once the best fit methodology has been chosen, it will need to be modified to meet the constraints and conditions imposed on the project by the project's characteristics, and to continuously adjust that best fit methodology as the project work commences and those conditions change. The characteristics that suggest modifications to the best fit methodology, and which have had an impact on the chosen PMLC model in my client engagements, are:

- **Project Characteristics**
  1. Risk
  2. Cost
  3. Duration
  4. Complexity
  5. Goal and solution clarity
  6. Team skills and competencies
  7. Completeness of requirements
- **Internal Characteristics**
  8. Business value
  9. Technology used
  10. Client involvement
  11. Organizational stability
  12. Organizational velocity
  13. Number of departments affected
- **External characteristics**
  14. Market stability
  15. Business climate
  16. Competitor behavior
  17. Breakthrough technologies.

For example, the best fit PMLC model for your complex project might be to use Scrum with the addition of a senior project manager, instead of a Scrum Master directly participating as a member of the Scrum team, and a senior level BA or Business Process Manager in the role of Product Owner. All of these adjustments to the standard Scrum model will have been driven by the project characteristics and the environment in which the project is to be conducted. So, to be successful, your project management approach is unique to the details of the project and its internal/external environment.

Every project is continuously impacted by one or more of these characteristics, and therefore, the best fit project management approach is likewise impacted. Furthermore, it is not a "once and you are done" impact. As the project changes and the solution begins to emerge, and any one or more of the internal or external characteristics changes, so could the best fit project management approach also change. If we are to effectively manage this ever-changing environment, we need a framework to guide our decisions on choosing and adjusting the best fit approach. That framework is the ACPF.

**Advice For Complex Project Managers**

The best advice for the complex project manager is to "do what makes sense." After all, complex project management is nothing more than organized common sense.

# STEP 7: CHOOSE AND MODIFY THE SPECIFIC PMLC MODEL

The choices for a specific PMLC model come from among approaches such as Waterfall, Scrum, and many others. I have included 12 specific PMLC models in my ACPF/kit. An organization will have its own carefully chosen portfolio, which is customized to fit its needs and project types. Organizations will have a preference, and skilled and experienced potential team members to adequately staff their preferences. Scrum is an extremely powerful and popular choice in many organizations, but it requires a senior level developer, who can work without supervision in a self-managed situation. That puts a strain on many organizations, whose developers are often less experienced.

## Which Specific PMLC Model is the Closest Fit?

Based on the *project* characteristics, which specific PMLC model is the closest fit? The initial decision was made without a consideration of the environment in which it will be implemented. It is based solely on goal and solution clarity.

## Should the Chosen PMLC Model be Adjusted for Better Alignment?

Based on the internal and external characteristics, the chosen PMLC model may need to be adjusted for better alignment. A consideration in regard to this adjustment is, what is the best way to convey this information? Suppose the project is in the Adaptive category, and Scrum is the PMLC model choice. Scrum requires meaningful client involvement through their representative, the Product Owner, but such an individual cannot be identified. As an alternative, an iterative approach, such as the RUP or the Evolutionary Development Waterfall model might be used, the difference being that the project manager and a senior level BA can function as co-project managers.

Together, they can take a more proactive role than otherwise would have been done by the Product Owner.

In another example, consider a project that is best categorized as iterative, and the RUP would seem to be the best fit choice. However, past projects for that client were disappointing because the client could not fully participate. One alternative would be to step back and use an Incremental approach to compensate for the shortcomings of the client involvement, allowing the project manager and BA to take up the slack.

## STAGEGATE #2

*StageGate #2* is the approval of the project management approach for the given project. The need for this approval will be new to sponsors and clients because they will not have encountered it in any other PMLC model. Those who participate in this approval will need to understand that this is not just a formality. The approval includes the allocation of the infrastructure resources needed to support the adapted PMLC model. It is also a signal to the resource managers that they will be called on for that support as well.

## DELIVERING BUSINESS VALUE IN A COMPLEX PROJECT LANDSCAPE

Expected incremental business value is the primary metric used to validate, approve, and prioritize a project. Figure 5.21 is a conceptual illustration of the likely outcomes. It also offers a projected business value for comparison purposes across the TPM, APM and xPM quadrants.

First, understand that the business value that will be delivered from a project is an *estimate* provided by the sponsor and client to gain approval to conduct the project.

For TPM projects, all of the business value is delivered after the project is complete, and the variance of the estimate is *small* compared to APM and xPM projects.

For APM projects, the situation is different. At each iteration or cycle, specific business value will be delivered. The variance of the estimate increases over the project life span. For the example illustrated in Figure 5.21, the delivered business value may fall far short of the business value estimated, if the goal is achieved. It is also possible that the delivered business value *exceeds* what was estimated if the goal is achieved. Clearly, the risk of not delivering expected business value is greater for APM projects than for TPM projects, but the rewards can be much greater.

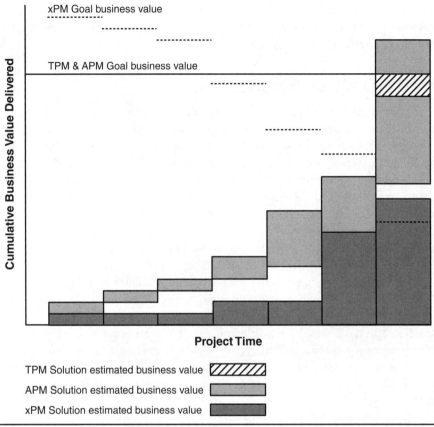

**Figure 5.21**   TPM, APM, and xPM solution business value

xPM projects are in a far different world than any APM project. In an APM project, the goal is clear. Hopefully, as the solution emerges, it will converge on the goal and deliver the expected business value, but there is high risk. In an xPM project, both the goal and the solution are not fixed. The goal may be an expression of a desired end state with no vision of how or even *if* that end state can be achieved. That is for the project team to learn and discover. As the solution emerges, the goal will change as certain aspects of the goal cannot be attained, given present technology and understanding of the solution space. That might account for the decreasing level of cumulative business value defined, as shown by the lowering levels denoted by the dashed lines in Figure 5.21. The goal and the solution in the xPM project are converging and delivering less business value than the project sponsor estimated from the beginning of the project. Hopefully, the goal and its solution will converge and produce business value. That business value may or may not be acceptable to the sponsor or the client. Again, we are dealing with a very high-risk situation.

## PUTTING IT ALL TOGETHER

The four steps in the Set-up Phase start with an approval to begin planning the project. No detail of how the project will be done has been discussed. The project must be classified in the appropriate quadrant of the project landscape (Step 4). Within that quadrant there will be several PMLC models to choose from. That decision process is embodied in Step 5. The ACPF does not assume that the chosen PMLC model will be an off-the-shelf solution to the project management approach. Rather, the chosen PMLC model might have to be adjusted based on internal and external characteristics within which the project will be executed. Those characteristics are assessed in Step 6 and any adjustments made in Step 7.

The Set-up Phase is a unique part of the ACPF. I like to refer to it as the "create the recipe" phase of a complex project. It is unlike anything you will find in a commercial project management model. In its uniqueness, the Set-up Phase brings a flexible and creative dimension to effective complex project management. But it comes with some baggage, too. The ACPF/kit defines the tools, templates, and processes available for the recipe. The ACPF/kit is your "pantry." That is fixed. The creative part is how you use that pantry.

I have identified a number of complex project characteristics that will influence the recipe. Some characteristics are known at the outset of the project and can be accommodated with the contents of the pantry. Other characteristics are dynamic and can change during project execution. That change brings into play a series of decisions that you will not have made from any other PMLC model. Do not expect these to be yes/no decisions. You will identify a number of possible actions and must choose from among them. In most cases, expected business value will be the criteria for making the choices.

# 6

## ADAPTIVE COMPLEX PROJECT FRAMEWORK: EXECUTION PHASE

> *You've got to think about "big things" while you're doing small things, so that all the small things go in the right direction.*
> —Alvin Toffler, American writer and futurist

> *Try several solutions at once. Maybe none of them, alone, would solve the problem, but in combination they do the job.*
> —Ray Josephs, President, Ray Josephs Associates, Inc.

> *Out of intense complexities intense simplicities emerge.*
> —Winston Churchill, UK Prime Minister

## CHAPTER LEARNING OBJECTIVES

This chapter will provide readers the knowledge or ability to:

- Gain a working knowledge of the five steps of Project Execution.
- Understand and practice version control.
- Know how to plan Probative and Integrative Swim Lanes.
- Interpret the size of the scope bank with respect to goal and solution convergence.
- Generate a work breakdown structure (WBS) from the requirements breakdown structure (RBS).

- Know the importance of the Cycle Build Plan.
- How to handle mid-cycle change requests.
- Understand the Client Checkpoint inputs, processes, and outputs.
- Conduct solution deployment and version close.
- Understand the contents of the post-version audit.

The Complex Project Execution Phase of the Adaptive Complex Project Framework (ACPF) is different than the project execution you might be accustomed to using. It uses a dynamic and continuously adjustable Project Management Life Cycle (PMLC) model, chosen and adapted for best fit by the project team during the Project Set-up Phase. The difference between a fixed "recipe" and the "ACPF recipe" is in its uniqueness: a specific instantiation of an ACPF PMLC model will never occur again. Furthermore, the ACPF Project Execution template presented here is robust—it can utilize any existing or adapted PMLC model.

Complex project execution draws on your ACPF/kit, except for one design feature unique to the ACPF: Probative and Integrative Swim Lanes. In its search for an acceptable solution, ACPF Project Execution uses experimentation in the form of Probative Swim Lanes. These are short term activities that are executable within a cycle, and are designed to test a hypothesis that a particular idea for a solution component is feasible and deserving of further investigation. This will often be done through additional Probative Swim Lanes until a decision can be made: a decision either abandons further exploration of the idea, or results in integrating the idea into the current solution through one or more Integrative Swim Lanes. What this accomplishes is the investigation of an idea without a heavy commitment or expenditure of resources or time, until the idea is validated to be part of the solution, and can be developed and integrated. Probative Swim Lanes are consistent with established "lean" practices.

You may already be familiar with Integrative Swim Lanes. While we did not use that term in previous chapters, these are the cycle builds in the Staged Delivery Waterfall model. They integrate additional functions, processes, and features into a working solution that is converging on a final solution. The difference in cycle builds between Traditional Project Management (TPM) projects and the ACPF is that the final solution cannot yet be defined. Like just-in-time planning, this is just-in-time building.

## STEPS OF THE ACPF EXECUTION PHASE

The initial PMLC model, delivered from Step 7: Modify PMLC model, is used to start Step 8: Define Version Scope, and is maintained and continuously realigned as a result of the analysis and deliberations that take place in Step 11: Conduct Client Checkpoint. This realignment is shown by the feedback loop from Step 11 to Step 5, as shown in Figure 6.1. As the solution becomes clearer and may be incrementally deployed, the project conditions change and often suggest that the adapted PMLC model should be reviewed for better alignment to the changing project needs. The purpose of this realignment is to deliver the maximum business value possible for the effort extended. The ACPF is unique in this regard, and structured so that the chosen PMLC model is not a barrier to the successful execution and completion of the project, but an enabler. Using a fixed recipe under the control of a project management "cook" would be a barrier.

The Complex Project Execution Phase consists of the following five steps, which are the final steps of an ACPF project:

1. Define version scope and create a high-level plan for this version.
2. Plan the next cycle, using your customized ACPF/kit.
3. Build the deliverables as planned, without any scope changes during the cycle.
4. With the full participation of the client, discuss the results from the just completed cycle and plan for the next iteration or cycle, if appropriate.
5. Close the project when the time and cost constraints have been reached or no further solution performance improvements or increased business value can be expected from this version.

These five steps are robust and I have used them on all of the 12 specific PMLC models included in the ACPF/kit.

TPM PMLC models are single cycle models, and so in these cases, there is no feedback from Step 11: Conduct Client Checkpoint to Step 9: Plan the Next Cycle. For TPM projects, the feedback loop remains from Step 11: Conduct Client Checkpoint to Step 5: Choose the Best Fit PMLC model. That step may seem out of place. Such changes are rare, but do occur (for example, when the TPM project is found to be off course and not likely to deliver an acceptable solution). Poor planning or faulty assumptions are often the cause.

One of the most common situations that I have encountered is when a Linear PMLC model was used to start the project, but soon it was obvious that the RBS was not complete, change requests continued at an increasing rate, and the plan was not going very well. A high incidence of change requests is the trip wire that signals this off-course condition. As a result, the client team and the development team could decide to switch to an Evolutionary Development Waterfall model with multiple releases.

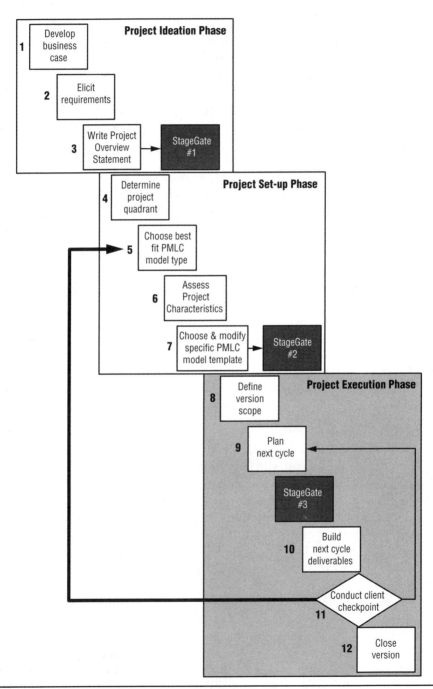

**Figure 6.1**    Complex Project Execution Phase

# STEP 8: DEFINE THE VERSION SCOPE

Using the term "version" is not a casual choice. Behind it is the assumption that in the complex project world, the best solution possible given the present situation is the solution that will be delivered. The business world is dynamic. A better solution will emerge as conditions change, as the result of practice using this version, technological advancements, marketing dynamics, and other factors not presently envisioned. In other words, an ACPF project will always be a work in progress, and each version is just another step in that journey. Project deliverables have a finite productive life. There will come a time when deliverables should be decommissioned, and replaced with a newer and improved version. Hence "version" has a specific meaning in the context of complex project management. The contents of the scope bank from the most recent version will be the major input to the decision to move forward with the next version.

In a complex project, there is no specific contracted solution. The solution is not known, except through the business value that an acceptable solution is expected to deliver. In more complex projects, the goal might simply be a desired end state and may not be achievable. For that reason, an ACPF project is a search for the maximum business value that the available time, cost, and resources can deliver. The burden of proof rests on the partnership of client and project manager. Working together, they will search for the best solution possible given the constraints. They are dependent upon each other for the success of the project. In complex projects, this partnership is a critical success factor (CSF). In Chapter 7, I will have a lot more to say about how you can create the conditions for establishing and making this partnership a sustainable reality.

## Defining the Goal of This Version

The goal of the ACPF version will be a simple yet definitive statement about what the project intends to do to address the problem or business opportunity, as described in Step 3: Write the Project Overview Statement (POS). It might be a total solution, but to be more realistic, it would be a solution that addresses a major segment of the problem or opportunity. I say this because, all too often, we define complex projects that are far too ambitious. Sure, you would like to cure all types of cancer, but be realistic. Maybe curing one form of cancer would be a lofty enough, intermediate goal. Having too ambitious a goal will open the project to frequent reductions as the project scope is framed a bit more conservatively.

Furthermore, there can be changes in the environment that render too ambitious a goal ineffective or unattainable. You run the risk of wasting resources or not delivering intermediate business value. By defining the goal of this version to be a reachable target, rather than a lofty or unattainable ambition, we protect the client and the team from scope reduction and significantly increase their chances of delivering business value. I am reasonably certain that ignoring this advice has a lot to do with the high incidence of project failure.

---

**Advice for Project Success**

It may sound pedestrian to some project managers, but you will be far more successful in the long run by biting off *less* than you think you can chew. Management did not appoint you as project manager expecting heroic efforts, just successful ones.

---

Getting an acceptable solution in place allows the organization to begin generating business value with the expectation that the present solution will set the stage for later versions and additional business value.

## Writing the Objectives of This Version

By way of analogy, think of the goal statement as a pie and the objectives statements as slices of the pie. All of the slices that make up the pie are the objectives statements. If you would rather have a mathematical interpretation, think of the objectives as necessary and sufficient conditions for the attainment of the goal. In either case, the objectives statements give a little more detail on how the goal will be achieved. They are the "boundary conditions," if you will. I would expect to see you write six to eight objectives statements to clarify the goal statement. Together the project statement and the objectives statements define the goal of the project.

Optionally, the set of high-level prioritized requirements generated in Step 2: Elicit Requirements may be a good choice for the objectives. I have had good success with this approach because the attainment of these requirements is easily verified. If the requirements can be linked to the success criteria, that is even better. However, that is not always possible.

## Prioritize the Scope Triangle Parameters

You might be asking: "Why prioritize the scope triangle parameters?" and, "Why now?" Those are fair questions. Here is the rationale: you want to avoid having to make these decisions when you are in the heat of battle. That seldom gives a good result. You will have to assign these priorities anyway, so do it now while in calmer times and when you can think clearly. A trade-off matrix like that shown in Figure 6.2 is a simple, yet elegant tool for facilitating the prioritization discussion, and can be a good reference later in the project when such information is useful during the Client Checkpoint Phase.

There are five parameters that define the ACPF Scope Triangle. They are prioritized into a list with no ties. The list is used primarily as part of the decision support for processing changes during the Client Checkpoint Phase. It is important to have these priority discussions as part of the version planning. Postponing such decisions until the Client Checkpoint Phase is not using best practices for complex project management.

## *Prioritize Requirements and Create the RBS*

The first deliverable from this phase is a prioritized list of the ACPF requirements. At this point, the RBS contains only a glimpse into the decomposition of the ACPF requirements. Both parties agree that this decomposition is incomplete and will change, but at this point in the project, the list reflects the best information available to the project team. There may be additions, deletions, or changes as the project work commences. Whatever process you use for prioritizing requirements, you must take into account:

- **Technical dependencies:** These must be maintained irrespective of anything else.
- **Business value:** To be releasable, the cumulative deliverables from the most recent cycle must provide sufficient business value.

| Parameter \ Priority | Critical (1) | (2) | (3) | (4) | Flexible (5) |
|---|---|---|---|---|---|
| Scope | | | | | X |
| Quality | | | X | | |
| Time | X | | | | |
| Cost | | | | X | |
| Resource Availability | | X | | | |

**Figure 6.2**   ACPF Scope Triangle example trade-off matrix

- **Release strategy:** Your cycle length might be four weeks, but you can't release deliverables every four weeks; maybe release them on a quarterly basis to align with existing enterprise release schedules.

The second deliverable from this phase is the mid-level WBS. Since the RBS is incomplete, the WBS will also be incomplete. If an RBS exists, it may be used as the starting point for defining the WBS. The RBS will specify *what* is to be done, and the WBS will further decompose the RBS to define *how* it will be done. For purposes of discussion, a mid-level WBS is one that shows the goal at level 0, ACPF Requirements at level 1, functions at level 2, and so on.

Generally, such a WBS would have a two- or three-level decomposition. The number of levels is not important. What is important is to have at least one level of decomposition to the work level for as many functions, processes, and features that have been identified. At this point, any more WBS detail is not considered useful. The reason for that will become clear during the Cycle Plan. The traditionalist would have a problem with this process, because the entire foundation of traditional project planning and scheduling is based on having a complete WBS. Trying to create a complete WBS at this stage is largely a waste of time.

Why plan for the future when you don't know what it is? In this case, the piece that is missing is that you are not exactly sure how you are going to deliver the functionality. You do know what functionality has to be delivered, and you are using that information to generate the mid-level WBS, but not the complete WBS. The complete WBS will eventually be generated when we know enough to generate it. That will happen within repeated iterations of Cycle Plan–Cycle Build–Client Checkpoint Phases. You will generate the complete WBS when you need it and not before; when you do generate it, you will know that it is correct and not a best guess.

---

**Caution about Assuming a Complete WBS**

Why plan for a future when you don't know what it is? In an ACPF project, looking too far and deep into the future is a waste of time. Guessing is to be avoided.

---

## Create a High-level Plan

Before planning the first cycle, a high-level plan should be built for the entire project. This plan uses the RBS (even though it may be incomplete) to create a high-level plan:

- Create a high-level WBS.
- Tentatively allocate known parts of the WBS to Integrative Swim Lanes within cycles.
- Tentatively assign potential Probative Swim Lane contents to the first few cycles.
- Establish a tentative number of cycles and average cycle length.
- Define milestone objectives.
- Assign a risk manager from among the development team members.

---

**Reminders about Plans**

- For TPM projects, the high-level plan is a complete project plan. Stage-gate #3 is the approval of the complete project plan to execute the project.
- For all complex projects, this will be a high-level plan to be followed by cycle plans. Each cycle plan may require an approval of a senior manager or sponsor.

---

## Create a High-level WBS

Some structure is needed to the project plan, recognizing that not much of the solution may be known at the outset. Beginning with the RBS and whatever detail is known about the functions, processes, and features, a high-level WBS should be built. The low-level WBS is built within the cycle, where those deliverables will be integrated into the solution.

## Tentatively Allocate Known Parts of the RBS to Integrative Swim Lanes Within Cycles

Put the emphasis on "tentatively." This information is more for the benefit of inquisitive stakeholders. In the absence of specific deliverables, it will provide somewhat of a road map for the sponsor and a glimpse into the future of the complex project for other interested parties.

## Tentatively Assign Potential Probative Swim Lane Contents to the First Few Cycles

These assignments are even more tentative than in the Integrative Swim Lanes. Probative Swim Lane intentions are very speculative. They can be nothing more than questions that need answers, a single function or process prototype to be built, or a short research project assigned to a team member.

Keep in mind that these are searches into an unexplored solution space and may provide sound direction or dead ends.

## Establish a Tentative Number of Cycles and Average Cycle Length

The sponsor will probably have specified the desired end date for the project. Using that date, the complexity of the project and the degree to which the RBS is complete, a tentative number of cycles and cycle length can be made. These estimates will depend on the PMLC model type:

- **Linear:** Only one cycle defines this model, and the cycle length includes the desired end date.
- **Incremental:** Cycles could be long or quarterly, if being aligned to established release dates. Alternatively, cycles could be short (less than 4 weeks) with releases less frequently.
- **Iterative:** Cycles are usually 2-4 weeks in duration.
- **Adaptive:** Cycles could be very short (1-4 weeks).
- **Extreme:** Cycle time varies.

---

**Advice about Cycles**

Shorter cycles should be used early in the project to engage the client and longer cycles can be used later. Shorter cycles help build client ownership, interest, and meaningful involvement.

---

## Define Milestone Objectives

Defining the milestone objectives will help put some "meat on the bones" of your ACPF project plan. These are tentative high-level descriptions of how you expect this project to progress. Promote the milestone objectives to your stakeholders as signposts along the road to discovering and implementing the project deliverables. Be aware that any dates you offer may often be seen by the sponsor and client as cast in stone.

## Assign a Risk Manager from Among Development Team Members

In a complex project, a risk management plan is a CSF. As complexity and uncertainty increase, it becomes more important that a team member be assigned the responsibility of managing the risk plan. This assignment begins before the risk management process is executed and continues until the project is complete.

## Establish Team Operating Rules

The best kind of team operating rules for a complex project are rules that are minimally invasive and do not add any significant non-value-added work.

### *Team Problem Solving*

When problems arise within an ACPF Cycle Build Phase that have to be solved within the cycle time-box, you don't have time to form a committee and launch an exhaustive study of the problem. You have to have a problem-solving model that can be executed quickly. The best model I have found to do that is one described by Couger (1995). The ideal application of Couger's model is a one-session solution identification and implementation within the cycle time-box constraint. In most cases, I would expect this model to be executable in less than half a day. The attendees at the problem-solving meeting are only those team members who have direct involvement with the problem, knowledge of the problem/solution, and a vested interest in its solution. Do not waste the time of team members whose involvement is not needed. They already have a full plate! Time is not on your side, so you have to act quickly. Couger's model is shown in Figure 6.3.

| Stimulus ⟹ | |
| --- | --- |
| **Step One** | Delineate opportunity and define problem. |
| **Step Two** | Compile relevant information. |
| **Step Three** | Generate ideas. |
| **Step Four** | Evaluate and prioritize ideas. |
| **Step Five** | Develop implementation plan. |
| | ⟹ **Action** |

**Figure 6.3**    An adaptation of Couger's creative problem-solving model

The ACPF Brainstorming Process is described in Chapter 4 and can be used in Step 3 of Couger's model.

## Decision Making

Every Client Checkpoint Phase requires a number of decisions. Either of the co-managers are authorized to make the decision. There are basically three approaches to decision making that apply in an ACPF project: directive, participative, and consultative.

### Directive Decision Making

There will be emergency situations where the development team manager or the client team manager will make the decision without any input other than what they already know. If the "enemy" is charging at you, do not convene a meeting to decide if or how to retaliate. The leader makes the decision on the spot, based on the information at hand. This is a forced decision, not an optional decision.

There are two considerations when using a directive approach:

1. If there is any doubt, and if there is time, another approach might be more appropriate. Do you feel that you correctly understand the situation? Do you have correct and complete information on which to base your decision? Find the missing information, if any.
2. The second consideration is the reaction of the other team members, especially the other co-manager, to your decision. The more critical the decision, the more likely the co-manager should be consulted. Obviously, this will be a judgment call. Are there points of view that differ from yours? Will any of the other team members be offended because they were not consulted? If they were not asked for input, they may be hesitant to support your decision. Again, if there is time, you might want to use another approach.

### Participative Decision Making

At the other extreme from directive decision making is the participative decision-making approach. Here, everyone has an opportunity to contribute their opinions. All opinions are carefully weighed and the decision is reached through group discussion. Since all are participating and all are heard, it is more likely that the team will be much more committed to the chosen decision and more likely to support it during implementation. In this approach, the co-managers make the decision consistent with the input and advice of the participants. They collect and weigh the input, and make the best decision possible. In most cases, they will clearly use some, but not all, input given.

## Consultative Decision Making

The middle ground between these two approaches—directive or participative—is the consultative approach. Here, the decision maker gathers input from all affected or involved parties, and then makes the decision. There is no discussion among those who are consulted. Their input may or may not be considered in making a decision. If time is of the essence, the decision maker can gather input from some of those who are most knowledgeable of the situation, and then make the decision.

## *Consensus Building*

In an ACPF project, arriving at a consensus might be the quickest way to decide what action to take, but it may not produce the best decision or ensuing action. A typical consensus decision might go something like this: Someone suggests the action to be taken and if no one seriously objects, that becomes the team's decision. Depending on the credibility of the team member who makes the decision, that suggestion might be taken or not. The record shows that many decisions made by consensus are not good decisions. In an attempt to please everyone, no one is pleased, and the decision may not be in the best interest of the project and the enterprise.

I recall a team member on a complex project that I was managing, whose behaviors were such that his suggested action might be good or bad but it was never determined if good or bad was the case. His name was "George" and if he is reading this book now, he will know that I am talking about him. That won't come as any surprise because he knows that I have singled him out for this before. Anyway, George is probably the most intelligent person that I have ever met. His mind operates at speeds I have never experienced with anyone else. On many occasions, the team was assembled to solve a problem. Before the team member could finish describing the problem, George was beginning to suggest the solution. He spoke first and was very aggressive. He demonstrated a command of the situation and the relevant facts. No one was willing to challenge him because they would lose the argument. So, most of George's suggestions were never challenged. They would appear to be the consensus opinion. Fortunately, George was usually correct. In an attempt to bring some openness to these sessions, I asked George to be the second person to suggest a solution. He knew that he dominated these sessions, and I showed him why it was so important to the team's morale that he do this. That worked—at least for a while. Old habits die hard!

## Daily Team Status Meetings

In an ACPF project, team meetings are held daily, usually first thing in the morning or at the end of the day; they last less than 30 minutes. Fifteen minutes is my strong recommendation for a meeting, and a learned behavior. There are no chairs to fall asleep on, and there are no handouts. Everyone who has a task open for work attends (even if by teleconference), and meeting facilitation is rotated among the attending team members.

These team meetings are typically not part of a TPM project. In an ACPF project, these are "no nonsense" meetings. Before the meeting starts, each task leader with a task open for work posts their status on a whiteboard in the team room and gives a verbal status report. Problem solving, decision making, conflict resolution, who wants to order pizza for lunch—none of these are part of a daily team meeting. The only open discussion that is allowed is for clarification purposes, and even that is very brief and controlled.

When a team is new to these types of meetings, the meetings tend to be clumsy at first, and they will usually run over schedule. With a little practice, the team quickly settles into a pattern and the 15-minute meeting becomes routine. For larger ACPF projects, the team is often divided into sub-teams. Each sub-team will be responsible for one or more activities, and for the sub-teams responsible for one or more tasks for an activity. Sub-teams will hold their own daily meetings. Less frequently, the sub-team managers might hold a meeting to coordinate with the other sub-teams that are working on the same activity. Even less frequently, the entire team will meet for general updates on the status of the ACPF project. The important thing to remember is that you do not want to overload the team with meetings. The cycle is short, and every hour spent in meetings is one less hour spent in building deliverables.

---

**Advice for Leading 15-Minute Meetings**

While one of the project co-managers might be the first choice for leading the team status meetings, this is not necessary nor even advised for complex projects. Rotating the person who leads team status meetings is a good idea. It gives others a chance to develop leadership skills and promotes team unification. It also allows the project co-managers to focus on the issues and not have to worry about running the status meeting.

## *What to Report in a 15-Minute Daily Team Status Meeting*

The 15-minute daily team status meeting is designed for complex projects, not for traditional projects. Status meetings for traditional projects should continue as they have in the past as far as frequency, length, and agendas. For complex projects, the situation is different. For some readers, this will seem like overkill and not something you want to engage in. You can already see the expressions on team members' faces when you announce that there will be daily team meetings. I remember the first time that I suggested daily 15-minute team status meetings. My team was not agreeable, but I quickly changed their minds, as I hope you will change your team members' minds. This is one of those "try it, you'll like it" cases.

For one thing, the meeting is short and everybody stands. The attendees are the task managers of all tasks that are open for work and are not yet completed. In other words, the scheduled start date for the task has passed, and the work on it is not yet complete. The only valid status report for such a task are as follows:

- I am on plan.
- I am $x$ hours behind schedule, but have a plan to be caught up by (give the date).
- I am $x$ hours behind plan and need help.
- I am $x$ hours ahead of plan and available to help with other tasks (it does happen).

There is no discussion of solutions to schedule slippages. There is no taking of pizza orders for lunch or other irrelevant discussions. Such discussions are taken off line and involve only the team members who are affected by the problem or issue being raised.

You will probably experience a learning curve for this process. My first 15-minute team meeting took 45 minutes, but the team quickly learned to bring the meeting time within the 15-minute limit, and within the next few meetings were inside the 15-minute window consistently.

I found it to be a good team development strategy to rotate the facilitator of the daily team meeting. That gives you a chance to observe future team leaders in action, and to develop their leadership and team management skills. Sometimes, it helps the project if the co-project managers step back from meeting facilitation and take an objective view of the project.

The project status is always posted in the Team War Room and is updated daily. Having a reserved and protected space for the Team War Room is ideal; absent a room, that space can be an electronic bulletin board. This space facilitates team members who are not co-located. Anyone who has an interest or a need to know can always go there for the details. Brief, written status reports should be available for the sponsor at milestone events, and more lengthy reports to senior management at the end of the version.

While the project is underway, we tend to place responsibility for status reporting outside of the complex project team and into the hands of the client. Placing it with the client maintains the core value of a client-focused and client-driven approach. Ownership is in the hands of the client, not in the hands of the project manager or project team. That is as it should be. The reason for this recommendation is that it puts the client in a position of responsibility for reporting the status of their project to the sponsor and to senior management. It now becomes a business-type report, not a project-type report.

## Scope Bank

The scope bank is the single depository for the current RBS, open change requests, the current solution, and all learning and discovery that has been accumulated from all cycles that has not yet been integrated into the solution. This includes all change requests that have not yet been resolved. The scope bank is an essential part of the ACPF/kit.

---

**The Scope Bank**

The scope bank is the only depository for the ideas for improving the solution. It will contain the updated RBS, new functionality, processes, or features not yet added to the solution. All of the ideas for solution enhancement are held for further consideration and prioritization.

At any point in time, the scope bank will contain the following:

- List of learning and discovery from prior cycles
- Change requests not yet incorporated
- Current prioritized requirements
- The known RBS decomposition
- Prioritized Probative Swim Lanes not yet acted upon
- Prioritized Integrative Swim Lanes not yet acted upon

---

I caution teams that nothing should be removed from the scope bank unless it is built into the solution. An idea once suggested and thought to be of no use early in the project might later turn out to be just the opposite. If it isn't in the scope bank, it will have been forgotten.

The scope bank is the primary input to the Client Checkpoint. Its contents are updated at the completion of each cycle. The contents include future Integrative Swim Lanes and ideas for future Probative Swim Lanes. Since there are fixed resources for the next cycle, the contents of these two types of swim lanes must be jointly prioritized. Depending on the degree to which the solution is complete, there will be a healthy mix of the two types of swim lanes, as discussed in this chapter.

The scope bank is posted on the whiteboard in the Team War Room or on an electronic board, and kept up-to-date by the responsible team members. At the completion of a Cycle Build Phase the scope bank becomes input to the next phase, the Client Checkpoint Phase.

The process of discovery and learning by the team is continuous throughout the cycle. Any new ideas or thoughts on functionality are simply recorded in the scope bank and saved for the Client Checkpoint Phase. The scope bank can physically be a list posted in the Team War Room, or some electronic form (spreadsheet or word processing document). Whichever form you decide to use, make sure it is always visible to the team.

The following fields are used to describe an item in the scope bank:

- ID
- Date posted
- Posted by (person's name)
- Brief description of the item
- Projected business value, if appropriate
- Estimated duration to complete the item
- Resource requirements to complete the item
- Team comments on the item
- Prioritization in appropriate swim lane

For the cycle just completed, the cycle plan called for a specific list of functions and features to be added to the deliverables through one or more Integrative Swim Lanes. No schedule or scope changes were allowed during the cycle, yet it is possible that not all the planned functions and features actually made it into the deliverables. There are several reasons for that, which we will not discuss. They are obvious reasons (e.g., schedule slippages that could not be recovered, a discovery that rendered the functionality unnecessary), which occur in all projects. The ACPF accommodates these anomalies without skipping a beat. Any functions or features not completed in the just-completed cycle are returned to the scope bank and prioritized for consideration in a future cycle.

## Cycle Scope Changes

In an ACPF project, the scope change process does not exist in the forms that you might be used to seeing. That should come as good news to the traditional project manager. That may sound strange, given what we have already said about the ACPF thriving on change. Scope change in an ACPF project occurs, but not like it does in a TPM project. Any thought or idea that the client team or the development team has, as to something different to do in the solution, is captured and stored in the scope bank. The major difference between TPM and ACPF scope change is that, in TPM, the scope change requests are considered one at a time on a first-come, first-served basis. Furthermore, in ACPF projects, scope changes become part of the project plan going forward, whereas in TPM they are an add-on to a project plan that already exists. It is easy to see that in a TPM project there is a lot of wasted time in revising a plan to accommodate scope changes. That does not happen in the ACPF because the plan going forward has not yet been prepared, and so there is no wasted time processing scope changes. In an ACPF project, resources are used to best business advantage on value-added work, whereas in TPM, there is no assurance that is the case.

### Bundled Change Request Process

If the project is subject to frequent change requests and these are processed on an as-received basis, significant resources can be wasted. Bundling change requests and processing them in bulk (say, at the end of a cycle or at milestone events) can avoid wasting resources and protect the project plan as well.

Regardless of the PMLC model you choose, you will have to deal with scope change requests coming from the client and from the project team. In some cases, you'll be expecting these change requests and be ready to process them. In other cases, you will not be expecting them (or at least won't want them), but that does not absolve you from having a way to process them. During project planning, I introduce the client to the Bundled Change Request Process and its benefits, and get their agreement to its use. So, the Bundled Change Request Process can be in place from the start of the project.

### The Bundled Change Request Process

It is difficult for anyone, regardless of his or her skills at prediction and forecasting, to completely and accurately define the needs for a product or service that will be implemented 6, 12, or 18 months in the future.

Competition, client reactions, technology changes, a host of supplier-related situations, and many other factors could render a killer application obsolete before it can be implemented. The most frequent situation starts with a statement that goes something like this: "Oh, I forgot to tell you that we will also need…" or "I just found out that we have to go to market no later than the third quarter instead of the fourth quarter." Face it: change is a way of life in project management! You might as well confront it and be prepared to act accordingly.

Because change is constant, a good project management methodology has a change management process in place. In effect, the change management process has you plan the project again so that it incorporates the approved changes. If your PMLC model requires a complete plan at the outset of the project, much of the time spent doing the planning will turn out to be non-value-added work, due to the time spent replanning to accommodate approved changes. Perhaps the use of a PMLC model based on just-in-time planning is a better approach, at least from a lean perspective. If you have to use a plan-driven PMLC model, incorporating the Bundled Change Request Process will be a good insurance policy.

An integral part of the Bundled Change Request Process is documentation. I strongly suggest that every change be treated as a major change until proven otherwise. To not do so is to court disaster. That means every change request follows the same procedure. Figure 6.4 is an example of the steps in a typical Bundled Change Request Process. The process is initiated, and the change request is submitted by the client, who uses a form like the one shown in Figure 6.5. This form is forwarded to the manager or managers charged with reviewing such requests. They may either accept the change as submitted or return it to the client for rework and resubmission. After the change request has been accepted, it is forwarded to the project manager, who performs an impact study.

Two documents are part of every good change management process: the Project Change Request and the Project Impact Statement. Here is a brief description of what each of these documents contains:

- **Project Change Request**—The first principle to learn is that every change is a significant change. Adopt that maxim and you will seldom go wrong. What that means is that every change requested by the client must be documented in a *Project Change Request*. That document might be as simple as a memo, but might also follow a format provided by the project team. In any case, it is the start of another round of establishing conditions of satisfaction (COS). Only when the request

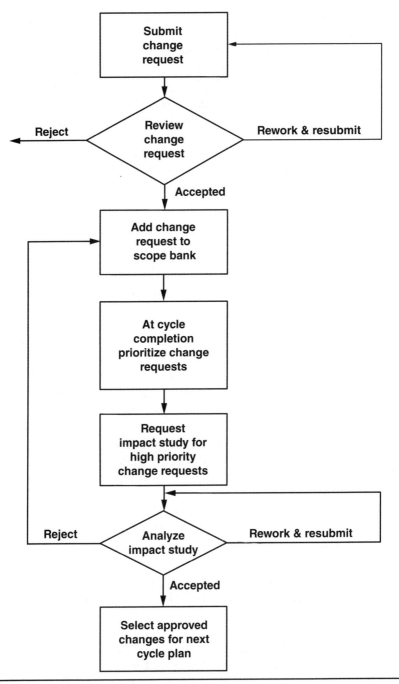

**Figure 6.4** The Bundled Change Request Process

| Project Name |
|---|
| Change Requested By |
| Date Change Requested |
| Description of Change |
| Business Justification |
| Action |
| Approved by                                              Date |

**Figure 6.5**   Change request form example

is clearly understood can the project team evaluate the impact of the change and determine whether the change can be accommodated.

- **Project Impact Statement**—The response to a change request is a document called a *Project Impact Statement*. It is a response that identifies the alternative courses of action that the project manager is willing to consider. The requestor is then charged with choosing the best alternative. The Project Impact Statement describes the feasible alternatives that the project manager was able to identify, the positive and negative aspects of each, and perhaps a recommendation as to which alternative might be best. The final decision regarding the choice of alternatives rests with the requestor.

The impact study involves looking at the project plan, assessing how the change request impacts the plan, and issuing the impact study, which is forwarded to upper management for final disposition. They may return it to the project manager for further analysis and recommendations, or reject it and notify the client of their action. The project manager reworks the impact study and returns it to upper management for final disposition. If they approve the change, the project manager will implement it into the project plan.

### *Benefits of Using the Bundled Change Request Process*

The major benefit is that the process will reduce the time wasted to process change requests. All meaningful analysis of the change requests is done at the completion of the current cycle. In a TPM environment, that means deadline dates for change requests are established. There can be more than one such deadline date imbedded in the plan-drive model. At these planned dates, all of the open change requests are analyzed as a package. The analysis includes a prioritization and scheduling of the approved change requests, so only one plan revision is done at these deadline dates, rather than one plan revision for every change request in the bundle.

## Issue Tracking and Resolution

Because of short cycle durations, the early identification and quick resolution of issues is critical in an ACPF project. Some issues will need resolution in the cycle in which the issue was first identified. Others may be more systemic and not as urgent. Examples of issues requiring immediate resolution are:

- The client is no longer meaningfully involved.
- One or more team members are consistently behind schedule.
- One or more team members have a habit of missing or being late for team meetings.
- The vendor has shipped the wrong product.

Any one of these issues can bring a cycle to a dead stop; until resolved, the cycle deliverables are at risk. In an ACPF project, you always have the option of delaying a deliverable to a later cycle. You do not have that luxury in a TPM project.

Some issues are not as critical, and may be resolved at some later time. For example:

- A team member will be leaving the company or reassigned elsewhere, and must be replaced.
- The major competitor has introduced a new product that will compete with the products being developed in this project.
- A new technology has just been introduced that impacts this project.

## Issues Log

In an Issues Log, the Issue ID could be a brief title with an imbedded date of discovery, perhaps. Something like Meeting Attendance or 090114 Meetings would be appropriate. The ID serves as a reference and a mental trigger. Who posted the issue, and who is responsible for taking action, are important fields, too. There is no reason to believe that these will be the same people. Table 6.1 is a template that I have used for issue tracking.

The Description in the Issue Log is brief and to the point. One or two brief sentences would be sufficient (for example, "The Client Team Manager is usually late for all project team meetings."). Assigned To is the project team member who is responsible for resolving the issue. While that person may require the help of other team members or even people who are not on the team, they are the responsible party. For example, the Assigned To person might be the Development Team Manager. In some cases, it might even be the person responsible for creating the issue. For one example, that would be the Client Team Manager.

Planned Action is a brief statement of what is to be done to resolve the issue, and Status is the current situation. It may simply be a statement of work underway against the Planned Action. A Status of Completed would indicate that the issue has been successfully resolved. The issue generally pertains to the current cycle and would be resolved in the current cycle,

Table 6.1   Issue Log template

| Issue ID | Date Posted | Posted By | Assigned To | Description | Planned Action | Status |
|----------|-------------|-----------|-------------|-------------|----------------|--------|
|          |             |           |             |             |                |        |
|          |             |           |             |             |                |        |
|          |             |           |             |             |                |        |
|          |             |           |             |             |                |        |

although on occasion a more serious issue may require more than one cycle to resolve.

The Issues Log is usually managed by the same team member who manages the Risk Plan. The log is posted in the Team War Room (a whiteboard or electronic board are appropriate technologies), and lists the problems and issues that the team has encountered during the cycle and those issues still open from a previous cycle. Because the list is continually changing, it should be handwritten (i.e., with nonpermanent marking pens) in a convenient location for the team. Handwriting facilitates the updating and keeps it always visible to the team. It contains the information shown in this Issue Log and is updated daily. The items in the Issues Log need resolution, and there should be a plan to resolve them. The person to whom the issue was assigned is responsible for developing that plan, and keeping the team informed by keeping the Issue Log up to date and visible at the daily team meetings. While there may be some discussion of an Issue Log entry at the daily team meetings, this is the exception, not the rule.

There will typically be a sense of urgency with an Issues Log Entry. If it affects the current cycle, something must be done ASAP. Here is where the prioritized ACPF Scope Triangle constraints help the team. The constraints help the team focus efforts at finding a solution within the constraints that are available. These constraints will save the needless wasting of time while pursuing solutions that are not feasible in the minds of the stakeholders and sponsor. The prioritized ACPF Scope Triangle should also be posted in the Team War Room or otherwise visible to the entire project team.

## STEP 9: PLAN NEXT CYCLE

The tools that you are already familiar with and use are directly applicable to cycle planning, but on a much smaller scale. A cycle is typically of 2-4 weeks duration, and composed of one or more swim lanes. The longest duration swim lane is the cycle's critical path. Any deliverables planned for this cycle and not delivered are simply returned to the scope bank for later prioritization and consideration. Unlike TPM projects, cycle length is fixed during planning and not extended for any reason.

### Swim Lanes

The basic component of a cycle is called a "swim lane." This should be familiar terminology to most project managers. One way to define *swim lanes* is that they are parallel streams of project work. Ideally, swim lanes are independent of one another, but that is not always possible. A number of swim lanes will be used to construct the cycle work plan. Each swim lane must have a total duration less than or equal to the cycle duration. The longest duration swim lane should command the management attention of the client team leader and the development team leader. This is the critical path for the cycle. These parallel swim lanes serve the same purpose as the tracks of concurrent work that make up the Rapid Development Waterfall model in a TPM project. They are designed to increase the amount of work that can be done in a fixed time box. In a TPM project, the swim lane approach is used to get deliverables into production faster. In an ACPF project, these parallel swim lanes are used to get to the final solution faster and to allow the project team to examine more alternatives for inclusion in the solution.

When you are planning to use multiple swim lanes in a cycle, it is good risk management strategy to construct them so that there is minimal or no technical or resource dependencies across the swim lanes. This allows for independent task scheduling and usually minimizes the risk associated with any potential resource scheduling conflicts. Figure 6.6 illustrates two types of swim lane configurations.

As shown in Figure 6.6, Cycle A is clearly easier to manage than Cycle B. There will be fewer problems with Cycle A than Cycle B. Except for resource constraints, each swim lane in Cycle A can be managed and scheduled independently of one another. The only scheduling requirement is that A7, A8, and A9 are all finished before the late start date for A10. Cycle B, on the other hand, has a number of schedule risks that may affect other swim lanes, due to cross-swim lane dependencies

There are two types of dependencies across swim lanes that can affect the schedule risk of a cycle: technical and resource.

## Technical Dependencies Across Swim Lanes

The work within a cycle is tightly scheduled. Having technical schedule dependencies across two or more swim lanes introduces the possibility that schedule delays in one swim lane will cause schedule delays in a dependent swim lane. Partition the tasks into swim lanes to minimize the possibility that delays will happen. If you can actually make the swim lanes independent of one another, consider yourself fortunate.

## Resource Dependencies Across Swim Lanes

Resource dependencies should appear in the dependency diagram and be displayed in a convenient location that is visible to the team. This dependency

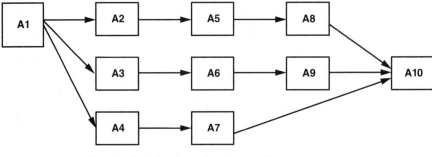

**Cycle A: Ideal swim lane plan**

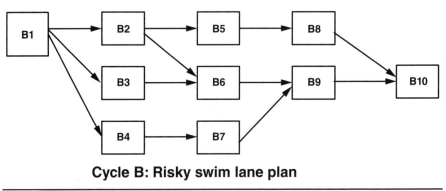

**Cycle B: Risky swim lane plan**

**Figure 6.6**   Examples of cycle swim lanes

can pack a double whammy. If the resource becomes unavailable for some reason, then two or more swim lanes are affected. Maintenance of the cycle schedule becomes more problematic, as well. Do not expect the swim lanes to be totally independent of one another. Consider independence to be the ideal. Depending on how you define "cross-lane dependencies," this may not show up in the dependency diagram. I recommend that they do because that will keep those constraints visible.

Another case of resources dependency arises when the resource falls behind schedule with a task in one swim lane, and may therefore be delayed in working on a scheduled task in another swim lane. The usual fixes when this occurs are the same as would take place in a TPM project. Those fixes include reassigning resources or requisitioning additional resources. In an ACPF project, you also have the possibility of reducing cycle scope without compromising the overall project schedule. Some of the lower priority work planned for this cycle can be put back in the scope bank for reprioritization and inclusion in a later cycle. That should give you a clue in planning the work of the current cycle. Try to complete the highest priority task and leave the lower priority tasks for later cycles if needed. If they are still important, they will be added to a later cycle. This option is not readily available in TPM projects.

## Types of Swim Lanes

In an ACPF project, there are two distinct types of swim lanes. I call them Probative and Integrative Swim Lanes.

### *Probative Swim Lanes*

"Probative" is the label I use for swim lanes whose purpose is to investigate new ideas or whether a particular variation of a function or feature could be part of the final solution, and what it might look like. New ideas are tested for feasibility in Probative Swim Lanes. Probative Swim Lanes are speculative, in other words.

Only as much planning and detail as is necessary for a decision is done for a Probative Swim Lane. Conserving project team resources is important. We want to save resources for Integrative Swim Lanes. If the decision is such that the potential function or feature can be part of the final solution, then either further Probative Swim Lanes would be planned to further analyze the function or feature, or an Integrative Swim Lane would be planned and prioritized for a future cycle. The decision as to which approach makes the most sense is subjective.

There could be several Probative Swim Lanes in one cycle, each investigating some new function or feature. You could even have several variations of the same function or feature running in concurrent Probative Swim Lanes. Your objective is to either eliminate one or more of the lanes from further consideration, or have one or more of them emerge as the one(s) to be integrated into the current solution. Hopefully, a new function or feature will be identified and will then be part of an Integrative Swim Lane in a later cycle. At some point, the deliverable from a Probative Swim Lane will be one or more alternatives from which the client will choose for development in an Integrative Swim Lane in a future cycle.

Conducting Probative Swim Lanes calls upon the problem solving and creative skills of the client and development teams. In the Integrative Swim Lanes, we are calling on the implementation and process skills of the development team. Different skill sets are needed for each type of swim lane. The challenge is to build a team that has both problem solving and creative skill sets.

One of the greatest benefits from Probative Swim Lanes is the meaningful and continuous involvement of the client. They are the decision makers in all activities, going forward. They are making decisions with full knowledge of what has taken place to date, and with the collaborative support of the development team. They understand how business value can be achieved by changes in functionality and they are in a position to take action. Their presence will be a constant reminder to the development team of the business aspects and value of what they are doing and what changes should be made to protect that business value. This ongoing client involvement is an important point to remember. It ensures that what is eventually built will meet client needs.

Probative Swim Lanes are unique to the ACPF. They have proven to be efficient strategies for examining ideas without the need for extensive time or resource commitments. With some practice, a lot can be learned with minimal investment. In my ACPF experiences, I have used three different kinds of Probative Swim Lanes: iconic, in-depth, and information gathering.

## Iconic Prototype Swim Lanes

These are models that represent a real situation: a model ship or a paper airplane, for example. These prototypes are built quickly to illustrate a function or feature. I have used prototypes to clarify with the client how a function or feature idea might be rendered in the solution. If this idea looks promising, then the prototype will have established a foundation on which more details can be explored in the Probative Swim Lane or in a later cycle. There have been situations where the idea does not look promising, but a variant of it might. The variant can also be explored in a later cycle.

## In-depth Discussion Swim Lanes

The result of a brainstorming session or other discussion might identify several options for consideration. A Probative Swim Lane can be used to discuss the details and establish specific directions for further investigation.

## Information Gathering Swim Lanes

In most cases, the organization provides the information needed for a project. Its collection comes in response to questions that have arisen during a previous Probative Swim Lane. Any team member can be assigned to the research task.

## *Integrative Swim Lanes*

"Integrative" is the label I use for those swim lanes that will be used to fully develop and integrate new functions and features into the current solution. These functions and features may have been known to be part of the solution from the start of the project, or may have been discovered in a Probative Swim Lane. They are in the scope bank, but their priority was never high enough to be integrated into the solution. The necessary testing and documentation is done as part of the tasks in an Integrative Swim Lane. At the end of every cycle, the deliverables from any Integrative Swim Lanes will be an updated working solution with functions, processes, and features added since the previous solution. This new solution and the updated scope bank are inputs to Step 11: Conduct Client Checkpoint for evaluation.

## Cycle Planning

There are two different planning situations in ACPF cycle planning:

- The first cycle plan, and,
- The second and all subsequent cycle plans.

## *The First Cycle Plan*

The first time the team enters the ACPF Cycle Planning Phase, it will have as input the deliverables from the Version Scoping Phase: the POS, the RBS, the PMLC model that will be used, the prioritized Scope Triangle, the mid-level WBS, a prioritized list of known requirements, the functions and features, and the high-level project plan.

For most ACPF projects, the first cycle should be short. I like to keep it to about two weeks, so do not plan on putting too much into it. At this early stage of the project, it is more important to get the client to have a vested and meaningful interest in the project, and to get the development team aligned to the project. To gain and sustain the client's interest and involvement, you need to show them something quickly. Consider using iconic prototypes. Since the ACPF team may be coming together for the first time as a team, you need to spend some time on team development. Who the team members are, why they have been assigned to this project, and their understanding of the project should be put on your agenda.

Depending on the depth to which the solution is known, there are five directions that the first Cycle Planning Phase might take: a project definition statement, a proof of concept, an iconic prototype, a current solution, or a prioritized list of functionality.

- **Create a Project Definition Statement.** The POS has been approved, but the entire project team may not have seen it. If that is the case, the Project Definition Statement is drafted by the project team to make sure that every team member is on the same page with respect to their understanding of the project. The Project Definition Statement is an expanded rendition of the POS from the perspective of the project team. It is the "insurance" that the team members all have the same understanding of the project, kind of like a mini-COS session. This is a one-day cycle and can be immediately followed by any of the following phases.
- **Make proof of concept the first cycle.** There will be cases where so little is known of an acceptable solution, or the likelihood of even finding one, that a proof of concept is done as the first cycle. This will often take the form of a prototype. The purpose of the *proof of concept* is to validate a direction to proceed in search of a solution.

  If little of the functionality is known, you may not be able to generate an initial solution that is useful to the client. A better choice for the first few cycles might be to start with a proof of concept and follow it with a prototype. The purpose of the prototype is to get a conversation going with the client and to begin identifying meaningful solution components. This prototype will be very high level and is not expected to contain much detail because details are not yet known. It can be done quickly and can be very informative. This is the approach I used for the first ACPF new product design project briefly described in the next section. Once a sufficiently detailed prototype is in place, the priority can shift to including Probative Swim Lanes.
- **Build an iconic prototype of the desired solution.** Building an iconic prototype is an alternative that can be used even when little of the solution is known. The high-level requirements will have been identified in Step 2: Elicit Requirements in the Ideation Phase. Proceeding from that knowledge, the development team should suggest several alternatives using an iconic prototyping tool. Several possible alternatives can be offered in a relatively short time. This is akin to a brainstorming approach.
- **Build the current solution, as it is known.** Building the current solution is the likely choice if enough of the solution is known to produce a meaningful part of the final solution for the client to begin

envisioning what the final solution might look like, and to begin working towards it. From the prioritized list of functionality created in the Version Scoping Phase, enough functionality for a short cycle of about two weeks would be taken, starting from the top of the list. Even if a reasonably complete solution is known, stick with two-week cycles for the first few cycles. Your goal in the first few cycles is to meaningfully engage the client, create a sense of ownership on their part, and begin the task of forming an effective team. Short cycles will make it possible to do that. At the same time, you will begin to deliver business value. Also, from the early short cycles, you might be surprised and discover that the solution was not what you thought it would be. Two-week cycles will keep the project heading in the right direction, and prevent you from wasting your time and your client's money jousting with proverbial windmills.

While building the current solution certainly is an approach for the first cycle, it is not high on my list of recommended first cycles for the following reasons:

1.  Building the current solution will make the first cycle too long and will hamper your establishing client ownership. Establishing meaningful client involvement from the very beginning of the project is the number one CSF for project success. We learned from The Standish Group's (2013) *Chaos Manifesto* the top ten reasons why projects succeed. Even when you know a lot about the solution, you still have to be patient. Establishing a solid client relationship early will pay dividends later.

2.  You might have guessed incorrectly as to what the final solution would include, and therefore, you wasted time. As learning and discovery take place in each cycle, your view of the final solution will change. Certainly more of the solution will be known, but so will earlier understandings change. What was once thought to be part of the solution may no longer be part of the solution. So, you will have wasted time integrating that part into the solution, and then backing it out of the solution. That is not consistent with the underlying lean principles espoused by the ACPF. Wasted time is the bane of all ACPF projects and to be avoided, if at all possible.

Instead of building the solution, I prefer to take a more pedestrian approach and work from the prioritized list. If your initial guess proves to be correct, then those functions and features will eventually find their place in the final solution and nothing will have been lost. The pedestrian approach reduces the risk of having made a bad decision as to the contents of the final solution at the beginning of the project and potentially saves a lot of wasted time.

- **Build from a prioritized list of functionality.** If your concern is about creating business value ASAP, you may have to lengthen the cycle duration in order to build enough functionality to attain even minimal business value. Be careful here because the longer the cycle, the more likely you will err on the side of including something in the solution that turns out to be not part of the final solution. Including Probative Swim Lanes in the early cycles are low priority when most of the solution is known.

### The Second and All Subsequent Cycle Plans

For the second and all subsequent Cycle Planning Phases we will have the current solution, an updated RBS, all the deliverables from the previously completed cycles, all learning and discovery that took place in those earlier cycles, and the scope bank that contains all the ideas for change accumulated over all previous cycles, but not yet acted upon. As you can see, these Cycle Planning Phases are moments of opportunity when the client team and the development team will come together to openly discuss, prioritize, and plan the work to be done in the upcoming cycle. These planning exercises should be lively sessions, where ideas are shared in a brainstorming fashion, discussed, challenged, and then brought to closure for exclusion or tabled for later consideration. Whatever their final disposition might be, all of the learning and discovery should remain in the scope bank for future reference. You can't possibly know what future courses the solution might take, and keeping the project team's cumulative knowledge at hand may prove valuable later on. It does not cost anything to keep it, but it may cost a lot to not have it, if it is needed later.

## Types of Deliverables in the Cycle Plan

There are two major types of deliverables from an ACPF Cycle Plan. The first is the decision as to what functions and features will be integrated into the current solution in the coming cycle to help converge towards the final solution. The current solution is always a working version of the then known solution. In the early cycles, not much integration may be happening simply because so little is known of the final solution. These form the Integrative Swim Lanes. In later cycles, this pattern will reverse as several functions, sub-functions, and especially features will be integrated in each cycle. A steady trend of integration should be the pattern. If not, there is serious doubt about the convergence toward a final acceptable solution. I will introduce some metrics in the Cycle Build Phase that will help you assess the extent to which convergence or divergence of the solution is happening. I have seen examples where the metrics indicate that the solution was diverging and would ultimately lead to project failure if some termination decision had not been made. Often, the decision is to terminate the project and start over in a different direction. Having an early warning system has proven to be a real strength of the ACDF.

The second type of deliverable is the choice of what new ideas in the form of functions and features are to be investigated for possible additions into the solution in a later cycle. These form the Probative Swim Lanes. These deliverables can start out as high-level descriptions of potential solution parts and be further investigated for as long as they seem feasible. At the completion of a cycle these discoveries will either be abandoned and returned to the scope bank, or added to the priority list for integration into the solution in some future cycle.

Just as with the Version Scoping Phase, the best way to introduce you to the Cycle Planning Phase is from the perspective of its deliverables. The Cycle Planning Phase includes these deliverables:

1. Update the prioritized functionality list.
2. Establish the contents of the next Cycle Build Integrative Swim Lanes.
3. Establish the contents of the next Cycle Build Probative Swim Lanes.
4. Create a low-level WBS for cycle deliverables.
5. Identify resource requirements.
6. Estimate swim lane duration.
7. Establish technical and resource dependencies.
8. Finalize cycle schedule.

Let's briefly discuss each deliverable.

### 1. Update the Prioritized Functionality List

The input to the prioritized functionality list is the prioritized list from the just completed cycle: any work planned but not completed from the previous cycle, any ideas or changes in the scope bank that have not yet been acted upon, and any new ideas or changes suggested by the client or the development team based on additional learning and discovery from the just completed cycle.

All of this information is best kept in the scope bank. The scope bank is the depository of all known functions, sub-functions, features, ideas, or suggested changes not yet acted upon. At the beginning of each cycle, all of the items in the updated scope bank are prioritized. From this prioritized list, the contents of the next cycle build will be identified.

## 2. Establish the Contents of the Next Cycle Build Integrative Swim Lanes

This is familiar ground for every project manager. The same vetted tools, templates, and processes used for TPM projects can be used here. Remember that cycles will be short (2-4 weeks typically for agile project management [APM] and extreme project management [xPM] projects), and so planning is not complex and does not need a lot of software support. For my purposes, white boards, sticky notes, and marking pens are sufficient!

The contents of the next cycle build will take the form of some number of Probative and Integrative Swim Lanes. You also have a preliminary estimate of the cycle time box for the coming cycle, and so you can determine the cycle contents based on what can reasonably be accomplished within that time constraint. If necessary, you might adjust that time box to accommodate the next item or items on the prioritized list. Apart from any dependencies between the functions, sub-functions, and features, the client team and the development team will jointly decide how much of the prioritized list the development team can deliver in the coming cycle. The duration of the cycle and the estimated duration of the functions and features to be worked on in this cycle is what you will use to determine the contents of what can be worked on in this cycle.

---

### A Caution about Overcommitment

Technical professionals tend to be optimistic about what they can accomplish in a given time box. There is something about the challenge that gets their juices flowing. That has no place here. ACPF projects are risky enough and do not need heroes on white horses arriving in the nick of time to save the project.

---

If this is the first cycle, don't be too ambitious, especially if your project team members have not had the opportunity to work together on an ACPF project before. Take the client team into consideration, too. Is this the first opportunity to work with them? What do you know about them? What is your previous experience with them? These are all factors to be considered regarding cycle content and length. How they have come together as a team may also influence planning for the coming cycle. If they are together for the first time, you should not expect them to be a lean, mean, fighting team. They will stumble at first. So do not burden the team too heavily while they are learning to work together efficiently.

You are constrained to a fixed time box for this cycle and the available resources of the project team. What can realistically be built within this time box, using the available team resources? As the project team gains experience through successfully completed cycles, you can get a bit more aggressive on what can be accomplished in the coming cycle. At that time, you will have direct and relevant experience working with the team on this project, and will have a better grasp on what they can be expected to accomplish.

Inside the cycle, think about using tools, templates, and processes from your TPM experiences. For example, you might use the Standard Waterfall model, Staged Delivery Waterfall model, or Rapid Development Waterfall model to maximize the deliverables that can be produced in a swim lane in this cycle. You should be on familiar ground here, and know what makes sense. When you have identified what will be built in this cycle, you can complete that part of the WBS down to the lowest level at which activities that define how you will build the functionality and features are clarified. Remember that even this part of the WBS may not be complete. For a given function, not all of its features will be known until some later cycle, and you don't know that at this point in time.

The first step in establishing cycle contents is to work down the prioritized list of functions, sub-functions, and features, estimating the time to build them. How far down the list to go is a judgment call. (As a guide, you might use the total number of hours of labor available from the project team in the coming cycle. If you feel uncomfortable with this, you might reduce labor hours by some percentage, say 10%, and use that as your guide to cumulative duration hours available in the coming cycle.) The cumulative duration of the work you have estimated can be larger than the cycle duration if the team size is large enough, so that parallel work can take place. Do not spend time working far down the list past anything that might reasonably be included in the coming cycle. That could prove to be a waste of time. Where to stop is a judgment call, so just remember that the complex project manager does not waste time.

### 3. Establish the Contents of the Next Cycle Build Probative Swim Lanes

The less that is known about the solution, the more important it is to aggressively identify potential solution details. That is the purpose of Probative

Swim Lanes. I have often found it helpful to use an iconic prototyping approach in these Probative Swim Lanes to investigate these possible additions to the solution. Several iterations of the prototype can be completed within the cycle time box.

Whereas Integrative Swim Lanes are planned in detail using TPM tools, Probative Swim Lanes are more like xPM projects and do not have such plans, but rather depend on the creative process for their completion. There really is no limit to the approach used in a Probative Swim Lane. Prototyping, brainstorming, and problem solving have already been discussed earlier in this chapter, and are the three approaches I have used in past ACPF projects. The outputs from these three approaches fall into one of the categories discussed next.

Because of the volatile nature of the Probative Swim Lanes, be prepared to move resources to other cycle work as available, when you have:

- **Positive results—more investigation advised.** This idea looks like a promising direction to investigate, but more detail is needed. That detail should be left for a later Probative Swim Lane in their next cycle or even later, and so its description should be placed in the scope bank for prioritization.
- **Negative results—looks like a dead end.** This idea doesn't seem like it will produce any fruitful results. No further action on it is recommended. It should be returned to the scope bank for further idea generation. Do not throw any ideas away unless you are clairvoyant!
- **New ideas have surfaced.** Probative Swim Lane ideas will often identify other ideas for consideration. Depending on the extent of those ideas, they might be considered within the context of the current swim lane, or relegated to the scope bank for later prioritization and consideration.

### 4. Create Low-level WBS for Cycle Deliverables

You have identified the preliminary contents of the cycle from the perspective of priority and duration. It is now time to build out the WBS for the functions, sub-functions, and features chosen as the cycle contents, and to finalize what actually will be included. The list could be compromised by any resource or schedule dependencies between swim lanes. If there are Probative Swim Lanes to be added, they will require resources, and hence will further compromise the Integrative Swim Lanes that can be included in the cycle plan. We only develop the low-level WBS for the next cycle deliverables. Anything further is a potential waste of time in a complex project.

How many times have you managed a project where the activities that occur late in the project schedule are not even done? The reasons are many, and you are aware of them, so we don't need to spend time discussing them.

## Probative Swim Lanes WBS

The variety of Probative Swim Lanes is quite broad. For some, you can generate a WBS, but most will be very simple. For example, a Probative Swim Lane might involve:

- Gathering information
- Answering a few questions
- Researching a tool
- Testing a hypothesis with a focus group
- Building a simple prototype
- Executing a simple design of experiments

These do not require a WBS. That would be like killing a mosquito with a sledge hammer.

## Integrative Swim Lanes WBS

An Integrative Swim Lane WBS should be familiar ground for project managers. The process that they will follow for generating this WBS is exactly the process they would use for a Quadrant 1 project. To make sure we are all on the same page regarding this process, here is the completion criteria that I always use to generate a complete WBS, which you can do for all Integrative Swim Lanes:

- **Status and completion are measurable.** At any point in time while the activity is open for work, its status can be reported. Certainly, the percent of work completed will be of interest, but even more important will be an estimate of how much time is required to complete the task.
- **Each activity is bounded.** Each activity has clear starting and ending events. When these events occur, either work can begin on the activity or the activity is finished.
- **Each activity has a deliverable.** Something tangible is produced by the activity. That might be something you can hold in your hands, a signature, or a document.
- **Time and cost are easily estimated.** This is a relative term. "Easily" may mean it is an estimate that has been provided in an earlier project, or it may mean this is the simplest it can be and no further decomposition will make the estimate any easier to obtain.

- **Activity duration is within acceptable limits.** This is an organizationally determined limit. Two weeks (80 hours) is a common choice in a TPM project, but the situation may dictate a smaller or larger limit. In an ACPF project, the cycle length might only be 2 weeks, and so the limit would be much smaller. Three days is probably about right for an ACPF Cycle, but it is a judgment call in any case. Remember the cycle is short and tasks even shorter. A one week task in a complex project cycle is about as long a task as should be scheduled.
- **Work assignments are independent.** This is critical. It simply means that once work has begun on an activity, it can continue without interruption to get additional input. This has obvious scheduling implications.

Once an activity meets the completion criteria, we rename it a "task" and no further decomposition of the task is needed or advised. No other type of activity will have this property, and so the term "task" is a precise term in project management vocabulary. When this part of the WBS contains all tasks at the lowest level of decomposition, it is the complete WBS, but for the coming cycle only. The WBS for this cycle is now complete, and a dependency precedence diagram of the tasks can be constructed. This becomes the input to the partitioning of tasks into swim lanes.

### 5. Identify Resource Requirements

Estimating resources requirements for an ACPF cycle is different than the process you would follow for a TPM project. In an ACPF project, you already know the resources available to you. They are assigned (100% is ideal, but not always possible) to your ACPF project. In a TPM project, you have to estimate the people resources by skill level or by position title. You will not know the specific person until much later in the process. In the ACPF project, resources requirements are determined during the Version Scope Phase and are generally not repeated again in the project.

Who will be assigned to work on what is the major decision to be made here. As a first pass, I usually assign the best person to each task and worry about any schedule conflicts this creates once duration estimates and the dependency network is built. The person who is initially assigned to specific work will provide the input needed to plan the cycle schedule. At that point, there may be some reassignment to reconcile scheduling conflicts.

### 6. Estimate Swim Lane Durations

For each task, you would usually estimate the labor time (not the duration time) that it would take with normal resources to complete it. Do not get heroic here. This estimate is nothing different than the traditional project manager would do at this point.

In an ACPF project, however, you have the advantage of knowing who will be working on each task. That is not the case in a TPM project where all you know is the skill level required. You do not know what you will get for TPM staff. You might get the skill level you need, but you might not. You might get one person to complete the task, but you might not. You will probably get the full-time equivalent count you need, but you might not. All you can plan for the TPM task duration estimate is that you will get the average skilled person working on the task at a normal pace with all of the normal interruptions and so on that will get in the way. In these situations, both task labor time and task duration estimates are needed. You have the added burden of actually getting the staff when you need them. Resource managers have a lot of competing priorities, and you could be disappointed when the time comes for the person to report to your TPM project and they are not available.

For the ACPF project, the person who will be assigned to work on the task is already 100% assigned to the team and participating in cycle planning. They can provide the estimated duration better than anyone else. Since they are assigned 100% to the project, you do not have to worry about outside scheduling conflicts. Hence, the ACPF task duration estimates are considerably more reliable than those from a TPM project, and more likely to be achieved than their TPM counterpart.

### 7. Establish Technical and Resource Dependencies

Now, we are going to put all the pieces of the puzzle together for a first look at what we have. Arrange these tasks into a network diagram from left to right on the whiteboard, showing their dependencies with the marking pens. You will eventually want to scale the display on a time line so that you will know if you are meeting the cycle time box constraint. The high-tech folks will not be able to resist the temptation, and will go ahead and put these dependencies into a software tool. They will let the tool tell them about the critical path. That's fine. Just remember that the cycle duration is only 2-6 weeks, so the task list will be short. Be careful not to create a monster in your software tool, because you will have to feed it throughout the cycle to get any return for your investment of time.

The tasks are few in number, and you know the availability of your team members. The ACPF works best when the resources are assigned 100 percent to the cycle. If that is the case, you should have total control over their schedule. That means that you can create the cycle schedule with both dependencies and resources schedules taken into account. In a TPM project, the project manager seldom has that luxury.

By defining project tasks as those activities that meet all six completion criteria, you should have reached a point of granularity with each task so that it is familiar. You may have done the task or something similar to it in a past project. That recollection, that historical information, gives us the basis for estimating the resources you will need to complete the tasks in the current project. In some cases, it is a straightforward recollection; in others, the result of keeping a historical file of similar tasks; in others, the advice of experts.

Recording dependency relations and generating the initial schedule is done with sticky notes, marking pens, and plenty of whiteboard space. If you really have to have the comfort and assurance of a software tool, go ahead and use it. Just remember that you created the software monster and you will be responsible for its care and feeding over the life of the cycle. Having planned and managed many ACPF cycles using nothing but sticky notes, marking pens, and whiteboards, I found that using a software package is non-value-added work. In other words, it is a waste of time and complex project managers do not waste time!

The steps to building the dependency diagram can be found in any good book on project management. See, for example Wysocki (2014b) for a step-by-step process for generating the dependency diagram and calculating the schedule.

## 8. Finalize Cycle Schedule

Finalizing the cycle schedule is the first pass at building a staffed schedule for the coming cycle. Based on the dependencies between tasks that will be open for work in the coming cycle, we partition the tasks into sets of tasks, so that within a set there are task dependencies, but between sets there are few task dependencies. To the furthest extent possible, it will reduce the number of scheduling dependencies between your sub-teams. Once the partitioning is acceptable to the team and the client, you can begin to form sub-teams that will plan and implement the tasks in their partition.

Every task is assigned to one person who is responsible for getting the task done. This person is called a *task manager*. There might be others assigned to work on the task, but the task manager is ultimately responsible for completing the task. Figure 6.7 provides a worked example.

### *Minimize Cross-swim Lane Dependencies*

If done properly, minimizing cross-swim lane dependencies is a step that will minimize the risk of schedule and resource dependencies across swim

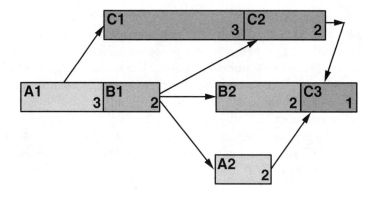

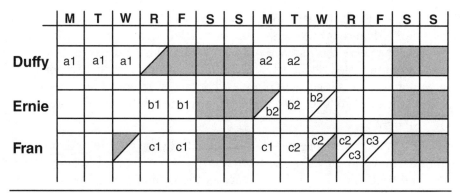

**Figure 6.7**   A task plan example

lanes. The total elimination of these dependencies is highly unlikely, but you must make every effort to minimize these occurrences. The process of minimization consists of observing the dependency diagram and partitioning it into independent streams of work, and then allocating those streams of work to different swim lanes.

## Task Plan

The task schedule can be built on the whiteboard as a time-scaled matrix. One row of the matrix is devoted to each member of the task team and the columns are the calendar days of the cycle. Each sticky note is a sub-task, and all you have to do is lay them out in the matrix (remembering dependencies) and you have the schedule. Later, when the cycle is underway, there may be a need to revise the schedule. Any changes that must be made due to slippages or other surprises are easily incorporated. Just move the appropriate sticky notes without violating any dependencies or over-allocating any task team member. Here is where sticky notes, marking pens, and white-boards really show their value. If you put the task team's work into per-spective, you will see the reason for my recommended approach. The cycle is short—just a few weeks' duration. The task team is working on a small set of sub-tasks, all of which must be completed within the duration of the cycle. If this cycle was the entire project, it probably would not even meet the basic requirements to be called a project. For a 2-4 week cycle time box, we do not need a high-tech solution. I have successfully managed three-year ACPF projects by using nothing more than these low-tech tools, so here is your low-tech solution:

### Step #1

The network diagram for this task is shown in the upper por-tion of Figure 6.7. Note that the network diagram is time-scaled. Please excuse the variance from convention I have taken to show the time-scaled dependency diagram. This time scaling is impor-tant because it is going to replace what otherwise would have been a schedule produced by a project management software package.

### Step #2

At another spot on the whiteboard (ideally, below the network diagram and on the same time scale), lay out a grid that shows the time line on a daily basis across the columns, and have one row allocated to each development team member. The resources for this example are Duffy, Ernie, and Fran. Show all seven days of the week on this grid. For any workday or half workday in this cycle for which a resource will not be available for cycle build work, put an X or some other indicator of unavailability (shading is used to indicate unavailability in the figure) in the correspond-ing cell or half cell. This grid is your resource calendar for this cycle.

Before finalizing the task plan, check to see if the initial schedule and re-source assignments allow the task team to complete their work within the allotted time box. You can do this by inspecting the scaled time line you created in the Cycle Plan Phase. If the current schedule does not meet the cycle time box, look for alternative resource assignments that bring the schedule inside the cycle time box. Resources that are not assigned for pe-riods of time are the place to look. They can either take over a sub-task or help another resource complete a sub-task earlier than currently scheduled.

What you are doing is manual resource leveling in a way that makes more sense than the approach taken by most software tools.

Once you have met the cycle time box constraint, you are ready to finalize the information on the grid. For each resource, simply transfer the information to the grid that shows what sub-task s/he is working on, what day s/he expects to start it, and what day s/he expects to end it. Every morning, you will have a 15-minute team status meeting, at which time you can compare what was completed the previous day with what the grid had scheduled for that day. Any adjustments to the plan are made on the grid. Resources can be moved to meet schedule delays. Because you still have the sticky-note network diagram on the whiteboard, you will be able to see if schedule delays will cause any other delays downstream in the plan, and you can adjust accordingly.

Let's look at a few important points with regard to Figure 6.7. First, when scheduling resources, try to keep them busy for consecutive days. That makes it easier if you need to replace an individual on the team. Second, notice when a resource is not busy (for example, Duffy is available for a half-day on Thursday of the first week). While this is early in the cycle, it may provide a resource that can help either Ernie or Fran or help the team recover from a slippage or a problem. Finally, note that in the second week, Duffy and Ernie are available to perhaps help Fran complete C2 when Fran is unavailable on Wednesday afternoon. If that can be scheduled, C3 may be able to be completed early. This means that the cycle would be completed ahead of schedule. Alternatively, that staffing adjustment might provide a way to make up for earlier slippages.

This grid should be permanently displayed in the Team War Room. It will be the focal point of daily team meetings. As status is being reported, the team can refer to this schedule and make any changes to the latter parts of the schedule. The most important benefit to having it displayed is that it is visible and accessible to the team. The only negative you have to worry about is that there is no backup for this approach. An electronic whiteboard or good digital camera would be a plus. The fact that the Team War Room is reserved for the exclusive use of the team and is secure will mitigate most of the risk but not all of the risk.

The reason that the use of sticky notes and the grid works is that the cycle length is short. The example cycle is only two weeks long, but even if it was three or four weeks long, the same approach will work. Just roll the grid forward at the end of each week. Even though I have used project management software packages extensively, I still find this low-tech approach to be far more intuitive and efficient than any software display. The entire team can see what's going on and can see how to resolve scheduling problems in a very straightforward manner. Try it.

## Develop a RASCI Matrix for This Cycle

The RASCI matrix (Figure 6.8) identifies the different types of interactions between complex project team members:

- R = Responsible
- A = Approval
- S = Support
- C = Consult
- I = Inform

In Figure 6.8, the rows correspond to the steps in the ACPF relevant to Project Execution. There are other applications, too. Any process can be represented by the steps that comprise it and these define the rows of the RASCI matrix. For example, the rows might be the tasks that comprise all or part of the WBS, and the columns would be the team members involved in those tasks.

# STAGEGATE #3

StageGate #3 is either the approval to execute the project (for TPM projects) or the approval to execute the next cycle. If it is for the project, it will include the resources agreed to by the plan. If it is for the next cycle, it is merely the agreement of the sponsor or client to execute the next cycle. The resources have already been approved.

# STEP 10: BUILD NEXT CYCLE DELIVERABLES

Work on the Integrative and Probative Swim Lanes is rather straightforward. A bit of housekeeping launches the build cycle in the form of assigning responsibilities just for this cycle. With that done, the actual work can begin.

## Execute the Cycle Build Plan

Work is now underway to build the functionality prioritized for this cycle. These are the Integrative Swim Lanes. Concurrently, investigative work is underway to explore the ideas represented in the Probative Swim Lanes. Even though the cycle is short and the build not very complex, things will

| ACPF Cycle | Stakeholder | | | | | | | |
| --- | --- | --- | --- | --- | --- | --- | --- | --- |
| | Sponsor | Co-Project Manager (Client) | Co-Project Manager (Develop) | Bus Analyst | Bus Proc Engineer | Resource Manager | Client Team Member | Develop Team Member |
| Plan Next Cycle | I | R/A | R/A | C | C | C | S | S |
| Conduct Integrative Swim Lane | I | A | A | C | C | S | I | R |
| Conduct Probative Swim Lane | I | A/I | A/I | C | C | S | R | R |
| Conduct Client Checkpoint | I | R/A | R/A | C | C | I | S | S |
| Close Version | A | R | R | C | C | I | S | S |

**Figure 6.8**  RASCI matrix for current cycle

not go according to plan. About this time, the complex project manager is thankful that not a lot of time was spent planning and takes the unexpected in stride. And the unexpected is sure to happen: a person gets sick or leaves the company; a vendor is late in shipping, ships the wrong hardware, or goes out of business. These are the same kinds of risks that the traditional project manager faces, but the results are far more catastrophic than they are for the complex project manager. The complex project manager will simply return unfinished work to the scope bank. If it did not make it into this cycle, perhaps it will still have a high enough priority to be included in a later cycle.

Depending on the severity of the unexpected event, the complex project manager either finishes the current cycle or, for the really major problems, cancels the current cycle and immediately moves into the Client Checkpoint Phase in preparation for the next cycle. Terminating the current cycle early is the result of some catastrophic event that may render continuation of the project in its present form to not be in the best interest of the organization. In rare cases, canceling the version and starting the project again, but by taking an entirely different approach to finding an acceptable solution, may be the best strategy.

## Ending a Cycle Build

A cycle build can end normally or abnormally.

### *Normal End-of-Cycle Build*

The normal end of a cycle occurs when the time box expires, and has nothing to do with the swim lanes being completed. Any planned work that is not finished is returned to the scope bank for reprioritization and consideration in a later cycle. If the cycle build plan has scheduled the development of the cycle deliverables based on their position in the prioritized list, then nothing is lost. The work not completed had a lower priority, and can be rescheduled as long as its new position on the prioritized list has placed it out of reach for a future cycle.

---

**Advice for Scheduling Tasks**

To the furthest extent possible, schedule the tasks in a swim lane in priority order. That priority order should be based on business value. Technical dependencies may affect the priority order. That gets the most business value into the solution if for some reason the swim lane tasks are not complete. Incomplete tasks will be low priority, and can be returned to the scope bank to be reprioritized for inclusion in a later cycle.

## *Abnormal End-of-Cycle Build*

There are two situations to discuss with regard to an abnormal end of a cycle build: tasks completed ahead of schedule and tasks not completed within the cycle duration.

1. **Tasks completed ahead of schedule.** First, all deliverables can be completed ahead of schedule. If so, end the Cycle Build Phase and proceed to the Client Checkpoint. For each of the swim lane teams, this means finishing their work ASAP. Just because you see you can finish early does not mean that you should stretch out the work to fill the available time. "Parkinson's Law" has no place in an ACPF project!

2. **Tasks not completed within the cycle duration.** It is the end of the workday on Wednesday and the current cycle is scheduled to end at the end of the 1st shift on Friday. Harry is managing an Integrative Swim Lane and he comes to you asking for a two-day extension so he can finish his scheduled integration testing at the end of the 1st shift on Tuesday. It would be nice to get the functionality integrated into the solution. Should you grant the extension? The answer is a qualified NO.

Cycle length is "sacred" for several reasons. If you said yes, should the rest of the project team just make work to fill the two days? That is a waste of time and ACPF-ists do not waste time. Should the rest of the project team work on another project? You might lose them, and then what would you do?

The unfinished work from a cycle is returned to the scope bank for reprioritization for a later cycle—for example, the next cycle.

## STEP 11: CONDUCT CLIENT CHECKPOINT

The Client Checkpoint Phase is the critical juncture of the ACPF project's past with its future. The past is defined by the updated solution from the just completed cycle and the current contents of the scope bank. The future will be drawn from the learning and discovery resulting from the just completed cycle. Early in the project, expect there to be several possible directions to consider. In this phase, the client team and the development team review everything that has been done and everything that has been discovered to craft the contents of the next cycle. There may be conflicting directions, so be prepared. This exercise must be done with care if the project has any hope of delivering an effective solution.

Without a doubt, this is the most important phase of the ACPF. For it is here that the future of the ACPF project is revisited. The client team and the development team come together and assess what has been accomplished, what has been discovered and learned from the completed cycles, and what should be done in the cycle to come. The client team and the development team jointly perform a quality review of the features and functionality produced in the just completed cycle. It is compared against the requirements, and its part in the solution and the overall goal of maximum business value. Adjustments are made to the high-level plan and next cycle work, as appropriate. The sequence Cycle Plan–Cycle Build–Client Checkpoint is repeated until the time and cost budgets for this version have been expended, the project should be terminated because it is not converging on an acceptable solution, or an acceptable solution has been reached for this version and this version of the deliverables is complete and can be closed.

Together, both teams will analyze what has happened in the project so far and jointly decide what will happen in the project in the next cycle. This is a very creative and challenging part of an ACPF project. Project deliverables from the just completed cycle are discussed with the full participation of all. This is a characteristic of what I mean by "client-facing." These discussions focus on what has to be done to maximize business value within the time and cost constraints established by the client (client-driven). I have often observed how the client and the team interact in these checkpoints. From those observations, it was obvious whether or not the project was moving along according to the principles and core values of the ACPF.

The Conduct Client Checkpoint Phase is a critical review that takes place after every Build Next Cycle Deliverables Phase is completed. During the phase, both the client team and the development team will benefit from several discovery and learning episodes. Variations to the version functionality will surface; alternative approaches to delivering certain functionality will be suggested; and, each team will learn through their continuous involvement with the other team. There is a definite synergy that will develop between the two teams. All of this must be considered along with the functionality that had originally been assigned to the next cycle. The result is a revised prioritization of functionality for the next cycle.

The most important thing to remember is not to speculate on the future. For the next cycle, prioritize only the functionality that you are certain will be in the final solution. That newly prioritized list will be input to decide on the Integrative Swim Lanes for the coming cycle. The learning and discovery from the just completed Cycle Build Phase will be input to decide on the Probative Swim Lanes for the coming cycle. The available resources and the resource requirements of the prioritized Integrative and Probative Swim Lanes will dictate the contents of the coming cycle.

There are a number of activities that take place during the Client Checkpoint. The clearest description is to use the familiar model: Input, Process, Output. Figure 6.9 is that model applied to the ACPF Client Checkpoint.

## Input Data

The input data consists of the items listed in Figure 6.9:

- Planned versus actual deliverables
- Learning and discovery
- Probative Swim Lane results
- Updated scope bank
- Status reports
- External environment
- Internal environment
- Updated RBS

### *Planned vs. Actual Deliverables*

At the end of a cycle, unfinished deliverables are returned to the scope bank for reprioritization. As a result of learning and discovery of the just completed cycle, unfinished deliverables may never get a high enough priority to be completed in a later cycle. This is quite common, especially when you consider the fact that the work of the cycle build plan should be completed according to its priority. The question then, is what is its priority with respect to other prioritized functions and features waiting in the Integrative Swim Lane list in the scope bank?

---

**Note about Formal Change Processes**

TPM defines a formal change management process that can be invoked at any time in the project. In the ACPF, a formal change process does not exist. The essence of a scope change process is imbedded in identification and prioritization of functions and features to be built or investigated in the next cycle. All of this takes place in the Client Checkpoint Phase.

---

## INPUT DATA

Planned vs. actual deliverables
Learning and discovery
Probative Swim Lane results
Updated scope bank
Status reports
External environment
Internal environment
Updated RBS

## PROCESS

ACPF project review
Is the team working as expected?
Is the client participating as expected?
Do cumulative deliverables meet expectations?
Is version scope still valid?
Prioritize remaining functionality
Brainstorm next cycle swim lane contents
PMLC model adjustments

## OUTPUT DATA

Reprioritized Integrative Swim Lanes
Reprioritized Probative Swim Lanes
Next cycle duration
Next cycle content

**Figure 6.9**  Client checkpoint input data, process, and output data

## Any Functionality and Features Planned and Integrated in the Previous Cycle

These are the deliverables from all previous Integrative Swim Lanes. In other words, the current solution. What was delivered will be used to update the solution through the RBS. So, the RBS is a hierarchical map of the current solution. It should be posted in the Team War Room. Through experience, I found that the updated RBS is one of the most visual artifacts produced in an ACPF project. I have also seen it used as an idea generator for planning Probative Swim Lane contents.

## Any Funtionality and Features Planned But Not Integrated in the Previous Cycle

A cycle ends when its time box expires, or if all planned deliverables are complete. What was planned in the Integrative Swim Lanes for the just completed cycle may not have happened for a variety of reasons. This is not the result of change. It is the result of running out of time or experiencing some other event that prevented the orderly completion of the cycle plan. Since the cycle time box is fixed, any schedule delays that cannot be recovered will result in some Integrative Swim Lane deliverables not being integrated into the solution in the just completed cycle. These incomplete deliverables will be returned to the scope bank for reprioritization and consideration in some later cycle.

## *Learning and Discovery*

The client will need some time to evaluate the most recent contributions to the solution. That evaluation has two aspects to it. The first aspect will be the experimentation with the newly expanded solution, paying particular attention to the functions and features added in the just completed Integrative Swim Lanes. Are other changes suggested from what was just produced? The second aspect is the results from the Probative Swim Lanes. Did you learn about any new functions or features? Are there any clues about other parts of the solution yet to be built? Will additional Probative Swim Lanes be needed to further define these discoveries, or can they be planned for inclusion in the solution through future Integrative Swim Lanes?

Learning and discovery will involve an unedited cumulative list, including ideas generated in the just completed cycle and all other ideas not acted upon. Once acted upon, an idea might end up in a future Probative Swim Lane or Integrative Swim Lane. Until then, the idea remains in the scope bank.

## Any Changes That Took Place in the Business Environment During the Previous Cycles

These changes will happen outside the control of the project team. A competitor introduces a new or upgraded product that competes directly with the deliverables you expect to produce in your project. This brings a TPM project to a screeching halt in almost every case, but that is not what happens on an ACPF project. Like a good athlete, the ACPF co-project managers anticipate such changes and can adjust accordingly. Whatever solution existed at the completion of the previous cycle may have sufficient business value to compete now. If not, all is not lost because the ACPF project can adjust deliverables going forward, and come into the market at a later time with expanded functionality and features.

Actual requirements are not static but, in fact, are quite dynamic. They can change several times throughout the life of the project for one or more of the following reasons:

- Changes in market
- Actions of a competitor
- Emergence of new or enhanced technologies
- Organizational priorities change
- Changes in sponsors
- Learning and discovery from a previous cycle

### *Probative Swim Lane Results*

The Integrative Swim Lanes are well-defined, and the development and the cycle build plan established. The Probative Swim Lanes are very different. They can be highly speculative, and can change depth of investigation and directions at any time. A good Probative Swim Lane investigation needs to be as adaptable as the situation dictates. The best return will be from a hands-off management style. Let the creative process unfold without any constraints except the cycle time box. The Probative Swim Lanes are designed to expand the depth and breadth of the solution. The major question is: Has anything been learned about further enhancements to the solution? A Probative Swim Lane has three results: integrate; modify and repeat; or abandon.

1. **Integrate: An enhancement to the solution has been identified.** Another piece to the solution puzzle has been discovered! It may have taken several Probative Swim Lanes spread over several cycles to reach that conclusion. The discovery may be so significant that a cel-

ebration is in order, but don't order the pizza just yet! The solution piece needs to be documented and placed in the Integrative Swim Lane queue for prioritization and consideration in a future Integrative Swim Lane.

2. **Modify and repeat: This direction may produce results and should be continued.** The idea shows promise. Continuing in the same direction or some other discovered direction will be appropriate. It needs to be documented and placed in the priority list for consideration in a future Probative Swim Lane.

3. **Abandon: Nothing new has been identified and this direction should be abandoned for the time being.** No idea is ever removed from the scope bank. What does not seem like a fruitful direction now may turn out to be valuable later in the project.

As work proceeds on a Probative Swim Lane, results may suggest that the basis for the swim lane does not seem like a fruitful direction to pursue. The less that is known about the solution, the more likely will be that result. From experience, my best advice is not to "throw the baby out with the bath water" too soon. I have experienced situations where a past Probative Swim Lane did not produce any immediate insight, but later provided an idea that did. Just remember to put all Probative Swim Lane results (both good and bad) in the scope bank for future reference.

### Search for New Functions and Features

The less you know about the solution, the more challenging the identification of Probative Swim Lanes and the higher the risk that you will not find that solution at all. Because the project team is journeying into the unknown, do not be discouraged by short-term results. Sometimes, it will take several false starts before a promising direction is discovered. Even then, it may take several additional Probative Swim Lanes to fully explore a discovery, and then implement it through one or more Integrative Swim Lanes.

### *Updated Scope Bank*

The scope bank is the depository for all information on past performance and the potential contents of future cycles. From a graphic perspective, the analysis of project performance follows from longitudinal reports. A simple graphical report is a primitive earned value analysis (EVA) like the one shown in Figure 6.10. The trend in the gap between "planned" versus "completed" is the important message contained in this report. But it is the effect and a deeper analysis that is needed to discover and correct the cause(s).

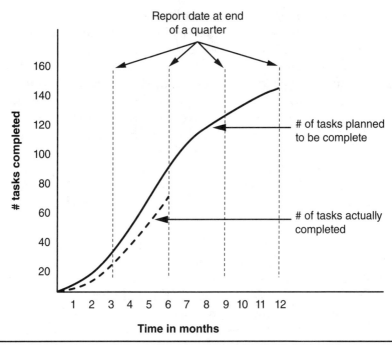

**Figure 6.10**   A primitive EVA of planned versus completed deliverables by cycle

The important questions to be answered here are: Did the cycle meet its objectives? Did the cycle meet its planned functional specifications? If no, where are the variances? The answers will provide input into planning for the objectives of the next cycle and the functionality to be built in the next cycle. Remember, you may have already specified objectives and functionality at a high level for the next cycle in the Version Scope Phase. So, we have the original scope and potential revised scope to review as we consider what the next cycle will contain.

A cumulative history of project performance metrics should be maintained. These metrics should inform the project team about the rate at which convergence to an acceptable solution is occurring. Frequency of changes, severity of change, and similar metrics can help. One metric that I have found useful is to track the size of the scope bank over each cycle. Figure 6.11 shows three trends in scope bank size that I have used in client engagements.

1. **Increasing at an Increasing Rate:** An increasing rate of client involvement is the trend displayed in Figure 6.11(a). It indicates a client whose involvement has increased over time, and it probably indicates that the solution is diverging instead of converging. Changes beget

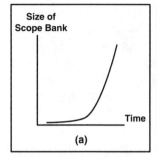 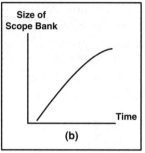 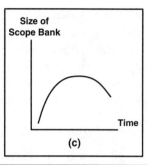

**Figure 6.11**   Tracking scope bank size

changes, and those changes beget even more changes. Sometimes, a change reverses an earlier change! Although it is good to have increased client involvement, it may have come too late for this example. If you see a pattern like this, it may be too late for any corrective action to be taken. Your intervention should have come much earlier so that you would have a chance to work with the client to increase their involvement earlier in the project. The solution would have been to put some trip wires in place as early warning signs that client involvement is below expectations. If this increasing at an increasing rate pattern is what you are experiencing, you may have a runaway project. Whatever the case, you have a problem that needs immediate attention. Further analysis of the underlying causes is needed.

2. **Increasing at a Decreasing Rate:** Figure 6.11(b) shows that the size of the scope bank is increasing at a decreasing rate. That may be a good sign in that the size of the scope bank may eventually turn to an actual decrease. The fact that it is still increasing is not good. Like panel (a), it might be indicative that the solution is diverging. I would wonder if it were not too late.

3. **Decreasing at an Increasing Rate:** Figure 6.11(c) is the desired trend. It shows an exemplary level of client involvement early in the project and good solution convergence. The scope bank size should increase for a while. Sooner or later, as the solution is converging on the final solution, the size of the scope bank should start to decrease and continue decreasing until the project has ended.

### Tracking the Size of Probative Swim Lanes and Integrative Swim Lanes

The overall size of the scope bank is a good indicator of project performance, but it does not tell the whole story. For that, we need to look at the relative sizes of the two swim lanes over time. At the next level of detail, I like to track the relationship between the Probative versus Integrative Swim Lanes over the history of the project. Figure 6.12 is an example of this type of report. It shows all four possible relationships between the two swim lanes: one is increasing and one is decreasing (a) and (d), both are increasing (c), or both are decreasing (b). Each pattern carries at least one interpretation.

## Scope Bank Status Reports

Scope bank status reports are longitudinal reports showing the changes and trends in the different contents of the scope bank. Changes and trends are simple concepts, but there is a lot of information here and a lot of guidance for future cycle planning. As the project progresses, the relationship between the size of the two swim lanes changes. Depending on those relative changes, the project can be in trouble or converging as expected toward an acceptable solution.

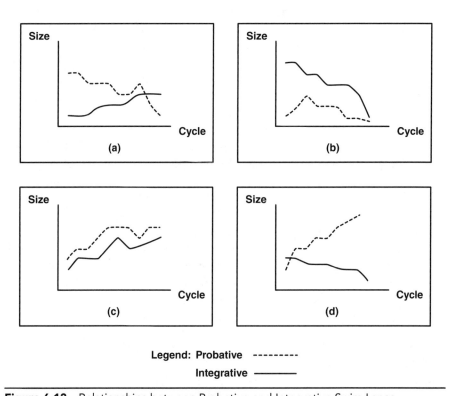

**Figure 6.12**   Relationships between Probative and Integrative Swim Lanes

Figure 6.12(a) generally denotes a successful project. The number of Probative Swim Lanes is decreasing while the number of Integrative Swim Lanes is increasing. In other words, ideas are being translated into actual solution components. This is the ideal situation. The size of the Probative Swim Lane will continue to decrease as the solution is nearing as complete a solution as is possible for this version. It remains to be seen if the success criteria have been met and business value achieved. There are still a number of Integrative Swim Lanes that are prioritized for inclusion in future cycles. At some point in time, these lanes should begin to decrease and decrease continuously until the project ends. The project has all of the earmarks of being a success.

Figure 6.12(b) paints a different picture and can be interpreted as follows. Both swim lane sizes are decreasing. The numbers of Probative Swim Lanes are decreasing and are not producing usable solution parts, as reflected by a decreasing number of Integrative Swim Lanes. Nearly all Integrative Swim Lanes are complete. If the project is early in its history, the situation is not good. This may be the best that can be done. Either the solution will be acceptable for now, or more work needs to be done. This project is essentially complete, and the current solution may or may not be acceptable. If not, then terminate the project and transfer the resources to a more encouraging solution approach. On the positive side, the solution is nearly complete and that is the reason for the decrease in the size of the Probative Swim Lane. The remaining question is the business value delivered by this solution.

Thus, early in the project, the focus should be on Integrative Swim Lanes. As most of these parts are integrated, the focus will shift to Probative Swim Lanes. You should try to keep a good supply of Probative Swim Lanes in each cycle so that there will be a steady supply of function and feature additions being discovered and available for integration into the solution. You are trying to protect yourself from the risk of having an incomplete solution and no new ideas for functions and features to be added. As you get close to convergence on the final complete solution, or expending the time and money allocated to the project, the number of Probative Swim Lanes compared to Integrative Swim Lanes should diminish. Late in the project, you will want to get as much of the solution defined and operational as is possible.

An example should help to illustrate these concepts. This example is an ACPF project where most of the solution is known at the start of the project. For this example, the early cycles will consist mostly of Integrative Swim Lanes. As they are moved out of the scope bank and integrated into the solution, their numbers in the scope bank will decrease. As learning and discovery takes place, the number of potential Probative Swim Lane ideas waiting in the scope bank to be acted upon will increase. That increase is due mostly to learning and discovery about the solution from actually building the solution through the Integrative Swim Lanes. By spreading the Integrative Swim Lanes across the early cycles, you might also discover that the lower priority functions and features that were once thought to be part of the solution may no longer be relevant. You would not know that if you simply used the first cycle to build the entire then known solution. Give considerable thought to that situation. It may save you from wasting the precious time of the developers.

The co-project managers will want to keep a healthy balance between the two types of swim lanes so that there will always be functions and features to be added or discovered. Probative Swim Lanes grow the solution by feeding ideas with business value to the list of functions and features waiting for a priority in the Integrative Swim Lanes.

As the project commences, keep the relative number of ideas for each type of swim lane in balance. What is considered balanced is a subjective decision, something the co-managers get a feeling for as the project progresses. At some point in time, the numbers of each type in the scope bank will decrease. This means that the solution is stabilizing and no new ideas are coming forth. Hopefully, the solution is stabilizing to a solution that has acceptable business value. That will always be the final question in an ACPF project. As the project completion deadline approaches, or as the budget is nearly exhausted, the effort should shift entirely towards planning Integrative Swim Lanes and away from Probative Swim Lanes. Your goal is to get as much of the defined solution implemented. Leave untested ideas for the next version.

This is the same interpretation as in the case of Figure 6.12(a). The only difference is that this pattern reflects a project that is much closer to completion than the one described in Figure 6.12(a). It is unlikely that the few remaining Probative Swim Lanes will introduce new solution features. This project is essentially complete.

Figure 6.12(c) shows both swim lanes increasing in size. This is the pattern you would expect to see for a healthy project. The list of functions and features to be integrated is growing, as is the list of ideas for future function and feature exploration. The Probative Swim Lanes are producing good results. If it is early in the project, the project appears to be healthy and should continue. As the project moves into the later stages both swim lanes should begin to decrease in numbers.

Figure 6.12(c) can also be describing a runaway project. Even though the size of both prioritized lists is increasing, the appropriate question may be related to solution convergence. Is the solution converging to something that will achieve the expected business value? If this pattern continues, that is a strong signal of solution divergence. If not, and the numbers in each swim lane begin to decrease, the project is healthy. A serious check on the COS and project scope is in order, in any case.

Figure 6.12(d) shows an increasing Probative Swim Lane size and a decreasing Integrative Swim Lane size, and has the following interpretation: the solution is about as complete as it is going to be for the approach taken. Missing parts of the solution continue to be elusive. The increasing number of ideas is not producing any meaningful additions to the solution. This project may be spinning out of control and another approach might have been more productive. You also have to admit that the solution has not been discovered. Either the problem is unsolvable or you may be looking for a solution in the wrong places. In either case, the project should be terminated.

There are two strategies that I have used successfully to manage project cycles. The first strategy is to have the first cycle focus on building a prototype followed by several cycles dominated by Probative Swim Lanes. If you have established good client relationships from previous ACPF projects, this can work quite effectively. If you do not have that client relationship, this strategy is not a good choice for the reason that it does not contribute to the early establishment of meaningful client involvement. For the second strategy, the less I know about the solution, the more I would lean towards prototyping for the first few cycles. Before you can effectively define probative initiatives, you and the client need a sense of direction as to where that elusive solution might be found. Early prototyping cycles will do the job and will also contribute to building that much needed client relationship.

In this example, little is known about the solution, and so the early cycles will be focused on discovering functions and features of the solution. Early brainstorming sessions should be conducted in the Version Scoping Phase and first few Cycle Planning Phases. You need to "stoke the fires" and get as many ideas as possible into the Probative Swim Lanes. Prototyping can be effective in the early cycles.

As Probative Swim Lanes successfully identify parts of the solution, they should be followed by Integrative Swim Lanes as soon as possible. It is important to get even a partial solution in front of the client. The most useful information about the missing parts of the solution will come from the learning and discovery by the client team as they work with the then solution.

Remember that the successful identification of solution components through the use of Probative Swim Lanes feeds the Integrative Swim Lane contents, and hence the convergence of the solution to the complete solution. It is the responsibility of the co-project managers to maintain a healthy balance between Probative and Integrative Swim Lanes so that convergence to that final solution is assured. That balance will change as the project progresses through the cycles.

Written reports that circulate among the team members do not exist in ACPF projects. They are a waste of time in an ACPF project. But your management and the sponsor may not share that same opinion and will require periodic status reports. You will have to accommodate their wishes; they pay the bills. All inter-team reporting is verbal and everyone on the team who needs to know, will know. There are reports that circulate outside of the team, but these are the responsibility of the co-project managers. In many cases, they will be exception reports or escalations of open issues and problems that are outside the span of authority of the co-project managers, and are then escalated to the appropriate senior manager or project sponsor. The co-project managers often will use the team meetings to quickly give the team the status of open issues that affect the project.

The monitoring and controlling functions pertain to the cycle build tasks. As part of that control function, the team collects whatever learning and discovery took place and records it in the scope bank. All change requests go into the scope bank as well. No changes are acted upon within a cycle. All changes and other learning and discovery are reviewed at the checkpoint. The review results in placing newly discovered functions and features into a priority list for consideration at the next or some future cycle.

## Internal Environment

The strategic plan drives the content of the ACPF projects, programs, and portfolios. An updated strategic plan drives the prioritization of projects and an adjustment of the contents of any programs or portfolios. For a strategic plan to be effective in the complex project world, it must be continuously updated.

For some organizations, internal change is a way of life. Management changes are probably the most common events that can have dramatic impacts on active projects. The new management team will have its own set of priorities, so your project may be in harm's way. The only protection is short cycles and cycles that deliver business value. That would tend to favor Integrative Swim Lanes, instead of Probative Swim Lanes. As a co-project manager team, you may want to build a strategy for approaching your new manager or sponsor to promote the expected business value that continuing the priority of your project will deliver. Program and portfolio managers face even more priority adjustments. They will need to understand the agendas that the new management team brings to the game and adjust their strategies going forward.

## External Environment

A significant external event may render continuing the current cycle a waste of time and/or money. A major competitor could make an unexpected announcement of the latest version of their product or introduce a new product. In both cases, it gives the client reason to rethink this project. An internal reorganization affects the process interfaces of your business process design project. That might be good reason to postpone your project until the dust has settled from the reorganization. In case of an event in the external environment, these are good questions to ask:

- **Should the project continue as scoped?** Upon further analysis, the client decides that the external event will not compromise the current project to the extent that a postponement or termination decision is warranted. Rather the current project will continue with a view toward using the next version to correct any anomalies caused by the external event. If the team and the client have done their due diligence in the analyses, their decision should be a no-brainer. If the tempo is increasing and there is sound evidence that the project is converging to an acceptable solution within the time and resource constraints, by all means the project should continue.

  On the other hand, if the opposite seems to be true that the project does not exude that confidence, maybe it is time to "pull the plug." Even if the current project is canceled, there may be sufficient evidence that a new project with the same goal, yet approached along very different lines, shows promise of producing the missing solution. The deliverables from the Probative Swim Lanes should provide some clues to an alternate approach. This is more of a research and development (R&D) situation, which may be entirely appropriate for some projects. Be advised that many R&D projects will straddle ACPF and xPM. It is all a question of goal clarity, as discussed in Chapter 3. All Agile PMLC models are structured so that a termination decision can be made at any Client Checkpoint Phase. The metrics that have been tracked since the first cycle, plus the client team and development team's comfort with the project, are inputs to that decision. If the project is not showing steady progress towards converging on an acceptable solution, it may be time to get out and cut any further losses. The changing contents of the scope bank may also provide clues to aid in that decision.

- **Should the project continue with significant revision?** If enough of the product design solution is in place, you might want to salvage that solution by revising the project goal. That will have an impact on the solution objectives of the now significantly revised project.
- **Should the project be postponed?** For process design or improvement projects, the best strategy will usually be to postpone the project and re-start it when an organization's reorganization is complete and stabilized.
- **Should the project be abandoned and restarted in another direction?** If the external event was catastrophic for this project, continuing the project would be a waste of time and money. Once the impact of the external event has been established, the project can be restarted, taking that impact into account. There may be some residual business value in the aborted project. If the success of this project is critical to the organization, the project should not be abandoned. So far, the experiences with the approach taken have not proved fruitful and some other approach is needed. Do not fall into the "Hope Creep" trap by expecting things to get well in some later cycle. In my experience, that is not very likely. The ACPF is a creative process and by its nature will self-correct. The collective efforts of the entire project team are what it takes to find that solution. Termination is a tough business decision, but it has to be made without the emotion and attachment some project team members will surely have. Based on what was known at the beginning of the project, the project team made the best decision it could as to the direction for the project. Now that you and the client have learned a bit more about the solution you might see that a different direction is called for. That is not failure. That is the nature of creative problem solving. Making the decision to terminate is not easy, and must be done in full collaboration with the client and with full disclosure of all the facts.

The next cycle will contain some combination of Probative and Integrative Swim Lanes. The exact allocation of team resources to each swim lane is a subjective decision. The only clues you will get will be documented in the cumulative history of the scope bank.

## Updated RBS

The RBS was first defined before any project work was done and was the primary input into the choice of best fit PMLC model. At each Client

Checkpoint, the RBS is updated with the deliverables from the just completed Integrative Swim Lanes, and any new requirements or requirements clarifications emerging from Probative Swim Lanes. Proposed changes can also impact requirements and requirements definitions. Remember that all of this learning and discovery is housed in the scope bank.

## Process

Process is the analysis phase that follows input data. The results of *Process* analysis establishes the actions to be taken (output data). The eight components of the Process are listed in Figure 6.9, starting with ACPF project reviews.

### *ACPF Project Reviews*

Project reviews have been used quite extensively in some TPM projects and have a place in all ACPF projects. A project review consists of the project manager appearing before a panel of peers to present an in-depth review of the project status. The review can take place at quarterly or semiannual points in time and at milestone events. Obviously, reviews should be scheduled at the completion of some ACPF cycle, but not necessarily every cycle. They might also be scheduled quarterly, or when one quarter of the time or the budget have been expended. If problems and their resolution have been discussed at previous reviews, the follow-up reviews might be scheduled at shorter intervals to check on the impact on status of the recommended corrective actions.

Those ACPF projects that are particularly complex, uncertain, or critical to the business are good candidates for project reviews. The strategy here is that the more eyes that can review the project and offer suggestions for improvement, the better the chance of project success. While these reviews can seem punitive at times, they are really designed to be prescriptive. The problem/opportunity being addressed is critical and complex. The primitive earned value (Figure 6.10) is a good conversation starter for these reviews. All help is welcomed, and sometimes it helps to have other points of view from outside the project offer their perspectives and ideas. An ACPF project review is an excellent window of opportunity!

### *Is the Team Working as Expected?*

Effective teamwork is a CSF in ACPF projects. A lot of worker empowerment is threaded throughout the ACPF. If you count the frequency of the use of the word "I," compared to the use of the word "we," you will have a pretty good metric for measuring team strength.

---

**Definition: Team Strength Metric**

Here is a tongue-in-cheek definition of team strength that you can have some fun with:

Team Strength = Number of We's/(Number of I's + Number of We's)

You would like to see this number hover near 1.

---

The ACPF team needs to work in an open and honest environment for this to happen. That means that every team member must be forthright in stating the actual status of their project work. To do otherwise would be to violate the trust that must exist among team members. The co-project managers must ensure that the working environment on the project is such that every team member is not afraid to raise their hand, say they are having trouble, and ask for help. To do otherwise would be to let their teammates down.

## Is the Client Participating as Expected?

Clients will range from those who maintain some distance from the project to those who will be fully engaged. Expect everything in between. The extremes are not good. We know the risks when the client does not meaningfully engage in an ACPF project, but there are also risks when the client is too engaged. Not being meaningfully engaged means that questioning and introspection won't take place and an acceptable solution won't be produced. Being too engaged has its risks, too. Here the client is always in your face, suggesting changes and using valuable development team resources on work that does not add business value. The client that is too engaged will have you chasing windmills rather than adding business value to the solution. That is why the scope bank entry "expected business value" is so critical to the decision-making process.

## Do the Cumulative Deliverables Meet Expectations?

There are two characteristics that speak to the viability of the progress the project has made to date: tempo and convergence.

The first characteristic of progress viability is *tempo*. Because the development team and the client team have partnered throughout all of the completed cycles, they should have already sensed if the project is gaining momentum as it discovers and learns about the solution and integrates the results. Morale should be running high. The entire project team should be excited about the progress to date. There should be visible signs of commitment on the part of all team members. The client team should be eager to be involved in the ongoing affairs of the project. That eagerness extends to solving problems and making decisions with the team. Those are good signs and will instill confidence that the project is a success waiting to happen. On the other hand, if the project seems to be wandering aimlessly, morale is down, and the client team is not really involved but rather is just being courteous, that is not a good sign. The project's future is in question. The metrics discussed above will provide the input to how solution discovery is proceeding.

The second characteristic of progress viability is *convergence*. Because of their close working relationship, the team and the client should know if the project is converging on an acceptable solution. That will be evidenced by a growing sense of clarity in the remaining functionality. The end is coming into focus. These are good signs that the project is healthy and should be continued. On the other hand, the deliverables from each cycle may not give any indication that the project is approaching the end. If the frequency of change requests is diminishing, that is one possible indicator of convergence. A closer inspection of the messages inherent in Figures 6.11 and 6.12 is advised.

### Is the Version Scope Still Valid?

Armed with the information discussed in the previous two sections, we now can ask a basic question: "Is the version scope still valid?" If yes, we are on the right track. If not, we need to revise accordingly. Revisions to version scope can be significant. In some cases, revisions may be so significant that the correct business decision is to kill the current project, go back to the drawing board, and start over. You can see that the cost of killing an ACPF project will always be less than the cost of killing a TPM project. The reason is that TPM spends money and time on functionality that may not remain in the solution. The ACPF, on the other hand, almost guarantees that all functionality that is built will remain in the application. Further to the point, TPM projects are often killed, if at all, very late in the game when all the money is spent. ACPF projects are killed at any point where it becomes obvious that the solution is not converging and will not be acceptable. That will generally happen while there is still money and time left in the budget. Cut your losses and allocate the time, money, and team to a more fruitful direction.

Ending a project is not a sign of project failure, and that is important. Terminating an ACPF project because of lack of convergence is nothing more than the realization that the current line of pursuit is not going to find that elusive solution. Resources need to be redirected in another direction.

Projects in Quadrants 3 and 4 are such that the goal may be changing as the result of learning and discovery from previous cycles. Changes in the goal result in changes in version scope.

## Prioritize Remaining Functionality

There are several sources of input to the reprioritization exercise. We have all of the new functionality requests that have been collecting in the scope bank during all previous cycles. There is the functionality that was planned for the last cycle, but not completed. And finally, there is the functionality that was identified earlier but not yet prioritized for any cycle. The same prioritization exercise that was done in the Version Scope Phase will be repeated here. The difference is that the development team and the client team are much smarter today than they were back on Day 1 of the project. That prioritization is much more informed because a solution is emerging from the efforts of the previous cycles.

## Brainstorm Next Cycle Swim Lane Contents

Brainstorming is a tool you will use frequently in an ACPF project. It is the best mechanism I know of for generating the creative input needed to successfully plan and execute an ACPF project. You will use it throughout every phase of the ACPF project. It is simple and quick, and that is why it is the preferred tool of choice.

A brainstorming session is simple to conduct and does not require any special training of either the facilitator or the attendees. All you need is an environment where no one is hesitant to contribute and no one is critical of the ideas expressed by others. Brainstorming sessions should be lively with lots of involvement, and therefore, are excellent team building experiences.

Brainstorming will be invaluable to the project team as part of the discussion on what to investigate through Probative Swim Lanes. The more complex and incomplete the solution, the more the team will depend on brainstorming. The ACPF Brainstorming Model discussed in Chapter 4 is well-suited here.

## PMLC Model Adjustments

The use of "adaptive" in naming ACPF was deliberate. Due to the complexity and uncertainty associated with complex projects, the best fit approach chosen on Day 1 of the project is not necessarily the best fit approach later in the project.

If the RBS has changed significantly since the last client checkpoint, the questions of the correct quadrant and PMLC model choice must be asked again. The answers may suggest a change of best fit model. The decision to change the best fit model is a significant decision. For example, sooner or later the project will be far enough along in the search for the complete solution that there will be the great "project epiphany" as the co-project managers realize they now understand what the complete solution will look like. The project is currently using an Agile approach, but could change to an Incremental approach because the solution is now known. So, the question is, "Should the management approach be changed to an Incremental approach?" Some of the questions the client and project manager will need to answer in preparation for making that decision are:

- What will the final scope of the project be?
- What incremental business value will be delivered?
- Can and should team membership be changed?
- What are the additional costs to the project if the approach is changed?
- When can the change to an Incremental approach be implemented?
- When will the project be complete?

You can see that the entire ACPF Scope Triangle is likely to change.

## Output Data

From the above input data and Process analyses, you can generate the following decisions to bring the Client Checkpoint Phase to a close: reprioritized list of Integrative Swim Lane contents; reprioritized list of Probative Swim Lane contents; next cycle duration; and next cycle contents.

### *Reprioritized List of Integrative Swim Lane Contents*

Any functions or features planned for integration in the previous cycle, but not integrated, will have to be added back into the scope bank list and reprioritized with all other functions and features not yet integrated. This is not unusual. Just remember that the functions and features not integrated in the previous cycle should have been the lowest priority in that cycle. From what has been learned in the previous cycle about the priority of functions and features to be added, those functions and features not integrated in the previous cycle may have a priority lower than the new candidates for integration. The failure to complete the previous cycle may not be a failure after all.

This decision will be an updated and prioritized list of the functions and features that have been identified as part of the solution, but not yet integrated into the solution. The more of the solution you can present to the client team the better. So, some priority should be given to an Integrative Swim Lane over a Probative Swim Lane.

### Reprioritized List of Probative Swim Lane Contents

The discovery and learning from the previous cycle will suggest further Probative Swim Lane ideas. These will be integrated with the current list of Probative Swim Lane ideas and the new list reprioritized. The criteria used to prioritize will have to account for the likelihood that a discovery or learning will actually result in an addition to the current solution.

This will be an updated and prioritized list of all of the ideas that have been identified, but not yet investigated. If the solution is mostly unknown and the Integrative Swim Lane list is sparse, some priority should be given to a Probative Swim Lane over an Integrative Swim Lane. The tie breaker will always be the capability of the project team to accommodate the mix.

### Next Cycle Duration

The decision as to cycle length for the next cycle is based on two prioritized lists: the functionality to be integrated into the current solution and the ideas to be investigated in the next cycle. Team resources are also considered because they place constraints on what can actually be accomplished within the cycle time frame. The actual contents of the two prioritized lists have to be evaluated subjectively to decide on cycle length. Remember to be true to the overall time box decision made during the Version Scope Phase if possible.

### Next Cycle Contents

The next cycle length is known and a new prioritized list of functionality is available. How far down the two swim lane lists can the team expect to get with this next cycle? There may be some give and take between next cycle deliverables and the cycle time box, but this should be minimal and easily resolved.

I had cautioned you that in the early cycles of a project, do not be too aggressive. As the team gets to the perform stage and the client team is more comfortable working with the development team, the list of deliverables for the next cycle can get a bit more aggressive. The ACPF has the luxury of returning undone functionality to the scope bank and reprioritizing it for consideration in a later cycle. There is still the temptation on the part of technical professionals to have a "steak appetite on a baloney budget." Do not set the client up for results that cannot be achieved. That would put a serious dent in a relationship that was hard earned.

## STEP 12: CLOSE THE VERSION

The Version Close step is exactly the same as the closing phase you are already familiar with from TPM experiences. It includes:

- How well did your deliverables meet the stated success criteria?
- How well did the development team perform?
- How well did the client team perform?
- How well did the ACPF and the project management approach work for this project?
- What lessons were learned that can be applied to future projects?
- What requirements can be further improved in the next version?

### Client Acceptance

In a sense, client acceptance of the deliverables is the StageGate that leads to the beginning of Step 12: Close the Version.

### Release Strategies

Release strategy alternatives are in common use:

- **The project is a TPM project and no releases have occurred:** One of the weaknesses of a TPM project is that business value is still an expectation, but all of the time is exhausted and resources spent before any deliverables are released. For some TPM projects, there is no option.
- **Releases have occurred according to an established organizational release plan:** APM projects will learn from releases that occur according to an enterprise release plan. That may not be in the best interest of the APM project, but it is in the best interest of the enterprise as it attempts to absorb change in the most effective and efficient way.
- **Releases have occurred as decided by the co-managers:** These are, of course, in the best interest of the project as it works to discover and integrate learning and discovery. The feedback gained from the intermediate release of deliverables is valuable. The issue is how effectively

the enterprise can absorb change and the ability of the project team to support those intermediate releases.

## Installing Deliverables

The second step of closing a version is to go live with the deliverables. This commonly occurs in computer systems work. The installation can involve phases, cutovers, or some other rollout strategy. In other cases, it involves nothing more than flipping a switch. Either way, some event or activity turns things over to the client. This installation triggers the beginning of a number of close-out activities that mostly relate to documentation and report preparation. After installation is complete, the deliverables move to support and maintenance status, and the project is officially closed.

There are four popular methods to install deliverables: the phased, cutover, parallel, and by-business-unit approaches.

### Phased Approach

The phased approach decomposes the deliverable into meaningful chunks and implements the chunks in the appropriate sequence. This approach would be appropriate in cases where resource limitations prevent any other approach from being used.

### Cut-over Approach

The cut-over approach replaces the old deliverable with the new deliverable in one action. To use this approach, the testing of the new system must have been successfully completed in a test environment that is exactly the same as the production environment.

### Parallel Approach

In the parallel approach, the new deliverables are installed while the old deliverables are still operational. Both the old and the new deliverables are simultaneously in production mode. In cases where the new system might not have been completely tested in an environment exactly like the production environment, this approach will make sense. It allows the new system to be compared with the old system on real live data.

### By-Business-Unit Approach

In the by-business-unit approach, the new deliverables are installed in one business unit at a time, usually in the chronological order that the system is used. Like the phased approach, this approach is appropriate when resource constraints prohibit a full implementation at one time. Similar to the by-business-unit approach would be a geographic approach where the system is installed at one geographical location at a time. This facilitates geographic differences, too.

## Conducting the Post-Version Audit

During the Version Scope Phase, you developed measurable business outcomes in discussion with the client. These became the rationale for why the project was undertaken in the first place. Think of these outcomes as *success criteria*. That is, the undertaking will have been considered a success if, and only if, these outcomes are achieved. In many cases, these outcomes cannot be measured for some time after the project has been completed.

Take the case of a project impacting market share. It won't happen next Tuesday. It may happen several quarters later. However, the time frame is part of the success criteria statement as well.

When the budget and time allotted to a version have been spent, that marks the end of the project. Some functionality that was planned to be completed may not have been completed. It will be archived in the scope bank for consideration in the next version. The main focus of the Post-Version Review is to check how you did with respect to the success criteria, to document what you learned that will be useful in the next version, and to begin thinking about the functionality for the next version.

What the client team and the development team believe to be the best mix of functionality has been built into the solution. The project is done. The deliverables are installed, and the solution is in production status.

The post-implementation audit is an evaluation of the project's goals and activity achievement as measured against the project plan, budget, time deadlines, quality of deliverables, specifications, and client satisfaction. The log of the project activities serves as baseline data for this audit. The following questions should be answered:

*1. Was the project goal achieved?*
- Does it do what the project team said it would do?
- Does it do what the client said it would do?

The project was justified based on a goal to be achieved. If either that goal was or was not achieved, the reasons for this must be provided in the audit. This achievement can be addressed from two different perspectives.

The provider may have suggested a solution for which certain results were promised. Did that happen? Conversely, the requestor may have promised that if the provider would only provide, say, a new or improved system, then certain results would occur. Did that happen?

### 2. Was the project work done on time, within budget, and according to specification?

Recall from the scope triangle, discussed in Chapter 2, that the constraints on a project are time, cost, and the client's specification, as well as resource availability and quality. Here, you are concerned with whether the specification was met within the budgeted time and cost constraints.

### 3. Was the client satisfied with the project results?

It is possible that the answers to the first two questions are yes, but the answer to this question is no. How can that happen? Simple: the COS changed, but no one was aware that they had. The project manager did not check with the client to see whether the needs had changed, or the client did not inform the project manager that such changes had occurred.

### 4. Was business value realized?

Check the success criteria to see if business value was realized. The success criteria were the basis on which the business case for the project was built and were the primary reason why the project was approved. Did you realize that promised value? When the success criteria measure improvement in profit, market share, or other bottom-line parameters, you may not be able to answer this question until sometime after the project is closed.

### 5. What lessons were learned about your project management methodology?

Companies that have or are developing a project management methodology will want to use completed projects to assess how well the methodology is working. Different parts of the methodology may work well for certain types of projects or in certain situations, and these should be noted in the audit. These lessons will be valuable in tweaking the methodology or simply noting how to apply the methodology when a given situation arises. This part of the audit might also consider how well the team used the methodology, which is related to, yet different from, how well the methodology worked.

### 6. What worked? What did not work?

The answers to these questions are helpful hints and suggestions for future project managers and teams. The experiences of past project teams are real "diamonds in the rough"—you will want to pass them on to future teams.

### 7. What was learned about the ACPF process?

The refinement of the ACPF is an ACPF project! I do not see this project as ever ending. If you think of the ACPF as a thought process rather than a fixed procedure, you will understand why the ACPF will continually change. In every project, you should be looking for ways to improve the ACPF. Discover and learn about the solution to an improved ACPF.

The post-implementation audit is seldom done, which is unfortunate because it has great value for all stakeholders. Some of the reasons for skipping the audit include:

- **Managers don't want to know**—They reason that the project is done and what difference does it make whether things happened the way you said they would? It is time to move on.
- **Managers don't want to pay the cost**—The pressures on the budget (both time and money) are such that managers would rather spend resources on the next project than on those already completed.
- **It is not a high priority**—Other projects are waiting to have work done on them, and completed projects do not rate very high on a priority list.
- **There is too much other billable work to do**—Post-implementation audits are not billable work, and people have billable work on other projects to do.

---

**Advice for Conducting a Post-Implementation Audit**

I can't stress enough how important the post-implementation audit can be. It contains valuable information that can be extracted and used in the next version of this project and other complex projects.

Organizations have such a difficult time deploying and improving their project management process and practice that it would be a shame to pass up the greatest source of information to help that effort. I will not mislead you, though: actually doing the post-implementation audit takes a commitment because it competes with other tasks waiting for your attention, not the least of which is probably a project that is already behind schedule.

Implementing the ACPF requires a continuous process and practice improvement program. Completed projects are your most valuable source of ideas for that improvement program.

---

The business outcome was the factor used to validate the reason for doing the project in the first place. If it was achieved, chalk that one up on the success side of the ledger. If it wasn't, determine why not. Can something further be done to achieve the outcome? If so, that will be input to the functional specifications for the next version.

There is also a lesson here for everyone. If projects are limited in scope and they fail, and there is no way to rescue them, you have reduced the dollars lost to failed projects. The alternative of undertaking larger projects is that you risk losing more money. If there is a way of finding out early that a project is not going to deliver as promised, cut your losses. The same logic works from cycle to cycle. If you can learn early that a version will not work, kill the version and save the time and cost of the later cycles.

In a traditional project, the client would find out a project was not working only after all the money was spent, and then a great deal of trouble might be involved in killing the project. The traditional thought went, "After all, there is so much money tied up in this project, we can't just kill it. Let's try to save it." How costly and unnecessary.

## Writing the Final Version Report

The contents of a final report are unique to each organization. Ideally, the co-managers would write a report on the final version, but assistance by the Enterprise Complex Project Support Office (CPSO) or the appropriate Division CPSO can be used.

## Celebrating Success

Public recognition of those who were responsible for the success of the project is good for the soul and a great morale booster, too. The most effective reward I have ever seen was a project sponsor arranging a videotaping of each team member at work and giving each member a copy. Tee shirts, coffee mugs, and even flags displayed on the team members' work stations works, too. Be creative! You don't have to spend a lot of money, either—"It's the thought that counts."

# OBSERVATIONS ON THE NEXT VERSION

Project deliverables, whether products or services, have a finite productive life. The challenge to management is to know when that life will expire and when to begin the project for Version 2. The Version 2 project should begin sufficiently in advance of the estimated expiration date for Version 1 so that its deliverables are ready for prime time.

The contents of the scope bank from Version 1 should be preserved and will make good input for the Version 2 project.

## PUTTING IT ALL TOGETHER

The Project Execution Phase adapts many of the processes familiar to the traditional project manager:

- Defining Version Scope is exactly the same as Defining Project Scope except there is an implication that this version does not define the final solution. That is not implied in the Project Scope.
- Planning the Next Cycle consists of the same process used by the traditional project manager and the ACPF project manager.
- Build the Next Cycle is the same for both project managers with one exception. All change requests are considered during the Client Checkpoint for the ACPF project. That is not the case with a traditional project.
- Conduct Client Checkpoint exists in both the traditional and ACPF projects. In the ACPF project the Client Checkpoint is a very detailed process whereas in the traditional project it may just be a formality.
- Close the Version is the same for traditional and ACPF projects.

The conclusion from this discussion is that the ACPF is an umbrella framework for managing any project. In particular, important aspects to remember are:

- All past, current, and future projects align with the ACPF and can be managed within the framework processes defined by the ACPF template, shown in Figure 3.1.
- All specific models (Waterfall, Feature-Driven Development, Scrum, the Rational Unified Process, the Dynamic Systems Development Method, and so on) are consistent with the ACPF template.
- Version Scope, Cycle Plan, Cycle Build, Checkpoint, and Version Close is sufficiently powerful to embrace all project management methodologies and most systems development methodologies.
- The ACPF is robust, and as the project work commences, the ACPF adjusts to maintain its alignment with the management needs of the project. Even so, in all cases, the ACPF template is fixed and there is no need to change it.

- At all times, the project manager and the client are in charge of the management approach. They are empowered to adapt it to changing project situations but should always exercise organized common sense.

# 7

## ESTABLISHING AND SUSTAINING MEANINGFUL CLIENT INVOLVEMENT

> *Clearly, no group can as an entity create ideas. Only in-dividuals can do this. A group of individuals may, how-ever, stimulate one another in the creation of ideas.*
> —Estill J. Green, Vice President, Bell Telephone Laboratories

> *We generally need someone to show us things which should be apparent to the eyes of all.*
> —Francisco Algarotti, Italian writer and scientist

> *It can be no dishonor to learn from others when they speak good sense.*
> —Sophocles, Greek playwright

## CHAPTER LEARNING OBJECTIVES

This chapter will provide readers with the knowledge or ability to:

- Establish and maintain meaningful client involvement.
- Understand how to manage meaningful client involvement.
- Comprehend how client ownership relates to complex project success.
- Know who the stakeholders are in an Adaptive Complex Project Framework (ACPF) project.
- Understand the stakeholders' roles in an ACPF project.

- Realize the importance of the co-project manager in complex projects.

If I could choose and deliver on only one critical success factor for managing a complex project, it would be meaningful client involvement. In the complex project world, the client is the best subject matter expert (SME) when solving unsolved problems and exploiting untapped business opportunities. Beyond the SME role, the client will be the owners of the project deliverables. Their meaningful involvement will produce a vested interest on their part in the success of the project. In a sense, their reputation and credibility are at stake. That success will be measured first by the business value the complex project team will have delivered, and second, by the successful execution of the process that created the solution. The ACPF is designed to deliver on both counts.

Client involvement is so important to achieving success that I devoted this entire chapter to it. In the context of the ACPF, we will involve anyone who either affects or is affected by the deliverables. These are otherwise known as *stakeholders*, and I include in our discussion a definition of who they are and how they interact with the ACPF project first at the requirements elicitation steps, and then throughout the entire project life span. Not all stakeholders should or will be involved directly as a team member. If they are, they must be meaningfully involved. Token sign-offs on any document produced by the project is not meaningful involvement. It will be seen more as a threat to the client and sponsor than to their meaningful involvement.

## THE IMPORTANCE OF MEANINGFUL CLIENT INVOLVEMENT

The complex project landscape is populated with unsolved problems and business opportunities that have not yet been exploited. None of these will be easy projects. Some may have been worked on before with less than satisfactory outcomes or no outcomes at all. If they are critical to the business, they must be successfully executed and produce the results for which they were undertaken. So, the best approach for an enterprise is to utilize a project management approach that brings the appropriate parties together into a true team environment and turns them loose to find the sought after deliverables.

The team must be comprised of professionals who have business process expertise (systems engineers and business analysts) and professionals who have subject matter expertise (managers and professional staff in their departments) in the relevant business areas involved in the project. It is not sufficient to just put them together in the same room and hope to get an acceptable business solution. There must be guidelines, tools, templates, and processes from which they will craft a *recipe* to manage such challenging projects. That is a role for the complex project co-managers supported by the ACPF.

> "It takes a village" to successfully deliver business value from a complex project.

Lack of client involvement has been identified by The Standish Group (2013) as the second most critical factor for project failure. In fact, without meaningful client involvement from the start of an ACPF project, it will fail with near certainty. I would add that it is not only important to have clients involved, but that involvement must be meaningful. Simply getting sign-off on an ACPF implementation, or on some arcane specification or confusing test plan, is not meaningful involvement. For the past 20+ years of consulting, I have utilized a simple homegrown practice that fosters an ownership position and encourages the client to do whatever they can to make the project successful! Remember that having an ownership position puts their reputation on the line to deliver business value just as the project manager's reputation is on the line to create and manage an effective process. Meaningful client involvement is purposely designed into the entire ACPF project life span.

Meaningful client involvement begins before the ACPF has been implemented. It begins at the point where the enterprise defines the desired end-state ACPF environment; extends through the implementation planning and execution, and continues through to the practice stage where the ACPF is used, and process improvement efforts are undertaken. In other words, meaningful client involvement is an effort that extends across the entire ACPF project from conception to birth to maturation. To get the continuing full benefit from the ACPF, the enterprise must commit to this effort. For most organizations, using the ACPF will be a complete evolution from how they approached the management of their projects, programs, and portfolios. It is one of the enabling factors for the strategic plan of the enterprise.

Chapters 3 through 6 defined the ACPF and established it as an enterprise-level resource for complex project management. The success of that implementation and its eventual practice is heavily bound in meaningful client involvement. To that end, I share my homegrown practice for creating and sustaining meaningful client involvement in an ACPF project and present a real-life example of that practice. I have used this practice as one of the founding principles of my business, which began in 1991. All I can say is that the ACPF works all the time, so I don't plan on fixing it. It will certainly be improved through feedback from clients and adopters. My hope is that you will be able to integrate meaningful client involvement into your practice and find your efforts consistently delivering better solutions with greater business value.

## A PRACTICAL MODEL FOR MEANINGFUL CLIENT INVOLVEMENT

Once upon a time, early in my career as a project manager, I invited my client to work with me on a particularly complex software development project that my team was getting ready to start for them. The solution we were looking for had been elusive for a number of years, and had reached the stage where it was affecting the business. The need was critical and something had to be done. Despite our best efforts, the risk was high that we would fall short of meeting the sponsor's objectives and their expected business value. We may not be able to create the best solution, but at a minimum, it had to be an acceptable solution from a business value standpoint. Later solutions could improve the original solution. We were facing a particularly high-risk assignment due to the complexity of the business processes involved. If I was going to be successful, I knew I would need the participation of the client far beyond the common practice of the time. And so, I extended an invitation to the client to get meaningfully involved with the development team. I did not know what reaction I would get.

The client's first reaction was that they didn't know anything about software development and did not understand how they could help. They balked at my invitation and it took some reassurance from me that I would need their expertise if we were to be successful. Fortunately, I had built a trusting relationship with them from previous project successes, and at last I convinced them to participate. It was clear that I was in a *show me* situation.

This all happened during the time when software developers spoke to other software developers in acronyms that few outside their immediate circle understood. The business process we were trying to automate had never been automated before. The only SMEs on those processes were the business managers and their professional staff. They had to be involved, or the project was destined for failure. That was obvious to me. But how could the technology support the business needs? It had always been done poorly, but now there was a way to exploit the newest technologies and assist the business process. This would be a new business system and my team was not sure how to design the decision support system process that it required. This was the first time I had ever heard a technical team ask for help from the client.

Project managers have learned (and The Standish Group has validated through countless surveys) that lack of client involvement is a major reason for project failure. I would add *meaningful* to the client involvement. I have known that for a long time, having discovered it myself as part of my learning experiences and education as a project manager. And that is even more significant now that we are firmly planted in the complex project environment, where achievable goals and attainable solutions are problematic. In this chapter, I share what I have learned about attaining and sustaining client ownership, and why I insist on meaningful client involvement in every ACPF project that I manage.

In the contemporary project world, clients are a heterogeneous group. It was not too long ago that they were seen by the development team as technically challenged and not able to contribute anything meaningful to the project. Their role was restricted to signing off on documents that they could not possibly understand.

Those days are gone, but the "sins of our fathers" remain. History produced end user computing and the tools that allowed the courageous client to build their own solutions (spreadsheets came first and were soon followed by so-called "fourth generation" tools like Ramis, FOCUS, Informix, FoxPro, SQL, RPG-II, and several others). Some clients could now confidently approach the developers with their own functional specifications and even production-ready solutions. If the client could not get the response that they expected, they could do it themselves. End user computing was born, and the courageous client could lift themselves by their bootstraps. The developers now had to deal with a different type of client—one who would not be ignored. They had become SMEs through their own devices and needed to be included in the efforts of the development team.

## What If the Client Team Does Not Understand the ACPF?

During the design and first applications of the ACPF, this is the reality you will have to deal with. Suppose that this is the first complex project this client will be involved in. You will be introducing them to a strange new project world. How will you prepare them to be productive members of the project team?

Here are some strategies to consider. Training, training, and more training of clients is called for. There are three training models that I have used, and all have been successful: commercial off-the-shelf facilitator-led; custom-designed instructor-led; and, real-time consultant-led. It all depends on what the client team needs and how best to interact with them.

### Commercial Off-the-Shelf Facilitator-led Training

Commercial off-the-shelf (COTS) facilitator-led training is mentioned mostly for the sake of completeness, but it has worked on occasion. Rather than bring the training inside, it can be taken by your team in open enrollment courses. If the client wants a little more personalization, bring the training inside. If the client tends to be proactive and likes to work things out for themselves, this might give them enough of a push to overcome their hesitancy. An outside facilitator is the critical success factor. It tends to be safer ground for the client than if an internal facilitator is used. The outside facilitator can offer a fresh perspective that an insider does not have. If the facilitator can field questions with specific answers applicable to the attendee's environment, it should work.

### Custom-designed, Instructor-led Training

Custom-designed, instructor-led training will cost more than the COTS training because of the time needed to understand the environment, conduct a needs analysis, and modify the course accordingly. It does have the added benefit that the content is to the point and not wasteful of the attendee's time and money. The majority of my training engagements have been of this type. They tend to have a consulting component, as well, and deliver maximum business value for the costs involved. In the end, the training experience will be more efficient and effective.

### Real-time, Consultant-led Training

Real-time, consultant-led training is an interesting variation on the custom-designed, instructor-led training. In this variation, the training is imbedded in the execution of the project. It might be an actual project or a project to design an ACPF environment with the client participating. The project itself becomes a case study, if you will, in how to conduct an ACPF project. An internal consultant can be most effective because they already understand the environment. If an outside consultant is used, this is obviously the most expensive of the three models. Remember, an ACPF project is complex and its success is critical to the organization. Failure is not an option. I have used this model three times as an outside consultant and twice as an internal consultant, and been successful in all five. This variation is the most expensive of the three, but it is worth the added cost. With few exceptions, it has become the approach of choice by my clients. I have even developed a workshop for any business process design project.

This approach is especially applicable to ACPF design, implementation, and process improvement projects. It occurs in two steps:

1. Customization of the ACPF template, based on the results of the needs analysis.
2. Further customization of the ACPF template during the workshop itself.

I call this approach the Blended Training/Consulting Workshop. I have used this workshop for several business process applications:

- ACPF design, documentation, implementation, and deployment
- Prevention/intervention process for managing distressed projects
- Continuous process/practice improvement model
- Resource constrained agile project portfolio management process
- Establishing and maturing a Project Support Office
- Project manager position family design
- Career and professional development process design

Put this approach in your ACPF/kit. See Chapter 8 for details.

## What If You Can't Get the Client to Be Meaningfully Involved?

Not being able to get the client to be meaningfully involved is a tough situation that you are going to have to face. Not having meaningful client involvement in a complex project is a showstopper.

In earlier days, I might have said I would find some way to work around and do the project without the meaningful involvement of the client. Now, with years of experience to draw on, I just would not do the project until the client was willing to be meaningfully involved. I have tried both strategies and had a few successes, but left a lot of blood on the trail behind me. I often won the battle, but lost the war. In general, neither strategy met with my satisfaction. Now, I tend to follow a more diplomatic route. The success of the project is critical to the continued operation of the business and is beyond your authority to cancel or postpone. On the assumption that the project will go ahead, what would you, could you, or should you do?

Of prime importance is to find out what barriers to meaningful involvement exist in the mind of the client and put a mitigation program in place.

There could be many barriers, as the following discussion illustrates. For each barrier, I will share my mitigation strategies if the client was burned by prior project experiences and is hesitant to get involved, and if the client wants to get too involved.

## What If the Client Is Hesitant to Get Involved?

If the client is hesitant to get involved, this is a problem; the technical professionals have inherited some significant baggage from their grandfathers. In former days, the customer was not really encouraged to get involved: just get the requirements document written and approved, and turn the project over to the development and delivery teams. The prevailing attitude was that the client would only slow the process down. Fortunately, that attitude has not survived, but the memory of it has. The client is much more comfortable minding their own business and leaving technology to the technical folks. The client gets involved, but only when the development and delivery team offers them a comfortable way to get involved.

The burden is on the project team to change this attitude. Depending on the particular circumstances that the client is facing, different initiatives on the part of the project team can be employed. Workshops, seminars, site visits, conferences, and other venues have been productive. One strategy that I have had excellent results with is to engage the client in concurrent workshops and seminars that are imbedded in the complex project and to use actual project team exercises based on the project. This is an effective twist on the "learn by doing" principle that underlies all successful complex projects.

## What If the Client Wants to Get Too Involved?

Yes, I have encountered this situation, but not very often.

Taking a cue from the days of end user computing of the 1970s and 1980s, there will be clients who aggressively promote their solution. They want to get *too* involved. They will push hard to get their own solution on the table and are reluctant to consider other ideas. You do not want to discourage them from sharing their ideas, yet, at the same time, you don't want to risk missing a better solution. They can be an effective team player and the best SME you might have, but their eagerness must be channeled.

I have borrowed process ideas from prototyping and brainstorming, as appropriate. For example, you might start solution design with their solution, and discuss ways it might be improved with other features and functions. Oftentimes, the client will not be aware of other systems and processes that can be used to advantage. Both prototyping and brainstorming can be used here to include these systems and processes in the client's solution with good results. Assuming the client has good suggestions, you can exploit this with discussions about more sophisticated solutions that engage them in generating even greater business value than their solution affords. Capitalize on the knowledge that the client has displayed through their input.

## Stakeholder Management

To put a finer edge on meaningful client involvement, I need to expand the discussion to a broader audience—the stakeholder group. Broadly speaking, a stakeholder is anyone in the organization that can affect or be affected by the project deliverables. A caution, however, is that not all stakeholders will even know that they are stakeholders. It is incumbent on the project manager to not only identify who they are, but also to establish a communications plan with them.

The stakeholders are the most important group whenever you are entertaining change to the project management culture from whatever it is to some desired end state. The stakeholders' support and involvement is essential. To not have their support can be devastating to the project. For the purposes of ACPF design and implementation, the clients are all of the stakeholders that either impact or are impacted by the resulting ACPF environment that is delivered. So the first step is to establish the ACPF environment for the enterprise. For that, you will need to use the Stakeholder Interaction model shown in Figure 7.1. A similar model was introduced in Chapter 4 (Figure 4.7) as an illustration of the Complex Project Ideation Phase.

### *Who Are the ACPF Stakeholders?*

The ACPF stakeholders range from the most senior-level executives (C-Level) to those who enable the ACPF through projects (the project management position family), and, of course, their clients. In essence, you might consider *everyone* in the enterprise as the stakeholder group. For the ACPF design and implementation project, the stakeholders are identified in Figure 7.1. They are:

- **C-level Sponsors**—The senior executives who will pay the bill for the ACPF design and implementation project.
- **Line of Business (LOB) Managers**—The beneficiaries of the deliverables from an ACPF project. In practice, the LOB managers may

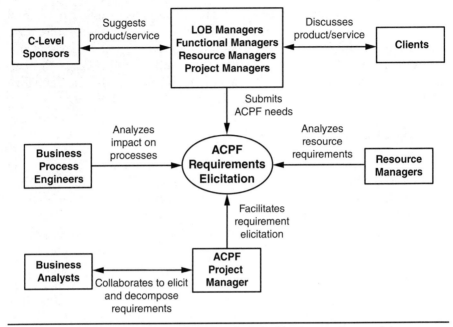

**Figure 7.1**   ACPF requirements elicitation Stakeholder Interaction model

originate the idea for an ACPF project, based on their own department needs. They have profit and loss responsibility for their line of business.

- **Functional Managers**—The department heads for such functions as marketing, finance, public relations, and other business functions. Their needs are usually for business process design and improvement. They do not have P&L responsibility. Rather, their responsibility is the first line tactical and operational support of the LOB managers.
- **Resource Managers**—These department heads manage the resource capacity of the enterprise. They support projects and business processes from a resource perspective. One of their major responsibilities is human resources, which is discussed in Chapter 8.
- **Project Managers**—The professionals who are the enablers in the enterprise strategic plan. They use the ACPF in their interactions with all stakeholders.
- **Clients**—The customers of the project managers. They represent the areas of the enterprise that are affected by, or that affect, the business areas involved in the project. They might use the deliverables directly, or provide the deliverables to the final customer.

- **Business Process Engineers**—Systems engineers and systems analysts who consult with LOB and functional business managers on items related to the business processes of the enterprise. Their responsibilities include business process design, business process performance monitoring and business process improvement from a technical perspective.
- **Business Analysts**—Professionals who understand the business of the enterprise. They act as consultants to LOB and functional business managers in matters related to the performance of the LOBs and their improvement from a business perspective.
- **ACPF Project Manager**—A senior project manager who is charged with the project to design and implement the ACPF version that will define the project management environment of the enterprise. Following implementation, they will also monitor ACPF performance with the goal of further process improvement projects.

## *The ACPF Stakeholders Interaction Model*

A Stakeholder Interaction model can be built for a variety of applications. For example, Figure 7.2 depicts how the Stakeholder Interaction model

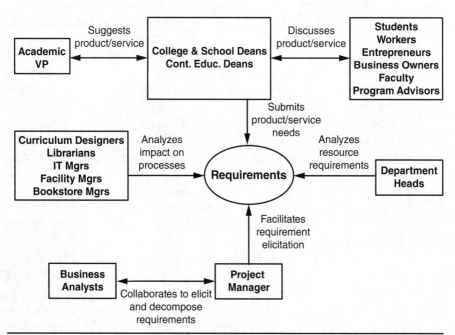

**Figure 7.2**   WBDC case study Stakeholder Interaction model

might look when an organization is considering a project where the ACPF is to be developed or customized for their environment. This model focuses on the requirements elicitation steps. Throughout the project, notice how stakeholders are involved for input, deliberations, and decision making. I have used similar processes in a variety of business process design and improvement projects. Figure 7.2 is the Stakeholder Interaction model from the Workforce and Business Development (WBDC) Case Study found in Appendix B.

The most important thing to note about the Stakeholder Interaction model is the collaborative and meaningful involvement of all stakeholders across the entire life span of this design and implementation project. From practice in similar situations, this model creates strong ownership on the part of all stakeholders. Ownership not only contributes to fewer implementation problems, but also to a better ACPF environment for complex project management.

## A REAL LIFE EXAMPLE

Here is another example of meaningful client involvement, taken from a real project that I managed. It occurred during the Ideation Phase of a $5M, three-year project to build a web-based, thin client decision support system. It was known that the solution would involve rather complex multidimensional algorithms in which business rules could not be defined clearly at the outset of the project. So, the client asked to have prototype algorithms built. The algorithms would be tuned during the course of the project, so prototypes would be useful.

Responsibility for the prototypes was given to the Chief Developer, whom we'll call "George." George was a brilliant technologist with a keen business sense. His problem was that he was impatient, not a team player, and usually added functions and features to the solution without discussing his ideas with anyone else—and that included me, the project manager. George reasoned that the client would obviously agree with what he had done. True, but his independent action and strong character prevented any other competing ideas from surfacing.

Initially, the client was somewhat reserved and not comfortable working collaboratively within a team of techies. The techies were uncomfortable having to dumb down their word choice. Everyone was jockeying for position in this strange setting. George's charm, brilliance, and sales abilities dominated the design process. We were searching for a solution that had not yet been defined and so an open and honest team environment with maximal client involvement was necessary if we were to explore every idea and encourage new ones. That could only happen if the client was offering new ideas during the prototyping process. George was unaware that he was short-circuiting that process. I wanted the collective wisdom of the team and the client to discover the best solution. George's approach wasted time and caused more rework than would have been needed if had he followed the agreed process.

It was clear that "managing George" was the key to getting meaningful client involvement. I was able to manage George with one simple practice. When problems or questions surfaced for team or client consideration, I had George agree to not be the first person to respond, and to encourage the client a chance to offer their thoughts first. The client seemed to defer to George, rather than contribute an idea that George might shoot down. George's delayed response eventually began working, but I just had to keep reminding him of our agreement.

It wasn't long before the client took over the prototyping sessions and George was making changes right in the prototyping session. The client became actively involved, and George took on the role of support to the client rather than leadership of the client. I could sense a more relaxed and open meeting as the client team members felt comfortable contributing without the feeling that George was waiting to pounce on what they said. The dynamics in the prototyping sessions were electric!

To the client's delight, the project finished successfully nine months ahead of schedule and $1.8M under budget. Readership of the "Job Opportunity Bulletin (JOB)" increased by 18,000 subscribers in the first six months, and with that came increased advertising revenues. The client was delighted!

## CHALLENGES TO ATTAINING AND SUSTAINING MEANINGFUL CLIENT INVOLVEMENT

Clients come in all sizes and descriptions. Some clients are a veritable fountain that continually spew ideas and changes. This may seem like an enviable situation, but don't overlook the need for convergence to a solution. Their behavior can cause the team to spend too much time on non-value-added work as they do their analysis of the scope implications and contribution to business value. A strategy to postpone some suggestions to Version 2 might work.

Other clients don't seem to have any ideas to share. Maybe they don't have any ideas, or maybe the project manager has not created the open and honest team environment that is needed. This is a dangerous situation, and will call upon all of the skills of the project manager and the development team. Change is critical in every complex project.

Let's consider some specific suggestions that I have used to attain and maintain meaningful client involvement: always use the language of the client; maintain a continuous brainstorming culture; use a co-project manager model; and, establish an open and honest team environment.

## Always Use the Language of the Client

Never use an acronym unless it is in common use in the enterprise. Clients will be wary of asking what you mean for fear of exposing their ignorance. If you find them nodding in agreement along with blank stares into space, you have lost them. The project manager, and especially the development team, have to be very observant. One trick that I have used comes from the conditions of satisfaction discussions, which is to ask the client to repeat in their own words what you just said. That will expose any misunderstandings. While this may seem to put them in a threatening position, that risk is better than the risk of not understanding. Both the client team and the development team have to work in an open, honest, and mutually supporting environment. Anything less exposes the project to risks that could have been avoided.

## Maintain a Continuous Brainstorming Culture

A continuous brainstorming culture puts the client team in a more relaxed mood and will encourage their input and willingness to accept feedback from the development team. These discussions are critical parts of the creative learning and discovery process.

## Use a Co-project Manager Model

Perhaps the most important advice that I can offer you is to adopt a practice in which the ACPF project is co-managed by you and a client representative with decision-making authority. That includes the ACPF design and implementation project and all the projects that utilize the resulting version of the ACPF. For it to succeed, the co-manager should be the highest level executive you can recruit from the client-side of the enterprise. That person must be capable and willing to get meaningfully involved. Token representation is not going to work. Unfortunately the higher you go in the enterprise, the greater the risk that you will end up with token representation and that would be the death of an ACPF project. Treat each case as unique, and proceed accordingly. You need someone who can provide ideas and visible support.

The co-project manager model is a founding principle of my consulting practice. I have used it in every project that my company has ever undertaken. One manager is me or one of my consulting partners, and the other is a high-level manager from the client-side. LOB managers, functional managers, and resource managers are often good choices. Both co-managers are equally involved and authorized to make all decisions, and share in the success and failure that flow from their decisions. Just think: if you put your reputation on the line in a project, wouldn't you participate in the project to protect your reputation and your business interests? You bet you would.

So, if the project is technical and the client is not, they will want to know why you want them as your co-manager. That's easy. Before the project was a technical project, it was a business project; it needs a business person as a major partner and decision maker. The project team should not be forced to make business decisions. As the technical project manager, you want every decision to be the best business decision possible, and your client is in the best position to make that happen. My client would hear me say that I wanted to do the very best job that I could, and it would not happen without their meaningful involvement as my co-manager on their project. In retrospect, my client co-manager participated in all decisions. They provided the product and business expertise while I provided the process and technical expertise, and we did this as co-equals!

You need to keep the client in the best possible position to make business decisions in a timely way. Given the need for a business decision, the project team can often present alternatives, maybe rank them, and even offer costs and benefits. Give the client whatever information you can to help them decide. Then, step back and let them decide, based on whatever business criteria they wish to use.

In the complex project world, holistic decisions that balance task feasibility and business value are important and critical. In these projects, either the goal or solution, or both, cannot be clearly defined at the beginning of the project. The search for an acceptable business outcome is what drives the project forward. Again, the client is in the best position to choose the alternative directions that lead to the deliverables that produce acceptable business value. The feasible technical alternatives are presented to the client and they choose the best alternative. These iterations are repeated until there is convergence on a goal and solution that achieves the expected business value, or the client terminates the project because it is not leading in a direction that will be fruitful. The remaining time, money, and resources can be redirected to a more likely goal and solution. This strategy speaks of a team/client partnership. Without it, success is unlikely.

## Establish an Open and Honest Team Environment

The team comprises two groups—the client team and the development team. They must work together openly and honestly if the project is to succeed. Leave your politics at the door. The team is your world during an ACPF project. The co-project managers have a critical role to play in establishing this environment.

# PUTTING IT ALL TOGETHER

The lessons that I learned from previous projects are clear. No one can claim to corner the knowledge market (i.e., more than one SME is needed), and the client and every team member must be given a chance to contribute openly in a brainstorming fashion to the solution. Creativity is a critical component, which must be openly encouraged and practiced. The technical team and the client team can form a formidable team, if given the chance, and exploit the synergy that results. George's behavior was an obstacle to that formation; correcting the behavior opened the door that allowed a successful outcome. Ownership of the resulting solution can only come from giving all of the stakeholders an equal opportunity to meaningfully participate in the development of the solution. I also learned that through ownership of the solution comes ownership of the implementation. Since it was their solution, they wouldn't let it fail. The client took the lead! How often can you claim that?

The practice that I have shared with you is simple, but implementing it takes project manager leadership and courage. For some clients, that required selling the idea because they were the ones who responded to my request saying they were not technical and couldn't contribute to a technical project. My selling proposition was that even though they may not be technical, I am not an expert in their line of business or business function. So, by combining our separate expertise, we can produce an effective solution and create the expected business value that justifies approving the project in the first place. They bring the business knowledge and experience to the table, and my team brings the technical knowledge and experience to the table. Together, we create the synergy needed to find creative solutions in the midst of a complex project world.

# 8

## IMPLEMENTING YOUR ADAPTIVE COMPLEX PROJECT FRAMEWORK

*Think before you act.*
—Aesop, Greek fabulist, 620-560 BC

*It is impossible for all things to be precisely set down in writing, for rules must be universal, but actions are concerned with particulars.*
—Aristotle, Greek philosopher and teacher, 384-322 BC

*Prediction is very difficult, especially about the future.*
—Niels Bohr, Nobel laureate in physics, 1885-1962

## CHAPTER LEARNING OBJECTIVES

This chapter will provide readers the knowledge or ability to:

- Understand the critical success factors (CSFs) and how an Adaptive Complex Project Framework (ACPF) environment can support them.
- Prepare the enterprise for the ACPF.
- Design an Evolutionary Transition Plan across the project landscape.
- Adapt the Blended Training/Consulting model for ACPF design and implementation.
- Understand the ACPF environment from the enterprise level.
- Understand the ACPF environment from the stakeholder perspective.

- Deal with the implementation obstacles.
- Understand the ACPF from the project team perspective.
- Deliver business value in a complex environment.
- Know the importance of aligning staff resources to complex project needs.
- Establish a Project Support Office (PSO) aligned with the ACPF.
- Design a complex project portfolio management process.
- Establish a complex project management position family and professional development program.

Implementing the ACPF can range from a nonevent to a major cultural upheaval, often burdened by several obstacles and resistances. It all depends on the current state of project management processes and practices in your organization and your vision of the end state of project management. Before you jump into the fray with a textbook version of a plan, you need to understand the stakeholders, the internal environment, the culture, and the tolerance for change.

For these transitions, how you handle the implementation will definitively impact the level of resistance to change that you are likely to experience. For example, one of my clients simply announced a new process and posted it on the PSO portal with a help function. Another client held several briefing sessions and brown-bag lunches, where they presented proposals and asked for discussion and input from their user community. The final version was completed and delivered in a series of workshops, and an extensive support structure accompanied that implementation. Any guesses as to which approach worked best?

You need to plan how you will develop an implementation plan. Among the tools that I have used and recommend that you should consider using to define this plan are force field analysis and strength, weakness, opportunities, and threats (SWOT) analysis. In this chapter, I will help you explore the realities of implementing the ACPF and offer a practical implementation plan for your use. In previous chapters, you have built a portfolio of tools, templates, and processes for the successful management of complex projects and the delivery of business value. In this chapter, we will build a plan for translating them into your new reality.

## OVERVIEW OF AN ACPF IMPLEMENTATION

This chapter presents a deliberate process for migrating from whatever project management framework your organization uses to a more robust framework for complex project management. The transition process is unique to every organization, but always includes the following components:

1. Current state of project management processes and practices
2. Desired end state for project management processes and practices
3. Transition plan from the current state to the desired end state

The first two components are data collection and data definition steps. They define the "as is" and "to be" states. The third step is the "how" step and presents a practical implementation plan. All three components are fully explained in this chapter.

Every organization will have to complete these three components specific to their organization and make this transition sooner or later. Some organizations have already done so, but many are mired in the confusion and need outside help. For those with a long history of practicing traditional project management (TPM), evolving to an Agile Project Management (APM) or Extreme Project Management (xPM) environment will probably seem chaotic and uncontrolled. The complex project mindset is very different than the traditional mindset, and some project management practices will have to be relearned. Other practices will have to be learned for the first time. Those who are new to project management have an opportunity to form robust practices right from the start of their careers. Whatever situation you find yourself in, the transition will be a daunting one, and its impact on the organization will be significant.

> Every ACPF implementation is a unique journey.

The desired end-state project management environment must be resilient. It must include a vetted portfolio of tools, templates, and processes to support every type of project the organization can expect to encounter. That includes the TPM processes currently in use. Your TPM processes and practices will probably remain intact. So, the transition adds or refines project management methodologies rather than replacing them. The transition also includes new processes that integrate all of the project management methodologies that result from the transition.

The robustness of the final project management environment comes from the fact that the specific project management approach you use for a given project is derived from the project characteristics rather than any preordained "management recipe." Project management is reduced to "organized common sense" rather than to prespecified recipes. In other words, just as projects are unique, so is the best fit management process for each of those projects. While all of this may sound like a lofty goal, such an environment can exist and must exist. I have had the opportunity to work with several clients to help them create their robust environments. On balance, the ACPF works and it has proven that it works.

Given that projects are rapidly evolving to a state characterized by increasing complexity and uncertainty, project management processes and practices must also evolve to remain effective in that evolved state. If this is obvious to your organization and it has decided to make the transition, I congratulate you for that decision. You have made a courageous step in the right direction. However, understand that even if done correctly, the transition will be anything but easy. It will require a new mindset about project planning and management, the nature of projects, and how to achieve the expected business value that justified doing the project in the first place. This chapter explores the best strategies that I can offer for making that transition. The strategies are cautious, based on deliberate planning and execution. Above all else, the strategies minimize the risk and disruptive nature of the pending organizational changes as much as possible. The velocity and extent of change is driven by the organization's culture, rather than by any timed schedule of events. That is important to every transition to the ACPF. In the end, the transition must be evolutionary and a good fit culturally.

## CHARACTERISTICS OF AN ACPF IMPLEMENTATION

An ACPF implementation project will have the following characteristics:

- It should be facilitated through an outside consultant in collaboration with your PSO.
- It must include the meaningful participation of a broadly defined stakeholder group.
- The transition to an ACPF environment should be an evolutionary transition.
- The organization must provide the infrastructure to support the ACPF.
- There should be a warranty period, wherein intermediate releases of the initial ACPF environment are tested under actual conditions for the purpose of improvement.

The ACPF project is best explained through the six questions shown in the left panel of Figure 8.1, which are mapped into the diagram of the evolu-

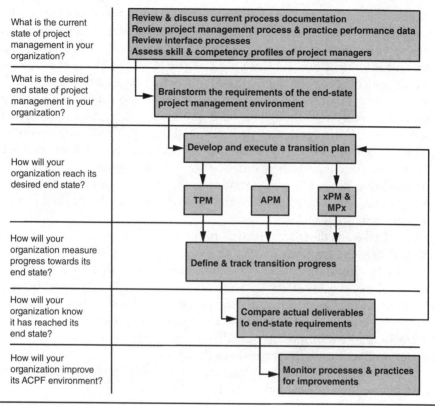

**Figure 8.1**    Evolutionary transition process

tionary transition process shown in the right panel of Figure 8.1. Whether your organization is mature in its approach to project management or is a project management neophyte, the transition process accommodates both maturity extremes. Figure 8.1 makes no assumption about the organization's project management maturity and, in fact, assumes your organization is a neophyte. More mature organizations can more easily make the necessary adjustments.

It is important to understand that the transition process is not one that necessarily replaces an organization's existing Project Management Life Cycle (PMLC) models. Rather, it may add PMLC models to the project management portfolio so that over the course of time, the portfolio becomes a much richer source for project managers. Once complete, the portfolio will have a collection of vetted tools, templates, and processes that can be adapted to any type of project. I have labeled that portfolio the *ACPF/kit* for easier reference.

Since you are heading into unknown territory and you don't know what to expect, my recommendation is that you take deliberate and well-planned steps as you converge on the final version of your desired end state. Your first reaction might be: "Why are we going so slowly? Let's speed this up." You are not going to get a chance to do this twice, so you'd better do it right the first time. Figure 8.1 shows the recommended planning template for that evolutionary transition. The basic premise in this template is that if every organization experiences projects in all four quadrants, then every organization will need more than one PMLC model to manage those projects. The evolutionary transition includes options for the organization to do that. The transition process is one that adds to the project management process portfolio through the evolution to the desired end state. It does not replace processes that are working.

Since I take a pedestrian approach to the transition process, the organization that uses the template process shown in Figure 8.1 will have an opportunity to develop those models at its own pace and add them to its portfolio. The transition process starts by assessing wherever your organization is in its project management processes and practices, and proceeds from there. If your organization is relatively immature, you should probably engage a consultant to help determine the specific planning steps that begin with your current state and evolve to your desired end state.

Let's now explore those six questions more closely. Each question is good to ask before implementing the ACPF.

## WHAT IS THE CURRENT STATE OF PROJECT MANAGEMENT IN YOUR ORGANIZATION?

Asking this question invites an honest and open assessment of how the processes of project management have been defined and how those processes have been practiced. I have used both SWOT analysis and force field analysis as parts of those assessments. For a more in-depth assessment, I developed a Project Management Maturity Assessment.

The current state of project management in the organization is usually assessed by a needs analysis that initiates the entire transition. An outside consultant would be my choice for conducting the needs analysis. Objectivity is critical. In my experience, with proper preparation, the needs analysis can usually be accomplished in one day, with a debriefing to senior management on the morning of the second day. The needs analysis should be a face-to-face meeting with a representative team of not more than 30 participants. The team should include representatives from the project and program manager family of positions, portfolio managers, human resource professionals, training professionals, and any other managers who either will affect or will be affected by the project management processes. The needs analysis has three parts: current state, end state, and the debriefing session. An agenda that I have used for describing the current state is:

- **Review and discuss current process documentation.** Typically, this review is done in two steps. The first step can be conducted by an outside consultant as part of their preparation for facilitating the needs analysis. The second step is the discussion. It is an agenda item for the needs analysis session. The strengths and weaknesses of the documentation can be related to the pain points in the above list.
- **Review project management process and practice performance data.** The documented and distributed performance data can further pinpoint systemic problems. Post-implementation audits can give invaluable insight into systemic problems, but unfortunately these are not commonly done. This review has to include the deliverables from an honest and open conversation among all parties that have earned the right to comment on the performance data. It is very difficult to pull off this conversation because the participants have to put their politics aside. I have tried several approaches to do this, but the only one that works well is a brainstorming session.
- **Review interface processes.** Whatever new project management processes will be put in place, they will need to interface smoothly with current input processes or provide the appropriate output to other processes.
- **Assess skill and competency profiles of project managers.** Formal assessments using one measurement from a variety of commercially available products should be used. The current data will provide the baseline measures. The assessments should be done about once a year to measure the changing skill and competency profiles of the project manager cadre. Once an ACPF environment has been implemented, the organization should give serious consideration to building its own skill and competency assessment instrument. This will have to be coupled to a complete position family definition and professional development process.

## WHAT IS THE DESIRED END STATE OF PROJECT MANAGEMENT IN YOUR ORGANIZATION?

The end-state definition of project management in your organization should be viewed as an ideal state. It is similar to the goal statement in an extreme project. It may not be attainable, but it is still a goal to be pursued. Here is an opportunity for the organization to dream of the desired end state of project management processes and practices without any constraints. The conversation might revolve around removing reasons for failure, the general health of the current state, obstacle and barrier removal, and addressing particular pain points. Specifying the end state sets the organization's stake in the ground and provides direction to the future evolution of its project management environment.

The agenda for the end-state definition is simple: brainstorm the set of requirements that the end state must meet. The ACPF Brainstorming Model (shown in Figure 4.2) should be used. Among other requirements, the set of requirements must contain:

- A robust approach that defines a best fit project management methodology for any type of project.
- An approach that must be adaptable to changing conditions that will occur during project execution.
- Meaningful client involvement throughout the entire project life cycle.

In developing the set of requirements, pay attention to the major obstacles to attaining the end state. The mitigation strategy might identify additional requirements. Some of the obstacles that you might encounter are:

- Project managers' resistance to switching from what they have been comfortable doing to an adaptive complex project management environment.
- Project managers must choose and continuously adapt their project management approach to the changing characteristics of the project, the client, the organization, and the market conditions (i.e., they must become chefs, not cooks).
- The need to learn new tools, templates, and processes and know how to choose and adapt them to the new complex project management environment (some project managers would rather have a recipe given to them than have to create their own recipe).
- Sponsor and clients accommodating a variable scope environment.

Knowing that project managers will have to work outside of their comfort zone, the best mitigation strategies will have to include providing a range of support services that extend across the entire project landscape and all PMLCs. Those support services should include project planning, requirements elicitation and gathering, risk management, problem solving, coaching, change management, and a comprehensive training curriculum that uses a variety of delivery formats. For the transition process to succeed, your PSO must be able to provide these services. If your organization does not have a PSO, start one and grow its support services in parallel with the transition process.

## A Successful ACPF Project Environment

However your organization envisions the end state, it must be such that it is the best end state for supporting its interpretation of what constitutes project success. The definition of an ACPF project, also given in Chapter 2, gives a good base for discussing project success:

> An *ACPF project* is a sequence of finite dependent
> activities in which successful completion results
> in the delivery of the net estimated business
> value that was developed to validate the project.

Note that "success" in an ACPF project does not follow from having met any constraints imposed by cost, time, or scope parameters. Exceeding those constraints is accounted for in the net business value. Certainly, a good project management process would meet those constraints and many organizations would consider those as necessary conditions for project success, but they are not sufficient. From the definition of an ACPF project, it is clear that there is an assumed causal dependency between having met the parameters and the eventual delivery of expected business value. Business value can be measured in several ways (see IRACIS in Chapter 4). We usually think business value is measured by money, but that is a profit-based metric. In a nonprofit organization, level of service may be a more appropriate metric. Ultimately, project success must include having met business objectives of the project. The delivery of expected business value is a surrogate for those business objectives. So, for some organizations, success is more a function of meeting process constraints than it is from meeting product constraints. In an ACPF project, product success is necessary; process success is a nice bonus.

In addition to supporting the CSFs, I recommend that the desired end-state ACPF environment consist of a balance among staff, process, and technology as described in the next section.

## Balance Among Staff, Process, and Technology

For years now, management gurus have preached that an effective organization is one where there is a balance among staff, process, and technology (SPT). The staff is smart, and of that there is no doubt. How many times have you heard an executive say, "Just put five of our smartest people together in a room and they will solve any problem you can throw at them." That may be true, but I don't think anyone would bet the future of their enterprise on the continuing heroic efforts of an anointed few. Technology is racing ahead faster than any organization can absorb, so that can't be the obstacle.

Process is the only thing left to improve, and it is to the business process that we turn our attention in this book. But it isn't just your normal, everyday business process. We have to look at a process that is really a process to define a *process*, rather than a staid and fixed approach—or "recipe," as I like to call it. Following the recipe analogy a bit further, I want to teach you how to create the recipe, rather than just blindly follow a predefined recipe.

As far as I know, no one has been able to build an assessment tool to measure the extent to which a balance among staff, process, and technology is present. The objective of this effort is to develop an assessment instrument that measures the project management balance in an organization with respect to the priority (and attention) it gives first to staff, then to process, and finally to technology. The assessment instrument should establish the current state and desired state, and suggest strategies for achieving the desired state. The proposed, underlying model is shown in Figure 8.2.

One project management model, using the SPT application, is depicted by a triangle with the three major dimensions of staff, process, and technology at each vertex. Each dimension has the maximum score of 200 at the vertex, and a minimum score of zero at the end of the line drawn perpendicular to its base. The score (0-200) for each of the three dimensions is derived from the questionnaire instrument, and represents perceptions of the current state of project management in a workplace setting. The total score adds to 200 in order to constrain all three data coordinates to the interior of the triangle.

The primary benefits to the organization of a balanced structure to its project management culture are:

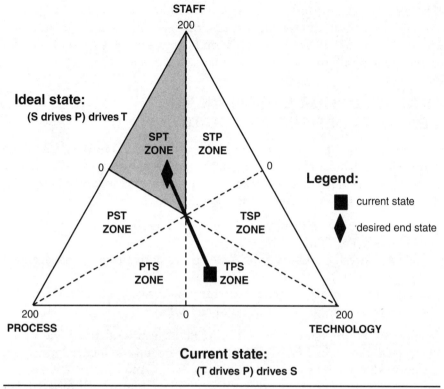

**Figure 8.2**   A model for transitioning from the current state to the desired end state

- Increasing delivered business value through improved project management practices by accommodating the three dimensions of staff, business processes, and information technology in the most appropriate and prudent manner.
- Creating a shared organizational vision and operational methodology for defining an effective project management culture with rewards consistent with the methodology.
- Empowering staff to develop and align themselves with project management processes designed to meet personal and organizational goals and objectives.
- Supporting the project management model with the appropriate information technology, at a reasonable cost, and for specific development and implementation strategies.

The SPT assessment instrument is quite robust and integrates well with continuous process improvement programs and project management maturity initiatives. See WAV™ for details on how to acquire a copy of the SPT Assessment Tool for your personal and organizational use.

## HOW WILL YOUR ORGANIZATION REACH ITS DESIRED END STATE?

Each organization travels its own path from the current to the desired end state. The path's starting point might be an immature state or a mature state. There are three distinct steps in the path that are followed in sequential order, depending on the organization's situation:

1. Achieve the end state for Linear and Incremental project management (i.e., TPM).
2. Achieve the end state for Agile and Adaptive project management (i.e., APM).
3. Achieve the end state for Extreme project management and Emertxe project management (i.e., xPM and MPx).

In most ACPF implementations, the ACPF/kit can be defined and nearly completed during the first step. These need to be fully defined, adopted, and supported by the PSO as they relate to the PMLC models that will be used in TPM projects. For some organizations, this will be straightforward. For other organizations, it will be a major challenge.

Some of the challenges in developing and executing the transition plan have been:

- **Plan projects to deliver requirements in several iterations.** During the transition process, I suggest that you minimize interim releases. To include interim releases complicates the design, implementation, and adoption of your incremental PMLC model. Many of the challenges listed below are minimized or eliminated altogether by suspending releases until the end of the project, just as you would in the Linear PMLC model situation. Once you have stabilized the Incremental PMLC model, interim releases can be added back into the projects as part of a new Incremental PMLC model.
- **Every release must deliver acceptable business value.** The chunking process must define chunks of sufficient size and completeness to deliver acceptable business value. That will protect the organization from premature or unexpected project cancelation, while still providing at least a partial solution that delivers some business value.

- **Requirements delivered in each iteration must be consistent with technical dependencies.** The sequence in which requirements are developed must be compliant with any technical dependencies between and among requirements.
- **Maintaining an intact project team between releases is difficult.** This situation arises because there will usually be a delay between the delivery of one chunk of requirements and the beginning of the next iteration. During that delay, a team member may be borrowed by another project with the promise of their return for the beginning of the next iteration. That's a risky promise.
- **Plan for added documentation between iterations.** Because of the potential loss of a team member, the project manager will want to input some protection if a new team member joins the project for the next iteration. That protection will come in the form of hand-off documentation to bring the new team member up to speed.
- **Each release will encourage unplanned scope change.** Whenever an iteration releases requirements to clients, they will usually find something about how the requirements were integrated into the solution that they would like to change or add.
- **Client confusion using deliverables can change from one release to another.** If the deliverables are a software solution, this confusion is common. If the client has to change how they use the solution from one release to the next, there will be problems.
- **Implementing and supporting interim products and services.** To address the potential problems from using a new release of the solution, the PSO will have to have support services in place. That could include documentation of the new release, training, and consulting support for the new release. The value of minimizing the number of releases is obvious.

Let's face it—implementing the ACPF in most organizations will be a big culture shock. Some organizations will have invested time and money to bring their project management culture to a position where they have Capability Maturity Model–Integrated (CMMI) Level 3 Maturity. Unfortunately, senior management has not seen the payoff in reduced project failures. Cost and schedule overruns are rampant. Clients and their sponsors are not satisfied with the business value that they achieve. Something is wrong, but no one seems to have the motivation or any ideas about how to improve the situation.

Other organizations are not as fortunate as the one depicted above. They are somewhere between CMMI Level 1 and 2 Maturity, and drifting aimlessly in a sea of failed projects and disgruntled clients. They are unprepared to find and implement a solution relevant to their station in life.

Regardless of the level of maturity in the organization, it will need help to plan and execute the transition to an ACPF environment. Rushing into a solution is not recommended. Preparing for and managing the pending change initiative is a big deal. In such pre-ACPF situations, I have often deferred to conducting workshops in parallel or jointly with the evolution from whatever project management environment is in place to an ACPF customized environment. To that end, I offer my Blended Training/Consulting Workshop template as a solution that has been very successful. For our purposes here, I have taken that template and applied it to implementing the ACPF.

The journey from your organization's current state to the desired end state with respect to a project management environment requires an infrastructure to be put in place in order to develop and support the transition effort. That is a three step process:

1. **Establish a PSO.** The PSO is the guide for the rest of your journey. It provides the basic structure and home base for the journey. In the absence of an existing PSO, an outside consultant will be needed. The consultant will guide the implementation of the PSO and facilitate ACPF implementation through the PSO.

2. **Develop and execute an evolutionary transition plan.** Figure 8.1 depicted the entire transition plan in terms of the six questions that would be answered by that transition plan.

3. **Mature the PSO to an ACPF PSO.** Step 3 consists of four parts:
   - Agile Project Portfolio Management (APPM) Process
   - Complex Project Manager (CPM) Position Family
   - Career and Professional Development Program
   - ACPF Project Review Process

   These are discussed in detail later in the chapter (see page 273) in the section "How Will Your Organization Improve Its ACPF Environment?" Recall that this is the 6th and final question in the transition plan defined in Figure 8.1.

These three steps define my recommended infrastructure to support the establishment of your organization's ACPF environment. The steps are discussed below.

## Establish a Project Support Office

I prefer the name "PSO" rather than PMO. PMO sends a message that it is a monitoring and compliance office. PSO sends a message that it is a support office. The PSO is a support unit. The PMO is a management unit.

The first step in an ACPF implementation is the establishment of a PSO. The ACPF requires an effective management structure in order to be successful (Wysocki, 2011). Having a PSO in place enables the stakeholder group to engage in the design, development, and deployment of their ACPF environment. Figure 8.3 is a model that I have used consistently with my clients to put a PSO into their infrastructure. The best way to define your PSO and plan for its realization is through the Blended Training/Consulting model.

## Form the PSO Task Force

I have seen too many organizations put a task force together whose members are a representative sample of project, program, and portfolio managers, and that's it! If you don't give the senior managers, sponsors, clients, and others who will interact with projects an opportunity to provide input, you are setting yourself up for failure. Managing successful projects is difficult enough. Why put the effort at risk needlessly?

## Assess the Current State

Assessing the current state involves four areas:

- Management's opinion of the role of project management
- Relationship between the business units and project management
- Analysis of the current project management process
- Analysis of the current project management practices

## Define the Desired End State

Just as projects are unique and changing so are their needs for tools, templates, and processes. So the questions the task force should consider as it defines the desired end state are:

- What are the future projects?
- What are the needs of the future projects?
- Is the vetted portfolio of tools, templates, and processes aligned to the needs of future projects? If not, implement the necessary corrective measures.
- What is the future staff resource profile?
- What is the expected gap between the current and future staff resource profile?
- How should that gap be managed?

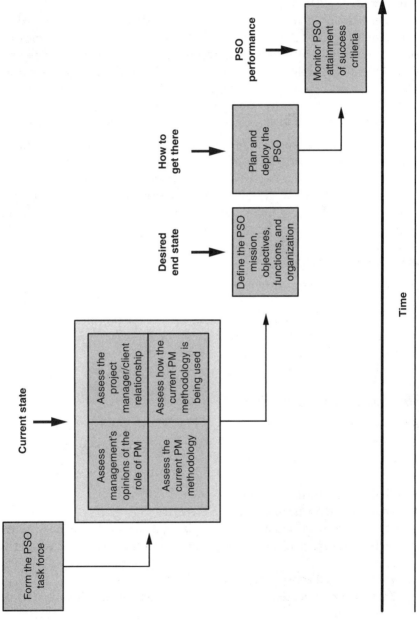

**Figure 8.3**    A plan to establish an initial PSO

## How to Get There: The Next Level

Figure 8.3 is a high-level look at the major steps involved in the creation of a PSO. The next level down might have these steps:

- Form the PSO task force.
- Establish the vision/mission/objectives statements of the PSO.
- Select and prioritize the services to be offered by the PSO:
  + Project support
  + Consulting and mentoring
  + Methods and standards
  + Software tools
  + Training
    o Training development
    o Training delivery
  + Project manager development
  + Project manager assignment
- PSO organizational structure
  + Enterprise
  + Division
- PSO staffing
  + Permanent
  + Rotating

The PSO is critical to help with the early implementation problems that an organization faces, especially if it had previously practiced traditional project management. The PSO is a prerequisite to the definition, implementation, and management support of the ACPF. If you want to do it right, this will be a multi-project, multi-year effort. In sequential order of priority, here are the high-level descriptions of each of the steps in the above list and shown in Figure 8.3. (For a more detailed discussion see Wysocki, 2007.)

## Form the PSO Task Force: PSO Performance

Don't fall into the trap of measuring PSO success in terms of product success, which is measured in terms of business value added. Business value is the responsibility of the product owners. Rather, process success is the responsibility of the co-project managers to execute, and the responsibility of the PSO to define and support. Rather than define quantitative metrics as you would for product success, I want to offer the attainment of the CSF's specified and tracked by The Standish Group for several years as a way to measure PSO success. The most recent CSFs in priority order, from most significant to least significant, as previously mentioned in Chapter 1, are:

- **Executive Support:** It is incumbent upon the PSO to provide the orientation and training that executives will need to not only understand what the ACPF is all about, but to understand the infrastructure that they will need to support for effective project management. In the end, it is the executives that set the priorities and approve the resources for every project. If an ACPF environment is to succeed, project sponsorship must be attained and sustained throughout the project life span.

- **(Meaningful) User Involvement:** I have added "meaningful" to user involvement. Having users sign-off on arcane specification documents is involvement, but it is useless. Clients, customers, and users will be the best subject matter experts (SMEs) available as we look for solutions that deliver acceptable business value. The ACPF co-project manager structure is the unique key to that involvement. I am not aware of any other methodology that is designed around a co-project manager structure. It not only creates a sense of ownership, but also allows the client to participate in project management decisions.

- **Clear Business Objectives:** These are embodied in the set of high-level requirements whose incorporation into the solution delivers the expected business value. These high-level requirements form a necessary and sufficient set of requirements for project success. The further description of these requirements follow from the learning and discovery opportunities built into each cycle. That translates into an evolving clarification of business objectives. These are translated into a hierarchical decomposition of functions, processes, activities, and features.

- **Emotional Maturity:** The ACPF team comprises a client team and a development team coordinated under the guidance of co-project managers—one from the client side and one from the development side. The project is approached as a business project to solve an unsolved problem or exploit an untapped business opportunity, and together these co-managers are responsible for the appropriate business decisions regarding the project and its management. Thus, every decision is both a technical decision and a business decision.

- **Optimizing Scope:** The scope of a complex project should not extend beyond the capacity of the organization to deliver business value. Projects that deliver business value only after long periods of time are not feasible in an environment of complexity and uncertainty. Unexpected changes can render a project obsolete at any time. That suggests short duration cycles that offer production-ready deliverables. In the end, scope is aligned with the delivery of maximum business value.

- **Agile Process:** The ACPF delivers not only an agile process but also an adaptive process. It is the only project management approach to have this designed into it. The result is a project management approach perfectly aligned to the needs of the project and the changing conditions in the internal and external environment in which the project is executed.
- **Project Management Expertise:** Complex project managers are chefs. They can take a specific situation and using the ACPF vetted portfolio of tools, templates, and processes, create a unique recipe for the effective and successful management of the project.
- **Skilled Resources:** ACPF implementation includes a career and professional development program that has been designed specifically to balance the supply of skilled resources against the demand for such types. To be successful with an ACPF project requires a village! The skills profile of the project team adjusts to project changes.
- **(Adaptive) Execution:** I added the word "adaptive" to execution of an ACPF project. In the ACPF, the Execution Phase is also adaptive to the changing conditions and needs of the project. Current project management models choose a model for the management of their project for whatever reason, and stay with that model until the project ends. The ACPF is not like that. The ACPF continuously adjusts the management model to the dynamics of the project.
- **Tools and Infrastructure:** The vetted tools, templates, and processes in an organization's version of the ACPF is honed over a period of time. It is designed specifically to meet the needs and culture of the organization. A PSO has been established to maintain and support that vetted portfolio.

## Develop and Execute an Evolutionary Transition Plan

### *Transitioning to the End-state TPM Environment*

The transition to this end state will be the starting point for most organizations. You will either have a Linear PMLC model in place, or you will have to define one. In any case, managing your projects using only a Linear PMLC model will be a short-term experience. For those organizations whose project management environment has not yet been defined, or is in an embryonic stage where each business unit or project team is free to approach project management in any way they deem appropriate, the organization needs to start the transition process by defining and implementing some form of Linear PMLC model. The primary goal of establishing a Linear PMLC model is to create a set of tools, templates, and processes that can be used across all projects.

Investing in the Linear PMLC model has a return. Having a Linear PMLC model is a foundation and point of departure for developing other models. Even though most projects are not linear, there will be a need for those processes. These tools, templates, and processes can be reused in projects in the APM and xPM quadrants. They are the initial contents for the ACPF/ kit to be completed later, during the transition project. For those organizations who have such a documented approach that is used by project teams, that approach will be their starting point from which they will transition to an Incremental PMLC model. For some organizations, establishing the starting point for a project management methodology may be a project for an outside consultant to direct. Consultants will have the knowledge and experience to not only get the transition process started, but also to direct the entire transition process to the end state.

The establishment of a repeatable and effective project management environment for the first time can be a traumatic event for an organization. If that is the case, first-line managers up to C-level executives must be prepared. The organization has to be positioned for the coming change. An outside consultant should be considered for this assignment. Some project managers will have come to your organization with a collection of tools, templates, and processes that they used elsewhere. The collection may contain quality practices that you will want to include in your growing ACPF/ kit. You will want the project managers involved in the team that builds your TPM end-state process. If you choose to ignore their input, they may be resistant to adopting the resulting models.

## *Transitioning to Your End-state APM Environment*

Once the TPM end state has been achieved, the organization initiates the second transition step: develop and execute an agile end-state environment. For some organizations, this will be their first foray into the agile world. It is a step into project situations where the goal is clearly defined, but parts of the solution are not known at the beginning of the project. These missing parts can be minor or major. Over this range, there are several Agile and one Adaptive PMLC models that align with minor through major missing parts. The Execution Phase of the ACPF is the one Adaptive PMLC model. I have categorized the APM PMLC models into three groups (Iterative, Adaptive, and Extreme), and list them from minor through major missing parts of the solution, as follows:

**PMLC models used when there are minor missing parts of the solution:**
- Iterative models
  - ✦ Prototyping
  - ✦ Evolutionary Development model
  - ✦ Rational Unified Access
  - ✦ Dynamic Systems Development Method
  - ✦ Adaptive Software Development
  - ✦ Scrum

**PMLC models used when there are major missing parts of the solution or goal:**
- Adaptive models
  - ✦ ACPF Execution Phase
- Extreme models
  - ✦ INSPIRE

An organization's ACPF/kit will contain the appropriate subset of these PMLC models. The appropriate implementation and application of their PMLC models will include a training component. The training will include courses that cover the Project Set-up Phase. While the first step might have been a minor disruption, the second step is not. Some of the challenges that arise during the second step of developing and executing an evolutionary transition plan have been:

- **Acceptance and accommodation of variable scope into the PMLC model.** Senior managers sometimes have problems with the acceptance and accommodation of variable scope into the PMLC model. As the sponsor, you are asking them to invest money, time, and human resources on a project where the outcome is not entirely known. The less that is known about the outcome, the greater the risk that the outcome will not deliver the acceptable business value that you used to justify doing the project.
- **Justification of the project based on estimates of expected business value.** Because scope is variable for projects in the ACPF quadrant, so also is the business value they will finally deliver. For the sponsor to get their project approved, it will have to estimate the business value that will result from delivering specified requirements. The more scope

change that can be expected, the greater the variance of those early estimates will be. Risk is high!

- **Gaining and sustaining meaningful client involvement.** The first step into projects in the APM quadrant puts clients in a different situation than those projects in the TPM quadrant. Now, they have to actively participate in the project in order to deliver on the requirements that they approved. If you are concerned about their possible lack of active participation, workshops specifically designed to help them understand their role and responsibilities in projects in the APM quadrant can help them make that transition.

- **Empowering project managers.** Iterative PMLC models provide a structure for the project manager that is absent in Adaptive PMLC models. The cook/chef metaphor sheds some light on those differences. The cook can be comfortable in the Iterative PMLC models because any changes to the recipe are simple. The cook is not at all comfortable in the adaptive PMLC models because there is not much of a recipe to fall back on.

- **Getting clients to be meaningfully involved and stay meaningfully involved.** Clients have been involved in the iterative PMLC models. In most cases, it was in a reactive mode, but that is not the situation in Adaptive PMLC models. Their involvement now accelerates to the level of SMEs. While the project manager could provide some SME support in the Iterative PMLC models, they would be hard-pressed to provide that support in the Adaptive PMLC models situation.

## *Transitioning to the End-state xPM and MPx Environments*

Some adaptive PMLC models can be used for projects that are in the xPM or MPx quadrants. However, there are certain practices and decisions that will be different, given the fact that the goal is not clearly defined. The fact that the solution is not clearly defined is not new. That has been the case with the use of adaptive PMLC models. So, the transition is not significant as far as learning new processes is concerned. The exit from adaptive models and the adoption of Extreme PMLC models is more a matter of convenience than need.

Most Adaptive PMLC models can also accommodate projects in the xPM and MPx quadrants. The process is virtually the same for both Adaptive and Extreme projects. The project management process is the same for projects in the xPM and MPx quadrants, but the interpretations of interim results are different.

Even though Adaptive PMLC models and Extreme PMLC models are quite similar, there are some differences that give rise to a few challenges:

- **Projects in the xPM and MPx quadrants have a much greater risk than projects in the APM quadrant:** This is obvious. The goal may be nothing more than an expression of a desirable end state. It may be fantasy, but that is not known at the beginning of the project. It can only be discovered by doing the project. As the project moves forward, the goal statement is usually revised and constrained. For example, the goal might change from curing cancer to curing melanoma to curing Stage 2 melanoma.
- **Projects in the xPM quadrant are research and development projects and will experience a high failure rate:** A process is needed to terminate those projects that do not seem to be making any progress toward goal attainment. The resources should be withdrawn from these projects and redirected toward more fruitful pursuits.

## HOW WILL YOUR ORGANIZATION MEASURE PROGRESS TOWARD ITS END STATE?

The current-state assessments that were done initially are the best benchmark that you have for measuring progress toward the end state. You will have assessed the gap between your current state and your desired end state. How that gap is closing is a nonquantitative measure of progress. Any shortcomings with respect to achieving the end state will show up and corrective actions can be implemented. Think of an ACPF implementation as a complex project. It has all of the characteristics of an agile project. Mid-project corrections of the implementation plan are not unusual.

## HOW WILL YOUR ORGANIZATION IMPROVE ITS ACPF ENVIRONMENT?

The initial version of the PSO was established to support TPM projects. It defined the support services for that purpose. The ACPF PSO utilizes those services, plus the:

- APPM Process
- CPM Position Family
- Career and Professional Development Program
- ACPF Project Review Process

These support services are discussed below.

## Agile Project Portfolio Management Process

APPM is a logical consequence of the agile movement. Agile projects are those that are continuously redirected to take advantage of the learning and discovery about the solution that arises from the work of the project. Extend that same concept to the portfolio. At regular intervals, the contents of the agile portfolio are changed and redirected to take advantage of the learning and discovery that arises from the performance of projects in the portfolio. The objective is to maximize the business value of the portfolio. Figure 8.4 is the APPM process life cycle.

The APPM life cycle consists of the following five phases, as shown by the shaded boxes in Figure 8.4.

### 1. ESTABLISH a Portfolio Strategy

The first step in portfolio management is deciding the strategy for the portfolio. The portfolio strategy is an investment strategy. It follows directly from the corporate strategic plan. Once the portfolio strategies are in place, the enterprise will have a structure for selecting the investment opportunities that will be presented in the form of project proposals. This is really a type of strategic planning phase in which the portfolio manager or the portfolio management team decides how it will allocate the human resources available to staff projects to various categories of project investment.

### 2. EVALUATE Project Alignment to the Portfolio Strategy

This evaluation is a simple intake task that places a proposed project into one of several categories, as defined in the model being used. The beginning of the project intake process involves determining whether the project is in alignment with the portfolio strategy, and placing it in the appropriate "bucket." These buckets are defined by the strategy that is used, and each bucket contains a planned dollar or human resource allocation. After all of the projects have been placed in buckets, each bucket is passed to the next phase, where the projects that make up a bucket are prioritized.

### 3. PRIORITIZE the Project

The first step in every portfolio management model involves prioritizing the projects that have been aligned with the portfolio strategy. Recall that the alignment places the project in a single support category. It is those projects in a support category that you must now prioritize. When you are

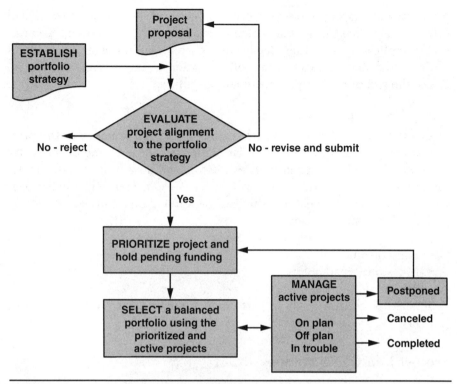

**Figure 8.4** Agile Project Portfolio Management process

finished, each support category will have a list of prioritized projects. Dozens of approaches could be used to establish that prioritization. Some are nonnumeric; others are numeric. Some are simple; others can be quite complex and involve multivariate analysis, goal programming, and other complex computer-based algorithms. My approach is to identify those methods that can easily be implemented and do not require a computer system for support, although sometimes a simple spreadsheet application can reduce the labor intensity of the process.

### 4. SELECT a Balanced Portfolio

You might think that because you have a prioritized list in each support category and you know the resources available for those projects, the selection process would be simple and straightforward, but it is not. Selection is a challenging task for any portfolio management team. The problem stems from the apparent conflict between the results of evaluation, the ranking of projects from most valuable to least valuable, the need to balance the portfolio with respect to one or more variables, and the availability of skilled professionals. These factors are often in conflict with one another. As a further complication, you may decide that partial staffing of projects makes sense. Partial staffing extends the total duration of the project, and can increase the risk of project postponement or failure.

### 5. MANAGE *Active Projects*

In this last phase, you continuously compare the performance of the projects in the portfolio against your plan. Projects can be in one of three statuses: *on plan*, *off plan*, or *in trouble*. You will see how project status is determined and what action you can take as a result. Here, the challenge is to find performance measures that can be applied equitably across all the projects. Two come to mind:

- Earned value
- Milestone trend charts

A detailed discussion of these performance measures is given in Wysocki, (2014a).

## Project Life Cycle Stages

The eight stages that define a project's birth to death life span are shown in Figure 8.4, where the project is:

### 1. Proposed

A proposed project is one that has been submitted to the portfolio with a request that it be evaluated regarding its alignment to the portfolio strategy. A project that does not meet the alignment criteria may be either rejected out of hand or returned to the proposing party for revision and resubmission. Projects that are returned for revision are generally only in minor noncompliance, and following the suggested revisions should meet the alignment criteria.

### 2. Aligned

A proposed project is aligned if it has been evaluated and determined to be in alignment with the portfolio strategy. Once it has been determined to be aligned, it will be placed in one or more funding categories for future consideration. At this stage, the proposing parties should begin preparing a detailed plan. The plan will contain information that helps the portfolio manager make a final determination regarding project funding and, hence, inclusion in the portfolio.

## 3. Prioritized

An aligned project is prioritized if it has been ranked along with other projects in its funding category. This is the final stage before the project is selected for the portfolio. If it is high enough in priority in its category, it will be funded and included in the portfolio.

## 4. Selected

A prioritized project has been selected if it is in the queue of other prioritized projects in its funding category and is awaiting funding authorization. This is a temporary stage, and funding is certain at this point.

## 5. Active

A selected project is active if it has received its funding authorization and is open for work. At this stage, the project manager is authorized to proceed with the recruiting and assignment of team members, scheduling of work, and other activities associated with launching the project.

## 6. Postponed

An active project is postponed if its staff resources have been temporarily removed. Such projects must return to the pool of prioritized projects and be selected, and its staff resources restored. The resources allocated to a postponed project are returned to the staffing category from which they originated to be reallocated to the next project in the queue of that project category.

There are two types of postponement: a project can be postponed indefinitely, or simply paused for some number of cycles and then resumed. The pause is a planned postponement and is often used when a higher priority project requires a few cycles for completion.

## 7. Canceled

An active project is canceled if it has failed to demonstrate planned progress toward its successful completion. Depending on the stage in which the project was canceled, there may be unspent resources. If so, they are returned to the resource pool from which they originated. They then become available for the next project in the queue of that category.

## 8. Completed

A project is completed if it has met all of its objectives and delivered business value as proposed. Even if it has not met all of its objectives, the decision may be to call the current solution acceptable and, hence, the project complete.

## Complex Project Manager Position Family

I have defined a robust position family across all five disciplines, as described in Figure 2.7. The position family includes eight position levels that range from team member through executive levels. I formulated definitions of these position levels so that they can be applied to all five disciplines. In order to fit your organization, you might define more or fewer position levels. I have chosen eight position levels because I believe that is justified by the needs of complex projects and the commonly accepted position levels across all four disciplines. However you choose to define your own position levels, I would suggest that you preserve the staff, professional, and executive distinctions as the highest level of classification in your schema.

The eight levels of the project life cycle encompass all professional positions that have some application to the management of complex projects. The two staff positions are project support positions. The five professional positions are most closely related to actual CPM positions. The Director position includes executive level positions that apply to either process management or practice management.

### *Staff Positions*

There are two staff positions: Team Member and Task Leader. The Team Member is the entry level into the CPM position family. Both Team Member and Task Leader positions are individual contributor positions. They are highly structured and depend on close supervision. They are not considered professional level positions. In a typical project, both positions can report to an Associate Manager, which is the lowest level among the professional positions. Once a Task Leader has acquired the experience and skills that qualifies them as a professional, they are ready for entry into the professional positions, beginning at the Associate Manager level. The Team Member and Task Leader positions are described as follows:

- *Team Member:* A Team Member is an entry level position into any of the five disciplines (project management, business analysis, information technology, business process management, or systems engineering). No prior knowledge or experience in any one of the disciplines is expected or required. A person entering this position will often come directly from completing a two- or four-year degree program with no full-time job experience in any business unit. At most, they will have limited experience as an intern or in a related part-time position as a Project Manager, Business Analyst, Information Technology

Professional, or Business Process Professional. In some cases, they may have as much as 18 months of full-time experience completely outside of the four disciplines. An IT programmer would be a typical example.

Typical Team Member positions will be assigned to a project in a structured and supervised role. In order to be productive in carrying out their first assignment, s/he will have to complete initial training in using the appropriate tools, templates, and processes to be able to carry out their assigned responsibilities. Once having acquired that working knowledge and minimal experience, s/he is expected to organize and plan the work to meet specified performance criteria under less direct supervision. S/he will quickly develop the skills to plan, schedule, and monitor his or her own work, as well as absorb new technical information as it is presented to them. Examples of position titles include documentation specialist, data analyst, and QA tester.

- *Task Leader:* A Task Leader is the upper-level staff position for those who are familiar with the scope of their tasks. After 18-24 months of experience as a Team Member, with experience in one or more of the four disciplines, s/he should be qualified for promotion to Task Leader. As Task Leader, s/he will perform tasks that s/he is qualified for and supervise the work of Team Members assigned to the same area of task responsibility. So, a Task Leader is a working supervisor position. Their position is distinguished from the Team Member by the depth and complexity of their technical knowledge base and the extent to which supervision is required. Task Leaders work with little supervision and are expected to meet the requirements of their assignment under their own initiative. They will often be required to provide initial guidance and training for the less experienced Team Members assigned to their task.

Task Leaders generally work unsupervised, and seek advice and support only when they feel the need for such help. Their assignments are given to them with the necessary specifications for satisfactory completion and they are expected to use the tools, templates, and processes needed for successful completion. They will have developed effective communication and problem-solving skills. They will begin to acquire skills and competencies related to their primary task assignments as a broadening experience in preparation for wider areas of responsibilities. They should begin to see the application of their tasks to broader functional areas and the business in general. Examples of position titles include business process analyst, risk analyst, acceptance test lead, requirements elicitation facilitator, and change request intake specialist.

## Professional Positions

The entry point to becoming a professional may require up to four years of preparatory experience and some validation of skills and competencies. The professional career path begins as an Associate Manager through the Senior Manager positions. As a Senior Manager, the professional will make a career choice to follow an individual contributor path as a Consultant and Senior Consultant, and finally, as a Process Director or to a general management position at the executive level as a Practice Director.

There are five professional positions: Associate Manager, Manager, Senior Manager, Consultant, and Senior Consultant, described as follows:

- *Associate Manager:* This is the entry-level position into the professional level. It is the lowest of three manager positions at the professional level. It will normally be achieved after clear evidence is available of full competence in a specialized role. At this level, full technical accountability for work done and decisions made is expected. The ability to give technical or team leadership will have been demonstrated, as well as a high degree of technical versatility and broad industry knowledge. An Associate Manager will often manage small projects or major parts of larger projects, and be responsible to the project manager. They work unsupervised and are accountable for specific results.

  The typical candidate will have about 12-18 months of successful experience in the role of Task Leader, and will have demonstrated the capacity to effectively manage simple projects and provide team leadership. They are responsible for managing the work of staff assigned to their projects, but do not have direct people management responsibility. Examples of position titles include Associate Project Manager and Business Analyst.

- *Manager:* A Manager is the mid-level manager position in the professional level. It will normally be achieved after 2-4 years of experience as an Associate Manager. The candidate will have demonstrated the capacity to manage projects of intermediate complexity and size. Complexity and uncertainty will characterize their assignments. Examples of position titles include Project Manager, Financial Systems Business Analyst, and Business Process Improvement Analyst.

- *Senior Manager:* A Senior Manager is the most senior of the three manager positions at the professional level. It will normally be achieved after several years of experience as a Manager. Service time as a Manager is important, but more important is the candidate's demonstration of full competence in a specialized role. At this level, full technical accountability for work done and decisions made is expected. The ability to give technical or team leadership will have been demonstrated, as well as a high degree of technical versatility and broad industry knowledge. The candidate will have demonstrated a capacity to manage the most complex of projects and programs, and often be responsible for managing the activities of Managers and Associate Managers, who function as project and sub-project managers. Examples of position titles include Senior Project Manager, Program Manager, Senior Business Analyst, and Business Process Owner.

- *Consultant:* A Consultant is the entry-level position to consulting in specialized areas of expertise across the organization. Candidates for this position are generally Senior Managers. The Consultant will often join a project team for a limited engagement as an advisor, and perhaps offer training to project team members in their area of specialization. They are a recognized professional having earned that respect as a Senior Manager. They work unsupervised, and receive only general directions and objectives from their manager (a Process Director). If the Consultant's discipline is project management, they are probably assigned to a PSO and report to the PSO Director. Examples of position titles include Enterprise Architect, Business Intelligence Consultant, and Business Architect.

- *Senior Consultant:* The Senior Consultant position differs from its more junior counterpart in that the Senior Consultant is called upon to advise the most senior-level executives in regard to the strategic aspects of their technology specialization. This strategic advice may be shared at large project or program levels, as well as at the enterprise planning levels. In either case, the Senior Consultant is recognized as "The Expert" by their colleagues and by executive management. Example position titles include Senior Business Architect, Senior Enterprise Architect, and Senior Business Intelligence Consultant.

## Director Positions

There are two types of director positions: Process Director and Practice Director. In most organizations, these two position types are usually part of the senior management team. Senior Manager or Senior Consultant positions are an entry point to either of these positions. The Process Director position manages all consulting and architecture practices for the enterprise in a specific discipline. The Practice Director manages the project assignments of all professional, and on occasion, staff-level positions in a specific discipline. The Process Director and Practice Director positions are described as follows:

- **Process Director:** The Process Director position represents the level associated with the mature, relevantly experienced, and fully capable consulting professional. Such a person is fully accountable for work quality as a technical specialist. S/he possesses the background knowledge and experience to make informed and responsible decisions, which are technically sound and take the needs of the organization fully into account. They will be expected to advise executives on strategic matters related to their technical expertise.

  In small organizations, there may be only one Process Director position, with director responsibilities for all business processes. As organizations grow in size and complexity, there may be one Process Director position for each major business process group or each business process for the largest organizations. When there are multiple Process Directors, their manager, VP of Business Processes, will be a member of the senior management team. Examples of position titles include Director of Enterprise Architecture, Director of Knowledge Management, and Chief Business Architect.

- **Practice Director:** The Practice Director is the most senior people management level position in the position family. It is the level occupied by the most senior manager of a business function or unit in organizations where operating effectiveness (and possibly survival) is heavily dependent on the function or unit, and where large numbers of practitioners are deployed. A wide and deep practical knowledge base is called for, accompanied by mature management qualities. Examples of position titles include PSO Director, Director of Projects, and Director of IT Project Portfolio.

## A Career and Professional Development Program

Documenting your organization's current state consists not only of the project management processes that the organization has in place, but how they are practiced and most importantly, how effective those processes and practices are in meeting the business goals. Documenting that effectiveness requires a comprehensive analysis of the project management environment of your organization. Documentation should be done through a needs analysis or a SWOT analysis (or both). This is an important first step in any serious transition plan and must be an unbiased effort. An outside consultant is highly recommended.

The current state of the organization is best described from three perspectives:

- The alignment of the supply and demand of staff skills and competencies.
- The appropriateness of the tools, templates, and processes to the project portfolio.
- The effectiveness of the staff skills and competencies to the needs of the project portfolio.

These perspectives are discussed below, along with a plan for creating the needed balance proposed.

### *Aligning the Supply and Demand of Staff Skills and Competencies*

The trend towards higher percentages of complex projects being proposed for the enterprise project portfolio puts a resource planning and acquisition challenge on resource managers. Nowhere is this more pronounced than staff development. The staff requirements for the portfolio of approved projects must align with the skills and competencies profile of the staff. The significance of this is clearly illustrated in the Resource Availability side of the Scope Triangle shown in Figure 2.1.

Having an effective ACPF resource inventory is more than just a random assemblage of skilled professionals. In an ACPF environment, that is not what is needed. What is needed is a development program that assures the alignment of the resource inventory with both the short-term and long-term needs of the project portfolio. Clearly, it is a constraining factor on the contents of the project portfolio. In the long term, projects must be undertaken to reduce any projected resources gaps. These gaps are a barrier to building the needed portfolios of projects and to the attainment of expected business value that results from that proper alignment. The ACPF requires having a resource management system that meets the following requirements for each resource type:

- The current skill and competency profile of each project team member
- The planned changes to that profile through the professional development program
- The planned utilization of each project team member based on the project portfolios

- The projected gap between the resource profile and its utilization over the planning horizon
- Resource alignment corrective action plans

I have done a recent search of the commercially available software packages and have not found any package that meets all of these requirements.

Clearly the successful transition to an ACPF environment must take into account the current staff skills and competencies profile and keep it aligned to the staffing needs of the projects. This alignment must parallel the needs of the ACPF as the enterprise transitions from its current environment to its desired end state. Consider the fact that the skills profile and schedule availability of the cadre of project managers is a constraining factor on the contents of the enterprise's projects, programs, and portfolios. That puts a significant burden on the enterprise to design and implement a professional development program that assures a continual supply of the appropriately skilled and experienced project managers.

Defining staffing needs over a planning horizon and delivering on those needs doesn't happen by accident and certainly won't happen by next Tuesday. The alignment problem and its solution are long-range efforts.

What is the reality of the alignment problem? Let's paint a hypothetical situation and see how it might be resolved. In my experiences, projects are approved based more on their business value and priorities among competing projects. Little regard for the skill and competency profile of human resources or their availability when their committed assignments are included. The result is a resource contention problem and the inevitable negotiations between the projects competing for the same resources. Among the solutions you will entertain are:

- Delay your project until the resource becomes available and can be assigned.
- Negotiate schedule changes to accommodate your project and the competing project(s).
- Replace the resource with lesser skilled resource(s).
- Adjust your project plan to remove the need for the resource.

Every one of these alternatives will reduce the expected business value of your project and any others that will have been party to the resource contention problem. There is a solution that avoids all of these consequences. I don't want to minimize the project of creating the staffing solution because it will also be a very complex project. It is also a project that the organization has not done before and will probably not be repeated again. The alignment solution project idea begins with a business case and the resulting decision regarding the viability of the project. The decision to invest in such a project will have long-term implications to the organization. If such a project is not viable, then the organization has to live with the contention problem realities listed above.

While the discussion that follows is at the complex project manager level the same applies to any complex project team member. The solution to aligning the supply of CPMs to staffing requirements of the complex project portfolio has a number of component parts. These include:

- Define your CPM position family.
- Establish a demand curve over time by type of CPM.
- Define the available staff resources over the same time frame.
- Assess the gap between the supply of staff and the demand for staff over the same time frame.
- Develop a system to analyze the staff supply versus demand gap.
- Develop a project/team profiling system.
- Establish a career and professional development program.

There are many moving parts to this problem and equally to its solution. The list above identifies the projects that are needed to put a solution in place. These are not simple projects! So don't expect the solution to be any less complex. To decompose the problem consider the demand/supply curve. The demand emanates from the projects approved for the enterprise's project portfolios. So, projects distributed across the project landscape is one dimension. For each project a timeline that reflects staffing needs by skills can be imbedded in the project plan. So the supply of skilled project managers and developers over time can be estimated for each approved project. Both the long-term demand and supply are variables. Demand can be controlled through the project approval process. Supply can be controlled through a professional development program.

This is not an easy situation to manage. But at the concept level it does define the solution. The practical level is another matter. I'm sure the HR Directors of most organizations will agree that this does define the solution but finding and getting organizational support for its implementation has not been forthcoming.

Having a solution in place has far-reaching implications into several other business processes and programs, including:

- Project portfolio management: the project portfolio is constrained by the available capacity to staff these projects.
- Human resource management: developing a staff inventory must align with the project portfolio.
- Professional development: a managed and mentored program for staff growth.
- Training curriculum: a portfolio of courses using various delivery models.

## *A System to Analyze the Staff Supply vs. Demand Gap*

Analyzing the staff supply versus demand gap is no small task. The first challenge is to define a skills profile that accommodates both the project manager and the project. The second challenge is to age the project manager cadre based on the current professional development programs and the staff recruiting plans. If short-term gaps can be filled by using outside contractors, that will relieve some of the staffing constraints, but should not be relied upon as a long-term solution.

I am not aware of an existing commercial off-the shelf system with this in-tegrated supply versus demand functionality. Perhaps an enlightened vendor will see the business opportunity that such an application provides. Figure 8.5 illustrates the dual career path available for project managers.

Professional positions begin at the Associate Project Manager level. These are usually achieved after four years of relevant experience. Once the Senior Project Manager position has been reached, the individual has a decision to make. They can continue as an individual contributor by following the Consultant path, or they can continue as a manager by following the Asso-ciate Manager path. Both paths lead to a C or VP-level position as a Process Director or Practice Director.

An effective and practical career and professional development program must align with the current and future needs of the complex project port-folio. The supply of appropriately skilled and experienced CPMs must con-tinuously align with the demand for such professionals. It is not an unusual situation for the demand for CPMs to exceed the supply. That should send the message that the complex project portfolio should be constrained by the current and future supply. Unfortunately, that is not the case. The poor performance of complex projects is probably the result that we are experi-encing.

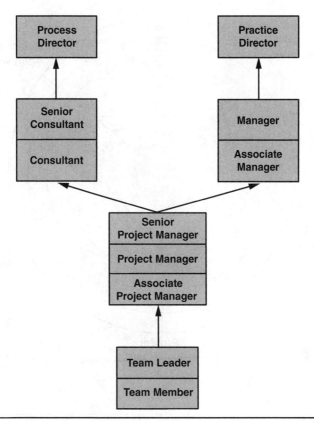

**Figure 8.5**   Dual career paths for project managers

At the team level, the same outcomes are at play. Scarce skills are over-committed. There are resource contention problems and schedules are compromised. Our focus is on the supply/demand gap at the CPM level, but the same arguments hold at the developer level.

## *A Project/Team Profiling System*

The Team Profile shown in Figure 8.6 has several uses. The first is to describe the CPM position family landscape and show the profile of a CPM across the five disciplines. The second use is a profiling tool for the team. By superimposing the individual team member profiles on the CPM position family landscape, a profile of the team emerges, as shown in Figure 8.6; the co-manager profiles are also shown.

In Figure 8.6, the heavy lines define the envelope that encloses the maximum skill level of any team member in each discipline. This team is

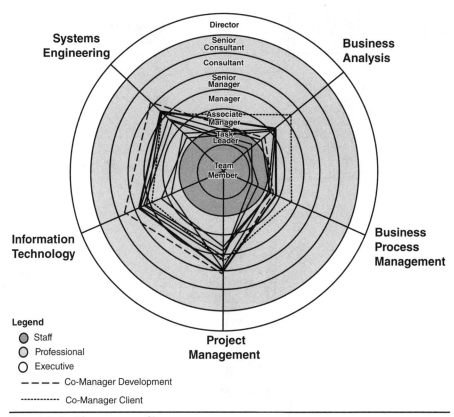

**Figure 8.6**   The team profile

strongest in Project Management and Information Technology, and would fit well with complex projects that place a high importance on those skills.

The third use of the Team Profile is as a tool to analyze the fit between the team and their assigned project. Figure 8.7 gives an example of this use.

The dotted line represents the skill levels required by the project. The Business Analysis and Business Process Management requirements of the project are not covered by the team. The team's greatest skill gap is in Business Process Management. To compensate for this gap, the PSO should be alerted to provide consulting help to the project team. The Information Technology and Systems Engineering disciplines are adequately covered, and may provide some support in the Business Process Management discipline. Reasons for analyzing the fit between a Team Profile and their project are:

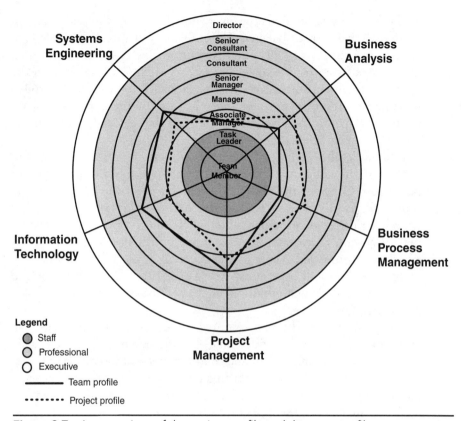

**Figure 8.7**   A comparison of the project profile and the team profile

- *Understanding the skill and competency demands of the current and future projects.* To understand these demands, the organization will need to establish the proper infrastructure. That infrastructure will include a two-level intake process. The first level asks for high-level information about a project. That high-level information helps the enterprise determine whether the project makes business sense and should be described in more detail. Describing that detail is the second-level of the intake process. Part of the information that is submitted at this level will identify, through the project plan, the skills and competency needs, and when those are needed. This builds the initial demand-side of the project staffing equation over time. Parallel to the demand over time is the supply over time.
- *Knowing the skill and competency profile of the current and future project managers and project team members.* This is the supply side

of the project staffing equation over time. Presently, the demand/supply equation is out of balance. The imbalance is mostly the result of a lag in the supply of CPMs and concurrent increases in the number of complex projects, due to several factors, such as those listed in the opening statement of this report. The demand side can be controlled to some extent by the business rules that are used to approve projects for the organization's project portfolio. But that can only go so far before it adversely affects the bottom line.

The availability of project managers or team members, or lack of it, constrains the contents of the project portfolio more than any other parameter. Consider the situation where the available project professionals are mostly junior level professionals with limited knowledge of complex project management, but where the proposed projects are mostly complex projects. The resulting project portfolio will be seriously compromised. Many of the complex projects that do end up in the portfolio will be at great risk. Those projects will be managed by professionals who are more likely to be "cooks" when the complex projects require "chefs."

There are several human resource management systems that can track staff availability down to single-day increments. These can easily border on micromanagement and may actually add too much management overhead to the whole staffing process. As a strong supporter of APM, I am not interested in adding non-value work to the project.

When analyzing the supply of skills and competencies, as compared to the demand for skills and competencies, there will most certainly be a gap between the supply and the demand for skills and competencies. With the appropriate management attention, that gap can be minimized. Since there are so many moving parts in this balancing act, it is unlikely that the gap can be removed, but it can be managed.

- *Knowing the skill and competency gaps, and how to reduce them with training and experience acquisition.* The organization's training curriculum must be responsive to the needed skills and competencies:

    1. **With respect to content:** Project performance data is the key to aligning content with deficiencies. That data applies to practice of the project management processes, but it also applies to the effectiveness of the processes.

    2. **With respect to availability:** Instructor-led training may be desirable, but not always accessible. The training schedule needs to align with the project staffing needs. Online synchronous courses can alleviate the problem.

In order to build an aligned cadre of CPMs over time, you need a program to plan and develop them. To be effective, that plan must align with the demand for CPMs over time as defined by the project portfolio. Just because a person hopes to become a CPM someday, they won't get there just because they are a nice person and happened to be hanging around the office when the opportunity arises. It can happen, but it is like investing in the lottery. Since the professional owns their career, no one is going to do this for them. They will have to develop and maintain a plan that will result in their career and professional development, which is targeted to their career goal position. That requires a concerted and diligent effort with the support of one or more mentors. I will call this plan a Professional Development Plan (PDP).

While an individual's career plan may extend over several years, the PDP planning horizon usually spans a single year with reviews on a quarterly basis or as needed. When used in a job situation, the temptation is to schedule a PDP planning session in conjunction with an annual performance review process. That is not a good idea. In practice, it is usually better to keep PDP development/updating and the performance review processes six months out of phase with each other. Conducting a performance evaluation and career planning session concurrently is strongly discouraged. The performance review is not a safe harbor for the individual. In a performance review, they are under pressure and often put in a defensive position. In a career planning session, they are in dream mode and don't need any pressure imposed on them from some other conflicting activity.

The structure of the career and professional development process is portrayed in Figure 8.8. First, note that the process is never ending. Well, I suppose it does end, but that will be when you are dead or earned so much money that you don't care anymore. Note that the plan is defined by doing nothing more than continuously answering the same four questions. Between each round of answering the four questions, your professional life can take several turns that justify reconsidering your answers from the previous round.

## The ACPF Project Review Process

Decisions regarding the future content of a project portfolio cannot be made without a review process that compares its projects on an equal basis. The Client Checkpoint (discussed in Chapter 6) evaluates the current performance of a complex project against the planned performance, and decides on the path forward. This is done on a project-by-project basis. With those planned futures in mind, the decision moves to the portfolio level.

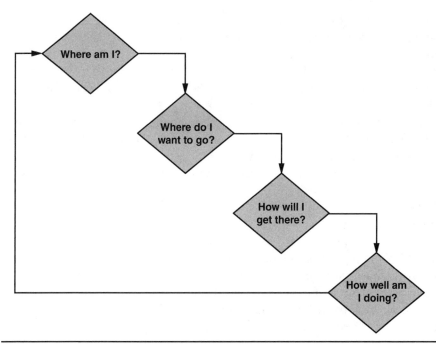

**Figure 8.8**   The structure of the PDP process

The question becomes how to allocate resources across all projects in the portfolio for the next review cycle. There are as many alternatives as there are projects in the portfolio. They range from withdrawing all resources for the next cycle to complete funding, and all variations in between.

## PUTTING IT ALL TOGETHER

Designing and implementing an ACPF environment in your enterprise is a challenging undertaking. In the complex project world, change is constant and so the project management world will constantly change as a result. I have shared my experiences and what I have learned over 20+ years of developing and maturing the ACPF. I have captured some of those experiences in this chapter.

Implementing change is a complex event. Some stakeholders will embrace the change as long overdue, while others will stand firm in their own practices. These are the extremes, and there are many variations between these extremes. Your implementation plan will succeed if, and only if, you anticipate all potential reactions to the new ACPF environment.

Designing and implementing your own customized ACPF is not a one-time event. In fact, it will be a continuous process improvement program. It is an agile process that has no end. The reason is exactly the same as the reason that a PMLC is not a static choice. Just as the project situation changes, so will the experiences your organization will have with its customized ACPF. Here are the more significant, early reactions that some of my clients have experienced with their own ACPF implementations:

- **Resistance to adapting or even changing the chosen PMLC model.** No matter how hard you may have tried, there will be project managers who would rather be handed a recipe than create their own recipe. I guess there is some comfort in basing their project management approach on something that has passed muster as a vetted process.
- **Fully engaging the client in decision making.** You should have already realized that the role of the client is different post-ACPF than pre-ACPF. The more radical the change, the more you will need programs that especially introduce the ACPF from the client's perspective.
- **Hanging on to old practices.** Some experienced project managers will take the view that what they are doing works and doesn't need fixing. You need to get these professionals on your side, and that is not hard to do. My solution is to ask them to present their practices to a small but representative group of project managers for the purposes of discussion and potential integration of their practices into the ACPF. You might end up expanding the portfolio of vetted tools, templates, and processes, and giving project managers the option of what approach makes the most sense, given the characteristics and environment of their project.
- **Training is not being implemented.** Lack of training implementation is not good, and must be aggressively addressed. You will need to get to the root cause. The problem might be content or delivery related. If it is content, you might refer to the above paragraph for a solution. If it is delivery related, you can correct that through process improvement of either the training delivery system or the skills of those who deliver training. Neither of these issues is a showstopper.

The transition from the current state of project management processes and practices to a desired end state will be different for every organization. They all start in different states and they all define end states that align with their industry and culture. This chapter defines a multi-step transition plan that can be adapted to any organization. Some will be very immature with respect to project management processes and practices and will begin at an elementary maturity level that will require learning and discovery of the desired end state. This transition will happen iteratively. Others will be more mature but still require learning and discovery of adaptable processes to effectively manage the most complex of projects. The most mature among these organizations may be able to utilize a one-step transition to their desired end state.

# 9

---

# FREQUENTLY ASKED
# QUESTIONS

---

*I like people who can do things. When Edward and I strug-*
*gled in vain to drag our big calf into the barn, the Irish girl*
*put her finger into the calf's mouth and led her in directly.*
—Ralph Waldo Emerson, U.S. essayist and poet

## CHAPTER LEARNING OBJECTIVES

This chapter will provide readers the knowledge or ability to:

- Understand the practice issues encountered by adopting users.
- Understand the concerns and questions of interested parties.

Despite my best efforts to make the Adaptive Complex Project Framework
(ACPF) intuitive, the intuitive approach does not always materialize. Questions about understanding ACPF concepts and principles always seem to
come up. Sometimes, lack of understanding is my fault, and at other times
it is just the need for a minor clarification. In practice, the same thing happens. A situation arises that does not seem to be covered by the ACPF, and
it needs an explanation or an answer to a question.

## FREQUENTLY ASKED QUESTIONS

As clients and colleagues embark on an ACPF project for the first time, they are taking a leap of faith. Naturally, questions will arise. So far, the ACPF has held up to the promise of 100% success, all of the time. Below are significant questions that I have received about the ACPF. I pass my responses on to you because you will probably have the same questions. If your questions are not answered here, please let me hear from you at rkw@eiicorp.com.

**Q: You mean I'm going to ask my client for $1M and one year and I can't tell them what they will get?**

**A:** This is by far the most frequently asked question. It bothers senior managers as well as traditional project managers because it flies in the face of conventional thinking. The ACPF requires a whole new mindset—one that stands in stark contrast to traditional efforts. One is led to believe that this is a major weakness of the ACPF. It is not a weakness, and I'll explain why.

In a traditional project, scope is defined as part of project initiation and the client is given an estimate of the time and cost to produce the deliverables. That's fine, and would probably be OK if it weren't for the fact that the world does not stand still just because you are managing a project. Scope change requests are inevitable in complex projects as conditions change and the client learns that what they really needed is now different than what they originally said they needed. The final result can be a patchwork of changes and fixes. If that was not enough, the quality of the final deliverables has been compromised in order to accommodate the many changes. Much of the cost and time invested in planning and developing the original scope would have been wasted as it was replaced several times in order to accommodate the changed scope. In the end, the client is reasonably satisfied at best, and the project ends. The expected business value may not be achieved.

Let's take a look at what would have happened if the project had been approached as an ACPF project. First, the ACPF Project Management Life Cycle (PMLC) model is designed for projects that are looking for the solution to a critical yet unsolved problem, or to effectively take advantage of an untapped business opportunity. In both cases, we and the client are taking a step into the unknown and the final deliverables cannot be known at the beginning of the project. They can only be discovered during the execution of the project. Yes, you can't tell exactly what you will deliver at the end of the ACPF project but whatever it is, it will be the best that could have been delivered through leveraging the collective wisdom of you and your client within the constraints of the time and money invested by the client. You know that because the ACPF requires that you and the client participate in the decisions at every client checkpoint. If there was a better solution and your project did not discover it, the discovery of that solution will have to wait for divine intervention, or for someone with an insight you and the client do not currently possess. It might be that the solution you delivered wasn't all that was expected, but it was the best that could be done. In the end, scope is variable. That is a given in every ACPF project.

---

**The Short Answer**

Yes, you can't tell exactly what you will deliver at the end of the ACPF project but whatever it is, it will be the best that could have been delivered through leveraging the collective wisdom of you and your client within the constraints of the time and money invested by the sponsor and client.

---

Second, the time spent creating a detailed plan would not have been spent and would have been allocated to development. The only parts of the solution that were implemented were parts known to be in the final solution. No rework, and hence, no waste of time and budget on useless or unnecessary development. That time and money would have been spent on actual development of final deliverables. What this boils down to is the spending of time and money on the best business value that you and the client in a collaborative partnership could have identified.

It is critical that the client understand this, accept it, and do the best that they can in participating in the hunt for an acceptable solution. Clearly, their meaningful involvement is a critical success factor.

---

Remember: the project is complex, and its solution is not known at the outset. Still, reaching an acceptable solution was critical to the organization. You didn't have any choice. The project had to be done in the best way possible. There really was no other alternative than the ACPF.

---

**Q: Can the ACPF be used in an organization that frequently reorganizes?**

**A:** The ACPF is a perfect fit for such organizations. The ACPF is robust and adaptive. The choice of PMLC model should always defer to models that have short iterations with production ready deliverables at each iteration. As a result of reorganization, project priorities often change and shorter iterations increase the chance that a canceled project can still contribute some business value.

## Q: Can the client increase the budget or deadline?

A: Of course they can. The ACPF is such that at any client checkpoint, the progress to date and business justification of it should be revisited. You took the time to prioritize the Scope Triangle parameters. The decision to change the time or cost constraints can be made based on the best information available at that checkpoint.

You do not have this luxury in a Traditional Project Management (TPM) project because there are no business value considerations on which to base such a decision. In an ACPF project, that means increases, decreases, and even project termination are possible outcomes. Adding time and or money would follow if the project were converging on a solution deemed to be better than expected, but the time and or money wasn't sufficient to achieve that solution.

On the decreasing side, the picture isn't pretty, but it is the part of the ACPF that separates it from every traditional approach and most agile approaches. If the current solution is not converging on an acceptable solution, the client should pull the plug. Save the unspent money, time, and staff resources to take a fresh approach. Terminating the project permanently is not an option. Remember the successful completion of the project is critical to the enterprise. If the current approach is not showing some results early on, cancel the project, and come at it from a different vantage point. This is not a sign of failure. It is a sign that clear business value thinking and client focus are the important factors.

## Q: What if you can't get the client to be meaningfully involved?

A: This is a tough situation that you are going to have to face. In earlier days, I might have said that I would find some way to work around and do the project without the meaningful involvement of the client. Now with several years of experience to draw on, I just would not do the project until the client was willing to be meaningfully involved. I have tried both strategies and had a few successes, but left a lot of blood on the trail behind me. I often won the battle but lost the war. In general, neither strategy met with my satisfaction. Now that I have a few decades of experience behind me, I tend to follow a more diplomatic route. The success of the project is critical to the continued operation of the business and is beyond your authority to cancel or postpone. On the assumption that the project will go ahead, what would you, could you, or should you do? Of prime importance is to find out what barriers to meaningful involvement exist in the mind of the client. Options to fix this include commercial off-the-shelf facilitator-led training; custom-designed, instructor-led training; and real-time, consultant-led training (please refer back to this discussion in Chapter 7 for more details.)

**Q: What if the client team is not comfortable suggesting changes because of prior bad experiences?**

**A:** If the client's experiences have been mostly on TPM projects, they will have been conditioned to the fact that change is not welcomed. In an ACPF project, the reverse is the case, where change is expected and some unlearning must take place.

I have two suggestions for dealing with this situation. The first is to lead by example. Even if your ideas are not the best, they may encourage the client to begin participating. The second suggestion, and one that has worked well for me, is to question the client at each checkpoint. Your objective is to create a conversation with the client and ferret out their ideas for solution improvement. There will be a positive learning experience here that will benefit this and succeeding ACPF projects with this client. For this to be successful, the client has to be comfortable and not feel like they are being given the third degree or being asked to defend their position.

**Q: What if the client team does not understand their role or won't accept their role?**

**A:** You can always overcome a lack of understanding with training. If you have had previous successful experiences with other clients that this client can relate to, try getting testimonials or direct input from those satisfied clients. Having the client accept their role is absolutely essential to every ACPF project. I strongly advise that you assure yourself of their role acceptance before you embark on an ACPF project with them.

**Q: What should be done when the client team is passive and seems uninvolved in team meetings?**

**A:** You have to get to the root cause of the passivity and non-involvement immediately. Training, workshops, interviews, discussions with satisfied clients, or the use of mediators are all strategies that I have used effectively in these situations.

**Q: What if the client team won't risk making a bad decision?**

**A:** Not taking risks may be part of the organization's culture. The client needs to understand that you are both in it together, and both will take credit or blame for whatever happens. Assure the client team that to the best of your ability, you won't let them choose the wrong course of action. You will have done your homework and only presented them with feasible alternatives. Even though they will have the most important responsibilities in the project, you are not hanging them out to dry.

**Q: What should be done if the project team won't accept the client's new ACPF role?**

**A:** Project teams are accustomed to taking the lead in their projects. That is not what happens in an ACPF project. There is a joint ownership, with the client being the default decision maker.

**Q: How much planning do you do up front for the contents of the first few cycles?**

**A:** As little as possible. The secret to ACPF planning is not to try to guess the future. You can't guess the future, so don't waste any time on it and certainly don't put any planning effort into it. Stick with the artifacts you know will be in the final solution, and put your planning effort into those. These will be cycle-length plans (one or two weeks) and should be fairly simple.

As for ACPF planning tools, I prefer and strongly suggest the use of low-tech tools over high-tech tools. A one- or two-week planning effort does not need an automated tool. That's like killing a mosquito with a sledge hammer. White boards, marking pens, and sticky notes work just fine. I have successfully managed $5M, three-year ACPF projects with nothing more than these tools. And these are long ACPF projects! Tools like Microsoft Project are terrific and they have their place, but not in the ACPF. I always remind my clients that if you establish a project plan using an automated tool, then you have to maintain that plan as part of managing the project. Ask yourself if the added overhead is worth it.

**Q: Can a distributed team use the ACPF? How?**

**A:** Agile project management practices strongly encourage co-located teams and for good reason. Having the team within physical sight of one another is the foundation of a creative environment because it fosters immediate feedback and discussion of ideas. Not having that can be a major obstacle in your search for that elusive solution or way to exploit an untapped business opportunity.

However, what if the team can't be co-located, but the project is clearly an ACPF project? You use the ACPF, of course. This will be real test of its adaptability and a real test of your ability as a project manager to make the ACPF work. I know that the ACPF will work in a distributed environment because one of the early ACPF projects that I managed had a team of 35 technical staff spread out all over the globe. Eleven time zones separated the team members from one another. The secret to success is good and open communications. These were the communication aspects of this project:

- All project team status meetings were daily 15-minute audio teleconferences. They were limited to simple verbal status updates. No handouts were allowed. All other project meetings had timed agendas with meeting materials distributed ahead of time.
- Meeting times were adjusted to share the scheduling inconveniences as equally as possible.
- All team leaders gave a status report (on schedule, ahead of schedule, behind schedule) for tasks open for work only.
- If a team leader was behind schedule, it was discussed when they would be on schedule and if they needed help.
- All requests for help or to offer help were discussed outside the project team status meeting.
- Problem solving or issues resolution were discussed outside the project team status meeting and only involved the affected parties.
- Clients were routinely invited to all project team meetings.
- Team leaders posted their status for access by all project team members.
- No decisions were made or action items scheduled in daily project team status meetings.

By the way, these are the very same guidelines that are used for project team meetings when the project team is co-located. The ACPF is truly adaptive.

Besides these operational matters, there is the deliverables aspect of an ACPF project. First of all, the swim lanes, whether integrative or probative, should be independent of one another. Time zone differences can wreak havoc on the project schedule. I have also experienced situations where time zones can be worked to advantage. For example, at 6 p.m. EST, I can e-mail the description of a problem to a team member in Mumbai, India, where it is 4 a.m. the next day. He can work on it at the start of his day. He can forward any progress on finding a solution back to me at the end of his workday (about 8 a.m. EST on my next workday). Time is a precious resource and used sparingly.

**Q: Can part of a project use the ACPF? How?**

**A:** Yes. Refer to the ACPF variations section in Chapter 6 for the complete details on how to do this. It is fairly straightforward to integrate an ACPF component into either a Linear or Incremental PMLC model.

**Q: Do I have to worry about micro-management?**

**A:** When you propose an ACPF environment for your organization, keep in mind that you are taking senior management into strange and uncharted waters. You are taking them out of their comfort zone with a certain dose of "just trust me" bundled in. Getting senior management used to the ACPF creative environment, and how they should operate within it, will be a challenge. Burn charts and Earned Value Analysis are examples of the metrics they are used to seeing in TPM project reports, but these are not ACPF metrics. The ACPF metrics tend to be trend type metrics (the number of Probative Swim Lanes compared to the number of Integrative Swim Lanes over the history of the project, for example). And, even these metrics have different interpretations, depending on the status of the solution and how far you have journeyed into the life cycle of the project. The best management strategy for senior managers is to do whatever they can to facilitate and support the ACPF project team, and trust the team to make the best business decision they can. Otherwise, stay out of the way and let the process happen! More discussion about executive management support of complex projects is found in Wysocki (2011).

**Q: How do you implement the ACPF in an organization heavily invested in TPM?**

**A:** There are three strategies for implementing the ACPF that I can recommend. I have had direct experience or knowledge of all three, and with proper planning and leadership they work! The strategies are: bottom-up implementation, top-down implementation, and the CEO says "Do It!"

## Bottom-up Implementation

If you have one or more respected project managers who would fall on their sword for the ACPF, a bottom-up implementation approach can work. I have a colleague that uses this approach, but in a passive way. She uses the ACPF religiously on every project that she is assigned to manage for which the ACPF is appropriate. She does nothing overt to promote the ACPF, but rather depends totally on showing its power by way of example. Her success rate exceeds that of her colleagues by a substantial amount. She says nothing about how she does it. Her success speaks for itself in all performance reports that compare the performance of the 20 project managers in her PMO. At some point in time, her fellow project managers can't resist, and they have asked her how she is so successful while they are not. Her answer blows them away: she tells me that others are beginning to adopt some of her suggestions. So, she has planted the seeds of the ACPF. In time, they will grow.

Another bottom-up strategy is to choose two projects as demonstration projects for the ACPF. Because of the nature of ACPF projects this is a high-risk strategy. You want the projects to be unqualified successes or you will bury any chances for the ACPF in your organization. I would look for these demonstration projects in departments suffering a lot of pain due to their project failure rates.

### Top-down Implementation

If you have a sponsor whose leverage, credibility, sales ability, and power in the organization is without question, then a top-down approach can be made to work. That sponsor could be the CIO, VP of Product Development, CFO, or any other C-level executive. They have to sell the ACPF to the organization and appoint you the project manager for the ACPF implementation project. This is your chance and it will only come once. I would not use demonstration projects for this situation. Rather, I would appoint a representative task force staffed by project managers of all skill and experience levels. The task force should also have resource managers and key client representatives as well. The members should all have credibility in their business units because you want the deliverables from their efforts to be widely accepted in the organization.

### The CEO Says "Do It!"

The CEO saying "Do it!" won't happen very often, so consider yourself blessed if it does. You have been given a lot of power, so don't abuse it. The task force approach is still my recommendation. Keep the CEO and other C-level executives involved through a strong communications program. As part of that communications program, include frequent open invitation presentations on the ACPF, and your version in particular. Seek broad input, and make sure you provide feedback on all ideas received.

## PUTTING IT ALL TOGETHER

If questions come up that are not listed in this chapter, you can communicate with me at rkw@eiicorp.com. I will make myself available to help!

# Appendix A

## ACPF ACRONYMS

This Appendix brings together in one place all of the acronyms used throughout the book. It provides a convenient one-stop for information, and avoids the need to search through the book for the meanings of acronyms.

| | |
|---|---|
| AC | Avoid Cost (Part of IRACIS) |
| ACPF | Adaptive Complex Project Framework |
| APF | Adaptive Project Framework |
| APM | Agile Project Management |
| APPM | Agile Project Portfolio Management |
| ASAP | As soon as possible |
| ATP | Acceptance Test Procedure |
| B2B | Business to Business |
| B2C | Business to Customer |
| BA | Business Analysis, Business Analyst |
| BABOK | Business Analysis Body of Knowledge |
| BA | Business Analyst |
| BPI | Business Process Improvement |
| BPM | Business Process Manager; Business Process Management |
| CIO | Chief Information Officer |
| COS | Conditions of Satisfaction |
| COTS | Commercial off-the-Shelf |
| CPI | Cost Performance Index |
| CPIM | Continuous Process Improvement Model |
| CPM | Complex Project Manager; Complex Project Management |
| CSF | Critical Success Factor |
| DSDM | Dynamic Systems Development Method |

| | |
|---|---|
| ECPM | Effective Complex Project Management |
| EPM | Effective Project Management |
| EPPM | Enterprise Project Management Model |
| EPSO | Enterprise Project Support Office |
| EVA | Earned Value Analysis |
| FDD | Feature-driven Development |
| HRIS | Human Resource Information System |
| HRMS | Human Resource Management System |
| IIBA | International Institute of Business Analysis |
| INSPIRE | INitiate, SPeculate, Incubate, REview |
| IRACIS | Increase Revenue, Avoid Cost, Improve Service |
| IRR | Internal Rate of Return |
| IS | Information Systems |
| IT | Information Technology |
| LOB | Line of Business |
| MoSCoW | Must have, Should have, Could have, Wouldn't it be nice to have |
| MPx | Emertxe Project Management |
| PDP | Professional Development Plan |
| PERT | Project Evaluation and Review Technique |
| PM | Project Manager or Project Management |
| PMBOK | Project Management Body of Knowledge |
| PMI® | Project Management Institute |
| PMLC | Project Management Life Cycle |
| PMO | Project Management Office |
| PMP | Project Management Professional |
| PO | Project Office |
| POS | Project Overview Statement |
| PQM | Process Quality Matrix |
| PSO | Project Support Office |
| QA | Quality Assurance |
| R&D | Research and Development |
| RASCI | Responsible, Approves, Supports, Consults, Informs |
| RBS | Requirements Breakdown Structure |
| ROI | Return on Investment |
| RUP | Rational Unified Process |
| SDLC | Systems Development Life Cycle |
| SME | Subject Matter Expert |
| SPI | Schedule Performance Index |
| SWAG | Scientific Wild A** Guess |

| SWOT | Strengths, Weaknesses, Opportunities, Threats |
| TPM | Traditional Project Management |
| UML | Universal Modeling Language |
| WAG | Wild A** Guess |
| WBDC | Workforce and Business Development Center |
| WBS | Work Breakdown Structure |
| xPM | Extreme Project Management |

# Appendix B

---

## CASE STUDY: WORKFORCE AND BUSINESS DEVELOPMENT CENTER

---

This case study, Workforce and Business Development Center (WBDC), is hypothetical (Wysocki, 2010b). It is useful to gain further grounding in the Adaptive Complex Project Framework application.

### The Case Problem

In my view, American workers, entrepreneurs, small business persons, and the educational delivery system that should be supporting them are all in trouble. The US continues to slip in a number of rankings among the industrialized nations of the world. We could not be more in need of an economic and education overhaul than right now. It is time for a disruptive innovation that restores the US worker to the global family, puts business formation and development on a firm foundation, and aligns the education/training community to support them. To create this new environment is no small task. It cannot be done by incremental change. The economic world as we once knew it has disappeared, and no one is really sure what will replace it. The WBDC Case Study investigates an innovative solution, based on this rationale:

- It is time for a disruptive innovation in adult education and training.
- It is time for a disruptive innovation in the support of new business formation and growth.

- Current training and education models can be fixed by a complete replacement of instructor-centric models with team-centric models, and the integration of project/problem-based curricula.
- Businesses need to find creative and innovative ways to apply technology to product/service offerings in order to increase revenues, avoid costs, or improve services.
- To be successful, businesses will have to create new jobs or redefine existing jobs by leveraging technology in innovative ways, and do it before the competition does.
- To be sustainable, new jobs need to be designed so that they cannot easily be outsourced.

Many people will be looking for points of entry into a business world that expects varying degrees of technical knowledge and skill. Where are the points of entry, what skills are needed, and how are these skills acquired are all questions needing answers. Then, there is the underlying question of sustainability of these positions, too. Do these positions have any staying power? One thing that is common to all people is the need to identify and prepare themselves for positions that cannot be outsourced. Many of the more secure positions that offer growth opportunities will have some form of technology component.

One of the major obstacles is the need to extend the reach of education beyond presentation of concepts, theories, and principles to embrace real-world applications. The monolithic delivery model must give way to team-driven, project-based learning models.

## The Case Solution

A viable solution to workforce development must be comprehensive and adaptive. The solution will have many interdependent parts and will not be easily implemented, but it must be implemented. It will require a radical rethinking of how we educate students and train workers in the United States. Therefore, any WBDC model that claims to be comprehensive must:

- Exploit technology for sustainable business growth and job creation.
- Concurrently meet the needs of business, academe, and the worker.
- Continuously adapt and align to changing global and regional markets.
- Be based on the concept of a "classroom without walls."
- Include learn-to-work and work-to-learn components.
- Support entrepreneurship and business formation.
- Utilize team-centric learning and discovery models.

- Be based on a problem/project-based learning model.
- Be financially sound and create social value.
- Provide safe harbor for career development.
- Rekindle the US "spirit of innovation."
- Offer growth opportunities to every worker.
- Meaningfully integrate the business environment.
- Be scalable, replicable, and robust.

The proposed WBDC model, coupled with the concept of a Business Incubation Center (BIC), is a disruptive innovation that stands unique among such models. It will usher in a new and invigorating approach to career and professional development for every worker, regardless of their station in life, or their career and professional development goals.

## The Vision

The WBDC model is a lifelong career and professional development service designed to provide the one-stop resource for individuals seeking guidance and support for their lifetime career and professional journey.

## The Short-term Goal of the WBDC Model

The WBDC model will quickly become a self-supporting program, serving the career and professional development needs of its target markets:

- High school sophomores
- High school graduates
- Traditional college and university students
- Inexperienced adult workers
- Experienced adult workers
- Recently discharged military

These six groups are very different, with different levels of maturity, experiences, needs, and motivations. The WBDC model will be sufficiently robust to reach out to all of them through its unique project-based, team-centric learning and development model. The WBDC model architecture can be adapted to other disciplines and other types of businesses, such as family-owned product and services businesses.

## An Overview of the WBDC Model

I have crafted the WBDC model from my own direct involvement in career and professional development. I have seen parts of the model in application, and have some idea of what works and what doesn't work.

The WBDC model fully and meaningfully integrates academe, business, and business development to create a team-centric training and retraining experience. Each team is typically comprised of 5 to 6 students with common career, professional development, and business interests. An individual remains on a team until they complete their program. The team will be supported by a faculty advisor and mentor from the business community. Each team is attached to a single WBDC-owned nonprofit business or new business idea. More than one team may be attached to the same business. Team membership changes as students complete their programs and new students enter the program. New students to the program will interview to join a business, just like they will someday interview for a real job! Businesses operate in a team-centric mode, just as the WBDC model is a team-centric structure. The BIC is as much a microcosm of the real world as it can be! It provides as rich a source of learning and discovery opportunities as is possible.

There are three environments and three linkages that describe the WBDC landscape, as shown in Figure B.1.

## The WBDC Learning Environment

In the WBDC landscape, the classroom is not what you might think it is. The WBDC model is designed using the concept of a "classroom without walls." That is, the classroom is any place where learning needs to occur, can occur, and will occur. That space would include the traditional classroom as the focal point, but it is a much richer learning environment than that. Under the guidance and advice of their faculty and business advisors, the team will have identified a learning objective, and it is their responsibility to develop the plan to acquire it. They will have to go wherever they need to go, and get whatever they need to acquire that learning. It may be in the traditional classroom, but it might also be at a local business, on the Internet, in courses at another university, at a museum, or with an expert located anywhere in the world, including attendance at a conference or professional society meeting. The reward for meeting a learning objective is their motivation. A model that I have used successfully was introduced by Saul Gellerman (1973). I have adapted that model to the team environment and incorporated it in the WBDC model.

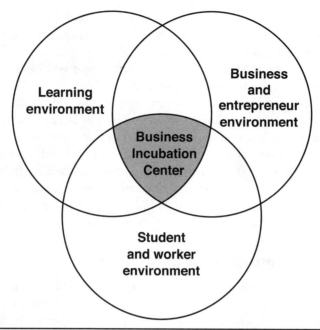

**Figure B.1**   Case Study: The WBDC model

The learning environment also encompasses a collaborative formed of participating high schools, community colleges, and universities. They will each contribute courses and programs to varying degrees of detail. Of prime importance will be the articulation agreements that describe the degree-granting relationship between pairs of participating institutions. A student from any of the participating institutions can take advantage of the WBDC curriculum to enhance and enrich their programs.

There will be a selection of core courses in all programs. These will be offered as part of the WBDC. Other formal courses will be drawn from existing courses offered by the participating institutions. In collaboration with the participating institutions, students will file and gain approval of degree or certificate programs, according to institutional graduation requirements. Due to the adaptive nature of the programs, there will be independent study and project-based learning components are still compliant with degree requirements.

In collaboration with the participating institutions, students will file and gain approval of degree or certificate programs, according to the program requirements of their home institution. Due to the adaptive nature of the programs, there will be a heavy reliance on project-based and problem-based courses. The content of these courses will be adaptive, but still maintain compliance to their home institution's program requirements. Because of the adaptive nature of the WBDC curriculum, these will be defined at the appropriate time in each student's program.

Please do not get the impression that the WBDC curriculum is a fixed and structured curriculum. Every course is adaptive because it uses project- and problem-based learning models. Courses derive their content and structure from the projects and problems contributed by businesses and others, but there is an underlying learning requirement defined by their program requirements. So, there is a standard that defines *what* disciplines, concepts, principles, and theories must be included in the certificate or degree program, but not *how*, that is included in the program.

## Business and Entrepreneur Environment

The business and entrepreneur environment contains two separate environments: entrepreneur and business owner. Each has a different perspective and motivation for using the WBDC. The entrepreneur wants to define a sustainable and profitable business, but needs help validating the business idea, and forming and launching the business. The business owner wants to stay in business, but needs process help and problem-solving support.

Local businesses contribute to the program in a variety of ways, such as:

- They are a resource to the learning environment through guest lectures, panels, etc.
- They invite students to visit their company for tours and attendance at business meetings, problem solving sessions, and a host of other situations.
- They may contribute equipment and other in-kind services.
- They will mentor and advise the teams as they work in their WBDC-owned businesses.

## Student and Worker Environment

Students and workers enter the program with some idea of where they want to go. (When the worker enters the WBDC program, s/he becomes a student and will be referred to as a "student" throughout this book.) The student may not have the specifics, but at least they know whether their future lies in growth in their existing position, continuing to work for others, or starting and managing their own small business. They look to the WBDC program to help them fill in the blanks and get their plan for career and professional development in place and underway. As they work on their plan, they will turn to the WBDC for support and guidance.

## Business Incubation Center

The BIC is the heart and soul of the WBDC. It does offer the support that you ordinarily associate with an incubation center, but it goes much further. The WBDC BIC is the meeting place of student teams, teaching faculty, entrepreneurs, and business owners. Student teams are looking for:

- Preparation for first-time entry or reentry into the world of work
- Practical application of learning on real projects
- The use of real projects to drive and motivate their learning program
- Advice and coaching from member business owners

Teaching faculty members are looking for:

- Participation from businesses in the learning process
- Projects from entrepreneurs and business owners drive the learning process
- Support in identifying Internet resources

Entrepreneurs are looking for:

- An unbiased review of the feasibility of their idea
- An evaluation of the proposed business
- Help in getting the new business defined, planned, and launched

Business owners are looking for:

- Help in researching a new line of business
- Process design and improvement assistance
- Leveraging technology to protect and expand market share

If you take a step back and look at the BIC, you will see that it is an ever-changing microcosm of the real world of business. The BIC is the heart of the WBDC model and it provides for the integration of the three environments, using the BIC as the bridge. It is the bridge that allows the three linkages to function as a living organism and produce the expected results.

At any point in time, the BIC will contain a wide range of projects that will be used by student teams to drive their learning experience and simultaneously meet the needs of the entrepreneurs and business owners who submitted them. The BIC project portfolio will include:

- Student and team-proposed new business ideas
- Entrepreneur-proposed new business ideas
- New product/service development projects
- Team-based nonprofit businesses owned by the WBDC
- Business owner member's process design/improvement projects
- Entrepreneur and business owner member's problem-solving projects
- Research-based contract work for member businesses

The number of potential technology-based business ventures in the BIC is limited only by the creativity of the WBDC students, business members, and other participants. Three ideas that come to mind immediately are:

- The automation of health care delivery systems, i.e., online meal ordering options, paperless operations, consolidated patient data collection and distribution
- The design and development of a web-based career planning system
- Applications of animated graphic solutions to specific business process design and decision-making models, i.e., dispatching and delivery, order entry, and order fulfillment

The BIC will be a microcosm of the real business world. It will house a number of nonprofit businesses at all stages of the business life cycle. These businesses will be managed by student teams under the advisement and mentoring of a faculty member and a manager from a member business. Teams will apply the principles and concepts delivered in class to actual business situations. Conversely, business projects and problems will arise that can be used in courses to drive and motivate the process of learning and discovery.

## The WBDC Model Linkages

The WBDC model contains the three environments described above. They form a fully integrated and interdependent set as defined by three linkages. Furthermore, these three linkages form a necessary and sufficient set for a comprehensive solution to be delivered by the WBDC model. Note that all three linkages are two-way linkages.

## Learning and Business Linkage

The learning and business linkage provides yet another venue for learning and discovery by student teams. It is a two-way linkage. Business executives will be invited to attend and speak in the classroom on topics of interest to the subject matter being studied, or observe and critique team presentations. Businesses will reciprocate by inviting teams and students to visit them in the workplace. The teams might be making presentations during these visits, or observing certain business meetings or activities. The students may be gathering data and information for the team for their WBDC project. Through this linkage, business and academe will be fully integrated into the process of learning and discovery.

## Learning and Business Incubation Center Linkage

The BIC is a living laboratory for learning and discovery. The needs of the student staffed business will drive the projects and problems studied in the classroom. Conversely, the concepts learned in the classroom will be applied to the businesses in the BIC. In effect, the BIC businesses become living laboratories for learning, experimentation, and discovery for all the students. The BIC functions as the clearinghouse for business projects and problems. It is these projects and problems that drive the learning and discovery processes of the WBDC curriculum.

The WBDC curriculum will be a project-based curriculum that is delivered in a team format. Projects may extend for more than a semester. In the criteria list below, projects and problems are interchangeable. There are specific criteria that an undertaking must meet in order to qualify as a project suitable for the WBDC model. Those criteria have been previously defined (Thomas, 2000) and are adapted to the WBDC model:

- WBDC projects are central, not peripheral to the curriculum.
- WBDC projects are focused on questions or problems that "drive" students to encounter (and struggle with) the central concepts and principles of a discipline.
- WBDC projects are student-driven to some significant degree.
- WBDC projects are realistic, not school-like.

## Business and Business Incubation Center Linkage

The local business community is a resource to the BIC businesses. Their advice and opinions will be actively sought. They have "been there and done that," and will be invaluable to the teams by bringing the real world into the BIC embryonic businesses and business ideas. Every business in the BIC will have a mentor from the business community and a faculty sponsor.

The BIC is also a resource for the business community. Here is the place where new business ideas can be tested in a "skunk works" setting. Student teams can be commissioned to research new business ideas, new/revised business processes, and other feasible ventures in a low cost and no risk setting for any of its business partners. Businesses can use the BIC as a permanent demo site, and a place to hold training for their employees and make presentations to their staff and customers.

## Features of the WBDC Model

The WBDC model is a unique and innovative idea that will rekindle the creative energies that built this great nation. To my knowledge, there is no equivalent model:

- The WBDC model offers a completely reinvented education/training delivery model.
- The WBDC model leverages the excitement of projects and problems to enhance learning.
- Through the BIC, the WBDC model provides a living business laboratory for learning, discovery, and rekindling of that "spirit of innovation" that President Obama has frequently spoken about. It is a benefit to all.
- The WBDC students are organized into teams coached by a faculty and business person.
- The WBDC model uses a team-centric learning model.
- The WBDC-owned, nonprofit businesses are team operated and professionally supervised.
- The WBDC model offers a fully integrated, state, certified curriculum at the high school levels.
- The WBDC model provides a fully supported environment for new business development.
- The WBDC curriculum can be integrated into existing high school and university programs.
- The WBDC students learn about the world of work in a safe environment.
- The WBDC model is scalable and can be replicated in other cities, states, and disciplines.

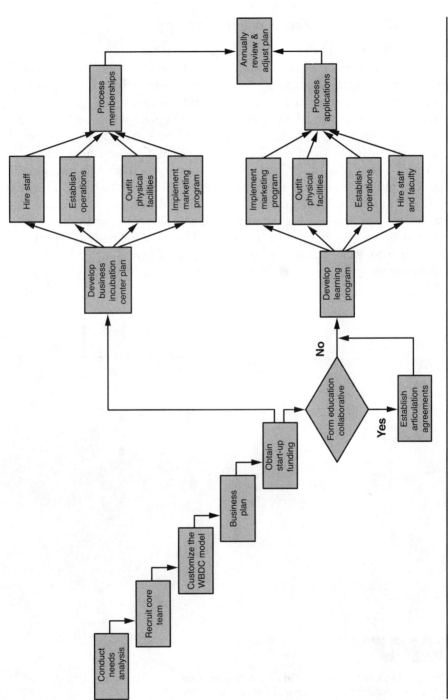

**Figure B.2**   Case Study: A typical WBDC model deployment strategy

## The WBDC Model Deployment Strategy

The transition to this WBDC model is significant. To consider implementing it, spend considerable workshop time with the key players (faculty, school administrators, local business owners, entrepreneurs, school boards, and local legislators), assuring that they understand the scope of the undertaking and the fact that it is an adaptive effort. Here is a place where an honest and open project scoping and requirements elicitation exercise is an essential ingredient for success. Figure B.2 illustrates a WBDC deployment process.

At the outset of a WBDC model deployment, there should be a significant community awareness program, utilizing all available media. This will include a number of presentations at Chamber of Commerce meetings, Kiwanis Clubs, professional society meetings, business clubs, and other appropriate venues throughout the market area. The bottom line in this program is to garner financial and in-kind support from the business community and private citizens. Creating visibility is a key to success.

# Appendix C

## REFERENCES AND FURTHER READING

The references listed in this appendix represent a collection of the publications cited in this book, as well as current publications from my personal library that provide background materials for further understanding of complex project management. Many titles are classics. All of these books will be of particular interest to professionals who have project management responsibilities, are members of project teams, or have a craving to learn about the basics of complex project management.

## REFERENCES

Couger, J. Daniel. 1995. *Creative Problem Solving and Opportunity Finding*. Danvers, MA: Boyd & Fraser Publishing.

Coad, Peter, Jeff De Luca, and Eric Lefebvre. 1999. *Java Modeling in Color with UML*. Boston: Pearson/Prentice Hall.

De Carlo, Doug. 2004. *Extreme Project Management: Using Leadership, Principles, and Tools to Deliver Value in the Face of Uncertainty*. San Francisco: Jossey-Bass.

Denning, Stephen. 2011. *The Leader's Guide to Radical Management: Reinventing the Workplace for the 21st Century*. San Francisco: Jossey-Bass.

Eckstein, Jutta. 2004. *Agile Software Development in the Large*. New York: Dorsett House.

Fowler, Martin, and James Highsmith. August, 2001. "The Agile Manifesto." *Software Development*, 9(8), 28-32.

Gellerman, Saul W. July, 1973. "Developing Managers Without Management Development." *The Conference RECORD*, 32-37.

Gray, David, Sunni Brown, and James Macanuto. 2010. *Game Storming: A Playbook for Innovators, Rulebreakers, and Changemakers*. Sebastopol, CA: O'Reilly Media, Inc.

Hass, Kathleen B. 2009. *Managing Complex Projects: A New Model*. Vienna, VA: Management Concepts.

Highsmith, James A., III. 2000. *Adaptive Software Development: A Collaborative Approach to Managing Complex Systems*. Somers, New York: Dorset House.

IBM, 2010. Capitalizing on Complexity: Insights from the Global Chief Executive Officer Study, GBE03297-USEN-00, Somers, NY.

International Institute of Business Analysis. 2009. *The Guide to the Business Analysis Body of Knowledge (BABOK Guide)*, Version 2.0. IIBA.

Kruchten, Philippe. 2003. *The Rational Unified Process: An Introduction*. 3rd ed. Boston: Addison-Wesley.

Maul, June Paradise. 2011. *Developing a Business Case: Expert Solutions to Everyday Challenges*. Boston: Harvard Business Review Press.

Palmer, Stephen R. and John M. Felsing. 2000. *A Practical Guide to Feature Driven Development*. Upper Saddle River, NJ: PrenticeHall PTR.

Poppendieck, Mary, and Tom Poppendieck. 2003. *Lean Software Development: An Agile Toolkit*. Boston: Addison Wesley.

Porter, Michael E. 1980. *Competitive Strategy: Techniques for Analyzing Industries and Competitors*. New York: The Free Press.

Project Management Institute (PMI). 2013. *A Guide to the Project Management Body of Knowledge*. 5th ed. Newtown Square, PA: PMI.

Robertson, Suzanne, and James Robertson. 2012. *Mastering the Requirements Process*. 3rd ed. Boston: Addison-Wesley Professional.

Schwaber, Ken, and Michael Beedle. 2001. *Agile Software Development with Scrum*. Upper Saddle River, NJ: Prentice Hall.

The Standish Group, 2013. *CHAOS Manifesto 2013: Think Big, Act Small*. Boston: Standish Group International.

Stapleton, Jennifer, ed. 2003. *DSDM: Business Focused Development*. 2nd ed. DSDM Consortium. Boston, MA: Pearson Education.

Tendon, Steve, and Wolfram Muller. 2014. *Hyper-Productive Knowledge Work Management*. Plantation, FL: J. Ross Publishing, Inc.

Thomas, John W. 2000. "A Review of Research on Project-Based Learning." Autodesk Foundation, San Rafael, CA.

Wysocki, Robert K., Robert Beck, Jr., and David B. Crane. 1995. *Effective Project Management*. New York: John Wiley & Sons, Inc.

Wysocki, Robert K., and Rudd McGary. 2004. *Effective Project Management: Traditional, Agile, Extreme.* 3rd ed. New York: John Wiley & Sons, Inc.

Wysocki, Robert K. 2007. *How to Establish a Project Support Office.* Arlington, MA: Cutter Consortium, 8(3).

Wysocki, Robert K. 2008. *Are You a Cook or a Chef? Succeeding in the Contemporary World of Project Management.* Arlington, MA: Cutter Consortium Executive Reports, 9(10).

Wysocki, Robert K. 2010a. *Workforce and Business Development Center: A Disruptive Innovation for Sustainable Economic Recovery.* Worcester, MA: EII Publications, LLC.

Wysocki, Robert K. 2010b. *Adaptive Project Framework: Managing Complexity in the Face of Uncertainty.* Boston: Addison-Wesley.

Wysocki, Robert K. 2011. *Executive's Guide to Project Management: Organizational Processes and Practices for Supporting Complex Projects.* New York: John Wiley & Sons, Inc.

Wysocki, Robert K. 2014a. *Establishing Meaningful Client Involvement.* Arlington, MA: Cutter Consortium Executive Reports.

Wysocki, Robert K. 2014b. *Effective Project Management: Traditional, Agile, Extreme.* 7th ed. New York: John Wiley & Sons, Inc.

## FURTHER READING

Anderson, David J. 2010. *Kanban: Successful Evolutionary Change for Your Technology Business.* Sequim, WA: Blue Hole Press.

———. 2012. *Lessons in Agile Management: On the Road to Kanban.* Sequim, WA: Blue Hole Press.

Cohn, Mike. 2004. *User Stories Applied for Agile Software Development.* Boston: Addison-Wesley.

De Grace, Peter, and Leslie Hulet Stahl. 1990. *Wicked Problems, Righteous Solutions.* Englewood Cliffs, NJ: Yourdon Press Computing Series.

De Marco, Tom. 1997. *The Deadline: A Novel About Project Management.* New York: Dorsett House.

De Marco, Tom, and Timothy Lister. 1999. *Peopleware, Productive Projects, and Teams.* 2nd ed. New York: Dorsett House.

Derby, Esther, and Diana Larsen. 2006. *Agile Retrospectives: Making Good Teams Great.* Raleigh, NC: The Pragmatic Bookshelf.

Dettmer, H. William. 1997. *Goldratt's Theory of Constraints: A Systems Approach to Continuous Improvement.* Milwaukee, WI: ASQ Quality Press.

Fleming, Quentin W., and Joel M. Koppelman. 2010. *Earned Value Project Management,* 4th ed., Project Management Institute, Newtown Square, PA.

Goldratt, Eliyahu M. 1997. *Critical Chain*. Great Barrington, MA: North River Press.

Goldratt, Eliyahu M., and Jeff Cox. 1992. *The Goal: A Process of Ongoing Improvement*. Great Barrington, MA: North River Press.

Graham, Robert J., and Randall L. Englund. 2003. *Creating an Environment for Successful Projects*. 2nd ed. San Francisco: Jossey-Bass.

Highsmith, James. 2002. *Agile Software Development Ecosystems*. Boston: Addison-Wesley.

———. 2009. *Agile Project Management: Creating Innovative Products*. 2nd ed. Boston: Addison Wesley.

Kendall, Gerald, and Steven Rollins. 2003. *Advanced Project Portfolio Management and the PMO*. Plantation, FL: J. Ross Publishing, Inc.

Kerzner, Harold. 2013. *Project Management: A Systems Approach to Planning, Scheduling, and Controlling*. 11th ed. New York: John Wiley & Sons.

Leach, Lawrence P. 2014. *Critical Chain Project Management*. 3rd ed. Boston: Artech House.

McConnell, Steve. 1996. *Rapid Development: Taming Wild Software Schedules*. Redmond, WA: Microsoft Press.

Office of Government Commerce. 2009. *Managing Successful Projects with PRINCE2, 2009 Edition Manual*. Norwich, Norwalk: The Stationary Office.

Rose, Kenneth. 2005. *Project Quality Management*. Plantation, FL: J. Ross Publishing, Inc.

Schenhar, Aaron J., and Dov Dvir. 2007. *Reinventing Project Management: The Diamond Approach to Successful Growth and Innovation*. Boston: Harvard Business School Press.

Schonrok, Johanna E. 2010. *Innovation at Large: Managing Multi-Organization, Multi-Team Projects*. Berne, Switzerland: Peter Lang GmbH.

Schwaber, Ken. 2004. *Agile Project Management with Scrum*. Redmond, WA: Microsoft Press.

Thomsett, Rob. 2002. *Radical Project Management*. Upper Saddle River, NJ: Prentice Hall.

Verzuh, Eric. 2011. *The Fast Forward MBA in Project Management*. 4th ed. New York: John Wiley & Sons, Inc.

Ward, J. LeRoy. 2011. *Dictionary of Project Management Terms*. 3rd ed. Arlington, VA: ESI International.

Wysocki, Robert K. 2006. *Effective Software Project Management*. New York: John Wiley & Sons.

———. 2006. *How to Establish a Project Support Office: A Practical Guide to Its Establishment, Growth, and Development*. MA: EII Publications.

————. 2006. *Distressed Projects: Prevention and Intervention Strategies*. Arlington, MA: Cutter Consortium, 7(8).

————. 2006. *Managing a Multiple Team Project*. Arlington, MA: Cutter Consortium, 7(4).

————. 2006. *Managing a Project That Involves Multiple Teams*. Arlington, MA: EII Publications.

————. 2011. *The Business Analyst/Project Manager: A New Partnership for Managing Complexity and Uncertainty*. New York: John Wiley & Sons.

Yourdon, Edward. 1999. *Death March: The Complete Software Developer's Guide to Surviving "Mission Impossible" Projects*. Upper Saddle River, NJ: Prentice Hall.

# INDEX